AIDS IN AMERICA

Susan Hunter

Foreword by Donald Trump

Preface by Alan Cumming

palgrave
macmillan

Also by Susan Hunter

AIDS in Asia: A Continent in Peril

Black Death: AIDS in Africa

AIDS IN AMERICA
Copyright © Susan Hunter, 2006.
All rights reserved. No part of this book may be used or reproduced in
any manner whatsoever without written permission except in the case of
brief quotations embodied in critical articles or reviews.

First published 2006 by
PALGRAVE MACMILLAN™
175 Fifth Avenue, New York, N.Y. 10010 and
Houndmills, Basingstoke, Hampshire, England RG21 6XS.
Companies and representatives throughout the world.

PALGRAVE MACMILLAN IS THE GLOBAL ACADEMIC IMPRINT OF
THE PALGRAVE MACMILLAN division of St. Martin's Press, LLC and
of Palgrave Macmillan Ltd. Macmillan® is a registered trademark in the
United States, United Kingdom and other countries. Palgrave is a
registered trademark in the European Union and other countries.

ISBN 1-4039-7199-4 hardback

Library of Congress Cataloging-in-Publication Data
Hunter, Susan.
  AIDS in America / by Susan Hunter ; foreword by Donald Trump ;
preface by Alan Cumming.
    p.   cm.
  Includes bibliographical references and index.
  ISBN 1-4039-7199-4 (alk. paper)
  1. AIDS (Disease)—United States.   I. Title.
RA643.86.H86   2006
362.196'979200973—dc22

                                                    2005056369

A catalogue record for this book is available from the British Library.

Design by Letra Libre

First edition: April 2006
10 9 8 7 6 5 4 3 2 1
Printed in the United States of America

CONTENTS

FOREWORD

Donald Trump

As a businessman, I have an intimate knowledge of the dynamics of risk and opportunity. *AIDS in America* presents us with the opportunity to intervene and stop the growth of this terrible epidemic, saving millions of people from suffering and harm. Ignoring it is an unnecessary risk.

AIDS presents us with a choice about our future. Will we make the choice to learn more about AIDS in America, so we can take the actions needed in our households, communities, and country to stop this disease? Susan Hunter has done thorough research to give us the opportunity to do so.

AIDS in America is giving us a vital wake up call. America now has the world's tenth largest epidemic—the largest of any country outside of Africa. In this book, Susan Hunter has given us the first comprehensive analysis of the epidemic in our country.

I say that it is always better to know than not to know. Education is a safeguard, and reading *AIDS in America* is a necessary first step in learning about a situation none of us can afford to ignore. Facts are important in any decision we make in our lives, and Susan is presenting us with the facts. Let us choose to be informed.

We think that AIDS can only happen to Africans as an epidemic, that it is serious there but will not affect us as a people and a country. By holding onto this myth, we are setting ourselves up for an unnecessary and perhaps disastrous consequence. It doesn't take prescience to understand that when it comes to AIDS, the whole world is involved, whether we like it or not.

We must widen our focus and include ourselves in the picture. Reading this book should be mandatory. It could save us from the disaster we are now courting, which is costing us so much already and could cost us as a country in the future. Taking a few hours of our time to learn about something that is so important, that is already affecting us economically and personally, is a smart investment. AIDS must not be underestimated or dismissed.

PREFACE

Alan Cumming

A very long time ago, I was obsessed with a board game called "Who's Had Who?" The premise was simple: you made your way across the board, landing on different well-known people's names, all of whom were connected by the fact that they had had sex with someone who had had sex with someone else, etc. Just like the song about the man who danced with a girl who danced with a girl who danced with the Prince of Wales, this game enabled you to see who had had sex with someone who had had sex with someone else who had had sex with, er, the Prince of Wales. It was fun. But then one day AIDS arrived and the next time I took it out of its box, the game had taken on a decidedly sinister hue: "Who's Had Who?" had become "Who Could Give AIDS to Whom."

Looking back on the twenty-five years since AIDS cases were first discovered, I mistakenly felt that we all have come a long way. But after reading Susan Hunter's book, I realized things are looking as bleak, if not bleaker, than they were in the halcyon days when "Who's had Who" held no portent.

I feel I'm one of the lucky ones. Not only can I remember my first sexual encounters as free from AIDS-related worry (because I'm old), but while America was suffering from the first wave of AIDS hysteria and deaths, and President Reagan was in utter denial about its very existence, my generation in Britain was subjected to one of the most intense and most successful public education programs ever that made condom carrying a matter of course and unsafe sex unthinkable. Fear tactics, when used sparingly and at times of direst need, work.

Sadly, today in America, there is no program of education that adequately explains the dangers and forms of prevention of HIV and AIDS to our young. Whilst Mr. Bush has pledged 15 billion dollars over five years to fight AIDS in Africa and the Caribbean, he is also allowing abstinence to be the only form of sex education that his administration funds in schools. Bigoted and outdated religious rhetoric is favored over hard facts that could save our children's lives. Aside from the stupidity, the loss and the ignorance of this situation, it is also (to speak, as it were, in the only language these people understand) a false economy: STD and HIV infections are skyrocketing, especially in the young. So maybe a little bit of education now might save some massive medical bills a few years down the line?

But that brings me to the next part in this sorry story that Susan's book highlights: the majority of Americans who are infected with AIDS don't have the money or healthcare to get the medication they need. And, as we saw when Hurricane Katrina devastated an economic group not unsimilar, Mr. Bush doesn't seem so quick to take action or to care. If he did, he would surely balk at the fact that treatment available in America is below levels of that in either Africa or Asia. I suppose he just has different priorities.

One of Mr. Bush's predecessors in the White House said the only thing we have to fear is fear itself. I think that is a great way to think of life: to live your life in the light and not the shadows. It's what I think of as the American dream. But right now I think there is something far worse than fear that we have to worry about: ignorance.

Ignorance, both in our governments' policies and in the minds of the generations they are betraying by them, is rife. This book, and the stories of the people in it, is a call to arms. We all need to be armed with this information so we can tell our friends and families and neighbors and shock them into action. Audre Lorde was right when she said "Your silence will not protect you."

INTRODUCTION

Despite large increases in reported AIDS cases over the last two years, most Americans believe that HIV/AIDS is "over with" in the United States, that our AIDS epidemic has been contained and controlled. The truth is otherwise. HIV is not going away, and it's not being confined to "high risk" groups. In recent years, HIV/AIDS has gained a lot of ground fast, making serious inroads along the hidden fault lines of our society. A new surge of HIV is on its way that will be much worse than the first wave in the 1980s.

While AIDS surges forward, our leaders rush back, shoving their Bibles between their knees and lobbyists' money in their pockets. AIDS is slipping through our public health safety nets, stretched thin by bad policy and mad budget cuts. The systems that are meant to protect us are failing, because they are underfunded, misused, and distorted by devious politicians bent on reelection or on lining their own pockets through complex deals hidden from the constituents they are supposed to represent.

In the process of writing this book, I interviewed far too many innocent Americans who have HIV because of the ignorance and greed of our conservative, right-wing "Christian" government. Their families have been broken or destroyed by a disease that is easily preventable if you know how to protect yourself and have the means to do it. I interviewed far too many Americans who didn't know the truth about HIV or their own sexuality until it was far too late to matter.

I left far too many young people and their mothers, sisters, fathers, and friends crying on the telephone, their anguished stories repeating themselves in my dreams. As I've learned in my work on the HIV/AIDS epidemic in twenty-eight other countries, AIDS in the United States is a family disease, a tragedy that strikes not only individuals but their kin, friends, and countrymen. This American family portrait of AIDS includes all Americans, portraying our strengths and weaknesses as a society, not just the HIV-positive people who share their lives with you in this book.

More than one million Americans are infected with HIV, the human immunodeficiency virus, and half a million have already died of AIDS, or autoimmune deficiency syndrome, the weakening of the body's own natural defenses caused by the virus. New infections surged between 2002 and 2003, adding a quarter of a million new cases to the rolls. The United States has the most severe HIV epidemic of any developed country. We are not immune. HIV/AIDS can infect anyone: every thirteen minutes another American becomes infected.

AIDS is the worst epidemic the world has ever known. It will soon become the worst epidemic the United States will ever know, yet it is virtually ignored by most Americans, their doctors, and our government because it has been deliberately identified with "problem populations." Despite what we have heard about the dangers of a bird flu pandemic since it was identified in 1997, it has caused only 76 deaths. The threat of SARS rocked our world in 2003; so far, it has killed less than 800 people. Ebola, disease-of-the-year from 2000 to 2002, killed somewhere between 700 and 1,000 people.

Meanwhile, AIDS trudges patiently on. Since it was identified in the mid-1980s, it has killed 37 million people. More than 40 million people are now infected, 14,000 *each day*. By 2010 projections from official data suggest that somewhere between 130 and 240 million people in the world will be infected or have died from the disease. There is no cure. There is no vaccine. The problem is in our heartland, our homeland, and the center of our souls as more and more Americans take their place in the family portrait painted by HIV.

All the conditions that contribute to epidemics of enormous scale in other countries are also present in the United States:

- Russia's prison system is a revolving door, an epidemic pump that pushes HIV, tuberculosis, hepatitis, and other infections out into the wider population. So is ours. The United States has one-quarter of the world's prisoners, giving us the world's largest revolving-door prison population, and their HIV rate is between five and seven times higher than that of the general population.
- The thriving sex business in Southeast Asia, which preys on young women and girls, is directly connected to the U.S. flesh trade. Our sex industry, worth at least $20 billion a year, is the largest in the world and the center of an international sex business that recruits U.S. teens and traffics women from other countries to meet an ever-growing demand.
- Drug users in Central Asia spread the disease to partners who are not using drugs, just as they do in every city and town in America. We have the largest number of heroin, cocaine, and methamphetamine users of any country in the world. New York City alone has more HIV-infected drug users than many of these countries put together.
- Poor Africans are not getting treatment for HIV or other sexually transmitted diseases, but neither are many of the inner-city poor in Atlanta, Baltimore, or any other large U.S. metropolitan area. We are withdrawing support for treatment, drugs, care, housing and food from HIV-infected Americans, increasing their infectiousness and throwing them out on the streets to support themselves by trading sex or drugs.
- Millions of China's peasants have been infected by faulty blood donation systems. Blood harvested from HIV- and hepatitis-infected inmates in Arkansas using illegal procedures and sold abroad by for-profit companies infected at least 20,000 Canadians, Irish, Spanish, and Japanese.
- Christian governments in Africa and Asia ally themselves with religious leaders to preach abstinence and spread misinformation about condoms and AIDS. American schoolchildren have not had frank sex education in their schools

since 1998, thanks to the Christian Right's collaboration with our own federal and state governments, and infection rates are already showing the impact.

The profile of the typical American with AIDS has changed drastically since the epidemic began. In the early years, homosexuality and drug use were the key driving factors. In the 1990s, racism and structural violence against minorities, gender violence and attacks on women's status, and religiously motivated ignorance and denial shifted the epidemic, spreading the disease to people with no identifiable risks.

Thirty-five years ago, you couldn't find an American with the virus. Now AIDS is in more communities than McDonald's, KFC, and Walmart put together, as ubiquitous as the hidden and often illegal behaviors it depends on to spread. AIDS is everywhere, from New York City to the most remote islands of the Aleutians, in Texas border towns and Native American reservations close to Canada. The infection has crept into every age group and affects families in every corner of the nation. AIDS is infecting all the branches of our American family tree and seeping deeply into its roots.

When I started to write this book, I had five questions:

- How bad is the AIDS epidemic in the United States?
- How can the richest country on earth be doing such a poor job containing the epidemic when much smaller countries are succeeding?
- Why don't Americans know more about their epidemic and the risks they are facing from it?
- Why aren't Americans outraged about HIV policy reversals promoted by the Christian Right and the disastrous effect they are having on our rights and our health?
- Where are the voices of responsible leadership needed to counter this plague?

To answer these questions, I decided to find out what AIDS looks like not just in the inner city but in the heartland of America. I set out to learn where the epidemic is going in the future—straight into white middle-class America—as well as where it's been. The answers I found were distressing.

International surveys show that Americans have sex more often and have a higher number of lifetime partners than people in any other developed country and most developing countries outside of Africa and Papua New Guinea, but they are not especially responsible about using protection. Americans also use more illicit drugs than do citizens of any other country on earth. Despite these facts, our HIV prevention programs are embarrassingly weak.

Even our government admits that our current prevention efforts are not succeeding. In fact, U.S. government-funded programs are throwing fuel on the fire. There is little in place to stop the epidemic, and what is in place is either being dismantled or is underfunded. We are not even close to a cure, antiretroviral treatments are failing for one-quarter of our patients, and vaccines are many years off. Emergence of highly drug-resistant HIV strains that convert to AIDS and kill in less than a year in five U.S. cities in 2005 suggests that mutant superstrains are developing, as many have predicted.

In the United States our drug approval process is a sham; our disease surveillance system is inadequate; Americans living with AIDS pay pharmaceutical companies as much as fifty times reasonable profit levels for the drugs they need; 48 million of us have no health insurance, so people with AIDS are forced into special programs that are now being cut; the U.S. prison system is getting larger by the day; and government "leaders" are accepting bribes (otherwise known as "campaign contributions") to do nothing about any of these problems although they are all easily fixed.

In collaboration with U.S. pharmaceutical companies and the World Trade Organization, the U.S. government also pays foreign legislators large sums of our taxpayer dollars to squelch innovative drug development outside our country, so that poor people with AIDS in developing countries (and in our own) cannot afford the medicine that keeps them alive.

When our politicians are not sitting on the sidelines for financial or political reasons, they are sabotaging the very measures that would contain AIDS in the United States and around the world. Our government has substituted disinformation for information about condoms on all government websites, including those of the Centers for Disease Control and the National Institutes of Health. It is dumping taxpayer money into abstinence-only sex education and just-say-no drug education programs for teens that are packed with erroneous and sexist information by the religious groups that provide them. It is paying religious leaders here and in other countries large sums to spread lies about condoms, buy Bibles as instructional materials for programs to prevent sexually transmitted diseases, and tell our young people that a woman's place is in the home.

None of these programs is evaluated, although secular programs and whistle-blowers are plagued with nuisance audits. President George W. Bush has even asked Congress to grant religious programs special dispensation from federal antidiscrimination statutes so they don't have to change their highly discriminatory hiring practices in order to qualify for federal money. Although avowedly interested in poking its nose into as little as possible, our government has its own website that provides patently false and sexist advice to parents and teens. We know nine ways to prevent HIV infection, but our government's single-minded advocacy of abstinence-only education is a textbook case of spitting in the face of a dangerous adversary.

Conservatives, pushed by right-wing hatemongers and aided by vote-buying liberals, are busy kicking the legs out from under programs to protect four groups that are highly vulnerable to HIV transmission: women, young people, gays, and minorities. We are also cutting programs that provide treatment, although other countries have demonstrated that free treatment (with cheaper generic AIDS drugs) saves money and reduces infectiousness, controlling the epidemic in a way few prevention programs can. We are pushing seriously infected people out on the streets by getting rid of housing supports.

Our government and corporate policies are knowingly promoting death, not life, harsh treatment for the weak instead of compassion, and suffering instead of comfort. We point our finger at corruption in other countries, yet wonder why we are going backward on AIDS and so many other tough policy issues. Outright vote buying and pandering to strong political interests on the right are hurting not just people with AIDS but everyone.

This same politics of convenience blocks solutions to other pressing American social problems, including the sex business, drug abuse, and prisons, all of which directly contribute to the spread of HIV. This lack of responsibility characterizes not only the battle against HIV/AIDS but most other areas of pressing social concern. We have put foxes in charge of the henhouse and walked away. It is time we took responsibility for our social problems, reclaimed our democracy, and halted the threat of AIDS to our American family.

It is difficult to find Americans who will talk on the record about the impact of HIV/AIDS on their families because AIDS is still very stigmatized. Not only was I lucky enough to find a typical, white middle-class American family brave enough to speak out, I was lucky to find one whose AIDS "family portrait" connects us to each part of the broader social picture. So I've centered my story—the story of HIV/AIDS in the United States—around them, and let them lead us through the maze of complicated and contradictory social factors that are increasing the number of Americans living with and exposed to this disease.

Paige "Big Sky" Swanberg of Billings, Montana, our lead character, grew up like many other rebellious American teens and learned she was HIV positive when she tried to enlist in the navy. In addition to most of the members of her family, whom we'll meet in later chapters, I also interviewed many other courageous AIDS activists who agreed to talk on the record. Tom Donahue and Susan Howe represent other facets of the disease and the changing demographics of AIDS as it creeps into our heartland. Many other people also spoke to me about their experiences but asked that their names not be used in this book.

As we pursue the lives of these ordinary Americans, the story of AIDS will take many of you into parts of America that you may not know much about, even though they have a major effect on how we live our lives. They are largely invisible to us although they might be very familiar to our teenage children or to other adults we know who keep their secrets close to their vests. If you're like me, you may be unaware of the darker side of your community—or maybe even the darker side of your partner, your family members, friends, or children. But they are there, and they are spreading AIDS to one more American every thirteen minutes.

The people you will meet in this book are by no means perfect. In their struggle with the difficult issues of AIDS, family, and community, they often stumble and fall short of their own ideals. But they are struggling courageously, trying to make sense out of their own lives and their society, like the one million other Americans who are now infected. The more than 20 million Americans who are their family members and friends are also struggling to fend off a killer they did not invite into their homes. They are fighting to provide care for those who have contracted the disease, and they are fighting to let other people know how to protect themselves before it happens to them.

All of these individuals have fallen prey to outdated and hypocritical social beliefs and values. They are HIV positive because of the failure of our government to do the simple things needed to protect them. As a society, we hold ourselves accountable to extremely high standards of behavior on many fronts, but unless we provide individuals the means by which they can uphold them, many of us will suffer this same sad fate.

Paige "Big Sky" Swanberg relaxes at a family picnic

Deputy Sheriff Gordon Grant and his "deputy" and grandson, Elijah Swanberg

Paige's kid sister, Lauren Swanberg

Lauren as First Runner-Up, Miss Montana Teen USA 2005 (third from left)

(below) Lindsay Swanberg cuddles her son, Jaden

Tamara Swanberg, mother of Paige, Lindsay, and Lauren

Elijah Swanberg, Paige's son, after making snow angels

Tom Donahue celebrates his second birthday, his second year of being alive after learning that he is HIV positive.

Susan Howe and her father enjoy a piece of pie together. At age 89, her father was blind, so Susan read his theology books to him and then they would go out for pie at his favorite diner.

1

PAIGE'S STORY

Paige Swanberg leaned into the cold wind that whipped around her body. The late January blow of Montana's high prairies gained speed as it whirled around the sandstone bowl that holds Billings at its base, nearly freezing the tears streaming down her face. Mixed with a light, cold rain, it sent her long brown hair flying around her head. She pulled up her coat collar, jammed her hair beneath it, and walked toward her old white Mitsubishi Gallant, its right front fender mangled by a small accident Paige had when she first got the car.

When she unlocked the door and climbed in, the sight of the recruitment papers scattered across the front seat sent fresh tears streaming down her face. She looked at the letter in her hand, trying once more to take in what it said. Collapsing against the steering wheel, she shut her eyes and cried out in despair. "Oh, my God! What am I going to do?" After a few minutes, the panic subsided a little. She started the Gallant's reluctant engine and pulled out from the curb, headed for her mother's house. "I was still crying." Paige recalls the day four years ago as if it were yesterday. "I was trying to see the road and the streetlights through my tears."

Paige had left for her induction into the navy in Butte the day before and was not supposed to be back in Billings. Tamara Swanberg recalls that she and her daughter were "on the outs" at that point and that it was "a very trying time in our relationship. Paige had come to the conclusion she needed to get her life together, which was wonderful. She was going to be sworn into the navy, but I didn't even know that she had gone."

Paige had ridden the bus from Billings to Butte, about four hours to the northwest, with six other inductees. That morning she'd been rousted from her hotel bed at 4:00 A.M. and was at recruitment headquarters half an hour later. "At that point I was under the impression I was in," she explained. "I was supposed to be sworn in and get my departure dates. I was pretty much figuring it was a done deal."

Induction is a slow process, so Paige waited patiently at first. "You can't sleep, you can't put your feet up. You have to sit straight all day." She remembers being puzzled when the names of the other six recruits from Billings were called and they disappeared through a door in the back without her. When the names of newer recruits who still needed their physicals began to be called, Paige went over to the desk officer to tell him she had already done hers. "What's taking so long?" she asked. "Why are all these other people going ahead of me?"

No one could tell her what was going on, so she sat back down, resigned to wait a few more hours. By midafternoon she again asked the receptionist to call the recruiters, but they were unable to get an answer. "So I sat there," Paige said. "They finally called me about 4:30 that afternoon, and instead of taking me in the back, they took me upstairs."

She thought it was a little odd that there was a military guard standing outside the room where they took her, but the captain invited her to sit. After he called a doctor in, the two men began to make small talk with her, asking about her son, her family, and her health. She was chatting, excited now that the induction process had finally started. "The job that I had picked was doing CIA-type stuff, investigation. Neat stuff."

She remembers that it felt very awkward in the room, and finally the captain interrupted her. "Your HIV test came back positive," he said. Paige gaped at him. "In my head," she remembers, "I'm thinking 'positive. Positive is good.' Then it hits me at the same time. 'No. Positive isn't good. Positive isn't right.'"

Paige remembers only too well what the letter they handed her said: "Dear Miss Swanberg: Your test for HIV was positive. This does not mean you have AIDS, but it does mean that you are no longer eligible for service with the navy. Seek medical treatment as soon as possible. We wish you the best in your future endeavors."

Paige sighs. "It felt like someone had just hit me in the chest. I couldn't breathe and I couldn't think straight. I had ten million questions running through my head. How long have I had it? How did I get it? What about my son? What about my family? All these questions, and they didn't have an answer for a single one." She sighs again. "They all tried to be understanding, and I'm sure they did the best they could with the information that they had, but it just wasn't good enough."

By the time the nurse drew some more blood for a confirmatory test, Paige was crying hysterically. "Why me? What happened? What am I going to do? Where do I go?" After a while, all she could think, over and over again, was "I'm gonna die." The navy had not counseled her before they gave her the test, one among a battery she had to have for induction. "They don't really say a lot about the HIV test, just that it's a standard precaution and you've got to take it. 'Sign the paper.' That's all I was told."

When they put her in another office to let her cry it off, she tried to call her mother. "I was in the office crying, and I didn't want to say it over the phone. I just said, 'I really need to talk to someone right now.'" Paige's mother recalls that she was working when her cell phone rang, so she didn't answer it. Tamara, who says she is "self-taught at everything," runs a local window-covering business and also sells real estate. That day, after her customers left, she checked her phone. "There was a message from her. She was in tears. She said, 'Mom, I've got to talk with you. I will be back tonight.'"

Tamara chides herself for not being there for her daughter. "I don't really remember exactly what she said in that short message, but I knew something was up and I knew it wasn't good. I attempted to contact her on her cell phone, but she was unavailable. I wasn't able to reach her. I felt so bad that I wasn't there for her when she needed me." Tamara, thirty-nine at the time, had been a single mom for Lindsay, Lauren, Paige, and Paige's son Elijah for five years after her divorce from David, a cosmetic dentist in Billings. Working two jobs spread her thin.

When Paige calmed down, the recruitment officers put her on a bus back to Billings. All the other Billings recruits were sent back on a different bus. "I was scared and felt alone, damaged." All the doors of possibility had slammed shut at once. "Now what am I going to do?" she thought. "I can't go to school and I can't go to work. What's the point? I'm just going to die. I felt like everything that I was starting to dream and plan just completely went down the drain. It sucked. I was so scared."

By the age of twenty, Paige had had enough of her hometown. Montana's largest city nestles between sandstone cliffs in the valley of the Yellowstone River. From the edge of the Rimrocks along the Black Otter Trail off the airport road you can see five mountain ranges: the Bighorns, the Pryors, the Beartooths, the Crazies, and the Snowies. Billings looks out over the Great Plains and is the hub of a huge, sparsely populated region consisting of eastern Montana, northern Wyoming, and the western Dakotas.

Tamara describes it as "a great little city, a little bit of everything, and a whole lot of nothing," like so many of cities of its size where most Americans live. Although its 100,000 souls make it the largest city between Spokane and Minneapolis and a business hub of the northern plains, its relatively small population can trap a young person. Caught up in the wrong crowd in her early teens, Paige found it hard to escape them and break old habits.

"I'd decided I was going to make some changes in my life and do something good for myself and my country," Paige said. Joining the navy would take her just about as far away from Billings as she could get. "I did the entrance physical. I was really excited and ready to go." The letter in her hand, brutal and plain, had closed that door with a loud bang.

When the bus reached Billings, Paige went straight to her mother's house. Tamara was upstairs in the family room when she arrived. As Paige walked in, she wondered, "How am I going to be able to do this? What am I going to say?" In the end, there was nothing she could think of to soften the blow. Paige brought her mother downstairs and handed her the letter. It's not difficult for her to remember the moment. "I'm having a hard time watching her without freaking out. I'm watching her eyes as they skim the paper, and they fill up with tears and then they close and open back up and they look at me. That pain. You can see the pain and you can feel the pain."

Tamara started to cry when she told me about it. "Paige walked in the door and she handed me a letter which basically just said that she was HIV positive, and I . . . I felt so sick about that. Especially that I couldn't be there to support her, and all I could do at that point was just hold her. She was very upset, obviously, just sobbing, and all she could say was 'I'm going to die. I'm going to die. I'm going to die.' And me having no education whatsoever, I had the same thoughts. Of course I didn't say that, but all I could think of is 'My daughter is going to die. I'm powerless to change it.'"

Every hour each day more than two young Americans are infected with HIV, but not all of them know it. On the same day Paige heard the news, twenty-seven other young people in the United States also learned they were infected, about half of the total. They are children of both sexes and all ethnicities. As Paige's kid sister Lauren says, "No matter who you are, no matter how old you are or what color you are, HIV/AIDS doesn't discriminate. It doesn't feel bad for where you live. It's like a bunch of terrorists dropped a huge bomb in the middle of the United States. Do you think that bomb is going to care if you live in Montana?"

No matter what age you are when you get it, becoming HIV positive changes your relationship to your past, your present, and your future; your partners, lovers, families, friends, and neighbors. "Initially it was devastating," Tamara said. "It was very traumatic. I was speechless. But I knew enough that Magic Johnson had it and he was okay, so there was this glimmer of hope. I was grateful at that moment that he was good enough to come forward and be public because that gives so many people that get this news hope. It's not a death sentence. He's brought a lot of people past that stereotype."

When Tamara recovered her composure she said, "We need to tell your dad." When they married, Tamara's second husband, David Swanberg, had adopted Paige, then age five, and her younger sister Lindsay, who was two. David is described by his family as a good provider but an emotionally absent husband and father, absorbed in his extremely busy and successful practice in Billings.

Paige's kid sister Lauren remembers the terrible sense of foreboding she felt as she watched her mom cradle her sister in her arms, both of them sobbing. "I asked them what was going on, but my mom just kept telling me to wait till my dad got there." Lauren's voice breaks and she starts to cry. "I was so frightened and confused." Tamara called David and said, "You need to come over." When he arrived, she handed him the letter "the same way Paige had done to me."

Lauren, who is fifteen now, is Tamara and David's biological daughter. Runner up in the Miss Teen Montana pageant last year, she has performed in national dance competitions and seems older than her age. "My parents are divorced," she explained, "so it was really weird because they are never in each other's houses or in the same room together. It just happens so seldom.

"My mom and sister were sitting on the couch and they were just crying. My dad was reading the letter, shaking his head. My mom asked me to come and sit by her. She said, 'We have to tell you something.' I was trying to figure out what it could be. Paige didn't usually react like that. I couldn't figure it out.

"My mom said, 'Do you know what HIV is?' I said I'd heard of it. 'Well, your sister has HIV.' I didn't know exactly what it was, but I knew it was really, really, really bad." Lauren says she regrets not learning more about it in school. "I think that while I was young, I should have known more about it. But it was still plain shock. I didn't feel anything. It was the worst feeling in the world, because I just felt my heart drop."

Paige says that her adoptive dad was impatient. "'What happened?' he asked her. 'You know, I was really hoping that the next time I saw you, it would be when you were coming back from the navy. But with you, it's always something else.' And that's pretty much all he had to say about it. He never said too much more. It was just 'Well, we'll have to handle this now too.' I felt like I was imposing on him because my insurance was through him."

Tamara recalls that later, her ex-husband told her, "'You know, that night I just didn't get why you guys were all crying and so sad. It's not like she didn't know what she was doing. She brought this all on herself.' I just cringed and thought, 'Another piece of ammunition.' He said to me, 'You know, every one of you have just embarrassed me except for Lauren.' She is still young enough. She hasn't done anything wrong yet. He doesn't really keep in contact with Paige. He doesn't ask. He's just not involved."

Lauren says, "My dad—he's really ignorant about it, a lot like most of America—he said: 'I can't believe you did this to me.'" Lauren is exasperated. "Paige didn't do it to anybody. It did it to her. She didn't do it to anybody. Then he said, 'Don't let anybody find out.' I love my dad to death. But I really don't respect him in the same way anymore because he said that. It's not meant to happen to anybody. Nobody deserves it at all."

At five foot seven inches and 150 pounds, Paige is a striking woman who looks more Native American than her adoptive father's name of Swanberg suggests. AIDS activists call her "Big Sky." When I described Paige as a pretty girl to her mother, she corrects me in a voice that has a touch of awe. "Oh, no. She's beautiful. She's a beautiful girl."

The bubbles that run beneath the surface of Paige's rich voice frequently break gently to the surface, sounding as if they surprise her as much as the listener. She is an animated speaker, plain talking, what we Americans love to call "down to earth." Occasionally she exaggerates a word or phrase, or imitates the voices of her past: her father's sternness, the voices of her recruiters, her own internalized parental voices. From time to time she raises her voice at the end of a sentence in the questioning lift so characteristic of adolescents, as if each assertion needs assurance. But most of the time Paige's voice is open, warm, and direct, with a wisdom and honesty that makes her a trusted guide to many teens. Sharing her story with them and with us is Paige's redemption, an act of optimism and grace that helps her make sense of her fate.

Her sister Lauren still talks in adolescent rushes, but is overall remarkably poised and well spoken. She thinks it is fortunate that Paige didn't listen to her dad and decided to go public with her HIV status because everyone who hears her story can learn from it. "She went out and she did what she knew she was supposed to do, which was to educate people about HIV," Lauren says. "I was really proud of the fact that she used it the best she could and made the best of it. We're all here to help her."

Studies show that people with HIV who are public about their status live longer than people who conceal it. The "flight" response in HIV-infected people who are shy or fearful releases the adrenal hormone norepinephrine in their bodies, boosting the virus's ability to replicate. Researchers have found that shy people carry up to ten times the viral load of more extroverted HIV carriers and that they respond less well to drug treatment. Like fear, mood can also have an effect on the progress of disease. One recent study showed that optimism can lower the risk of dying from heart disease by 23 percent.

Fortunately for Paige, the Swanberg women are a fiercely loyal bunch. Paige's sister Lindsay says that her mother had always been there for her, even when she messed up by getting pregnant in her sophomore year of high school. Her mom did a lot of the babysitting for Paige's son, Elijah, when he was small, and still helps when she can find time out from her two jobs. Paige says that her mom gave her one invaluable piece of advice that all the Swanberg women live by: their right to believe in themselves.

I asked Lauren if she's ever experienced discrimination because of her sister's status. She shakes the question off as trivial. "Yeah," she says, laughing. "But that just comes with it. Discrimination's just part of the job. I'm usually pretty good at ignoring that kind of thing. Me and my sister were both raised in a family where we learned—my mom really taught us—not to care what other people think and to be strong and to live for who you are. It's not about what other people say. It's about what you think of yourself.

"I think that Paige didn't deserve it at all, but I think she has the right set of mind and she's a strong enough person to have it," Lauren continued. "There's the people who have it and who sit on their butt all day and feel sorry for themselves. Paige did that for the first few weeks because that's just human nature. But now she's so good about it. She's a strong enough person to have it because she knows how to deal with it and she knows what she wants to do with her life now."

But it took a long time for Paige to make the adjustment. The first year of living with HIV was one of the longest years in her short life, the awful moment when HIV hits home. As Lauren says, "You never know how close it is until it hits your body or the body of someone you love," or how hard it will hit when it comes into your family. Paige was able to cling to denial for two weeks, until the results of her confirmatory test came back. "I had to pretend everything was okay. When people asked why I wasn't inducted, I just said, 'Medical stuff.' Or, 'They found out I have a bad eye.' I just made things up. I was scared and felt alone, like I was damaged."

In a few days, necessity forced her back to her job at Doc & Eddy's Casino in Billings. "I was hoping that the confirmatory test would come back negative. Like they said, some people's tests are false positive. Maybe it's just a mix-up. I still had that small hope. I was waiting and waiting for two weeks, calling my recruiter saying 'Where's my confirmatory test results?'

"I remember when he finally got it," Paige continues. "I called him from my mom's cell phone. She was taking care of Elijah because I was headed for my job. The recruiter said, 'Paige, I'm sorry to tell you. This one came back positive too.' I just said, 'Okay, thanks. If you can send them to my house, that would be wonderful.' I handed my mom her phone and I said, 'I gotta go.'" Submerged under the heavy armor of wannabe military brass for almost a year, the wounded, angry little girl in Paige finally got to show her stuff. The denial was over and anger kicked in.

"I jumped back into my Gallant and drove like a bat outta hell home. I was listening to the song 'Shit Can Happen' on a D12 CD. I was so mad and I was so frustrated and scared. I'm looking for this certain CD that I wanted at my house. All I wanted to do was listen to angry music. I was mad and yelling and screaming and I couldn't find the CD in my CD case, so I'm throwing them across the room. It was just like 'Screw it! I'm going to make a mess in my house. I don't care!' So I'm listening to this music getting myself all pumped up and I'm so mad and don't know where to direct my anger so I just like kind of totaled my bedroom. I grabbed the mattress and threw it against the wall and wore myself out to the point where I just fell asleep.

"I woke up to my mom. She's trying to crawl through my basement window because I had locked all the doors. I wasn't answering the phone and the music was blaring, and she's trying to climb through the basement window because she's afraid I'm trying to kill myself. I can understand that, because that's where I was at that point. I just didn't know how to react or what to do. It was pretty intense that day."

Suicide is an option too frequently chosen by people who have just learned they are HIV positive. Although treatment can extend the lifespan of someone with the virus for decades, most Americans still think of AIDS as the "gay plague" and believe it is basically untreatable. However, even with treatment—which many HIV-positive individuals don't have to begin right away—trouble adjusting to the medication brings on other illnesses, pain, insomnia, vomiting, and loss of appetite.

HIV-positive people say that their families and friends often reject them or don't know how to help. Financial problems can mount because of illness and the cost of medications. Depression is a common problem. "If a client gives us any indication that they're thinking about suicide, we stop the test immediately," a health educator told me. Suicide is now a concern for Paige in her current work as an HIV counselor at the Yellowstone AIDS Project. In this past year alone, she's lost five of her clients. Four died prematurely because depression accelerated HIV replication in their bodies, and one chose suicide.

While Paige still resents her mother for telling her son's father and parents that same day, it may have been the most important thing Tamara did. Paige had no time to dwell in her suicidal thoughts because she had to clean up and go to her mother's house. Tamara had "invited my son's father and his parents over to tell them. By the time I had gotten there, she had already told them, which really kind of upset me. They were speechless. They just hugged me and said 'We don't know what to say.' And that's just kind of how it was. For a while they didn't know what to say to me. They didn't know how to act around me. I felt like I'd failed them. I felt like I had failed everybody." Paige had gone public, ready or not.

When she took her two-and-a-half-year-old son for testing two weeks later, he was negative. Paige became afraid that she'd infect him. "The first time he cut himself on the floor in the bathroom and started bleeding, I couldn't give him the care he needed right away because I wanted to make sure there wasn't anything on me that would hurt him. I couldn't rush to comfort him, and that hurt. It still does right now when I think of it. I wanted to do everything I could to take care of my little boy, but it was just so scary that I couldn't handle it.

"I lived by myself, but I took him over to my mom's to get him bandaged up because I was too afraid to do it. I grabbed this towel and put it on his hand. It was a little cut. A Band-Aid and a kiss would have fixed it, but I felt like he had just busted his head open. That was how was my mind was going. Oh my God, it was scary. When they would draw my blood I would feel like a vampire, or like I was a reverse vampire. I couldn't stand the sight of my blood. I wondered, 'Is it going to be all full of bugs or something like that?'

"I felt really dirty and shameful at first. I couldn't look in the mirror and see a beautiful human being anymore. I saw this disease-infested thing. I would just look in the mirror and cry. Now I can hold my head up and look in the mirror and say, 'You're having a bad hair day, but otherwise you look pretty good. You're still here and people are still listening to you. So keep up the good work and go along with your day because it's another day you're here.'"

Paige nursed her anger, self-hatred, and guilt for over a year. Angry and confused, without guidance from professional counselors or health care personnel, she didn't know where to turn. Tamara says that "initially [Paige] was in denial. I think she was drinking a lot, trying to self-medicate. It was hard to watch. I try to be her friend and her mother, and the two conflict quite a bit. It's hard for me to support her and still be her mother."

Paige remembers a sense of burden and resentment. "My mom's birthday—her fortieth birthday—was just a couple weeks after I got the confirmatory test. I asked her what she wanted, and she said, 'I just want you to be able to see your fortieth birthday.' I didn't have time to think about my own feelings because I felt like I was supposed to be comforting her." Her mother helped her find medical care, but she had no one to talk to who actually had the disease.

It took Paige about a year to find the support services she needed. She went to her gynecologist first, and he referred her to Dr. Camilla Saberhagen, an infectious disease specialist then in Billings. Paige's life began an upswing when "Dr. Cam" pointed her in the direction of the Yellowstone AIDS Project (YAP). "I went in there on February 12th of 2001 to talk with them, and I was on the plane on the 14th to Dallas for the Ryan White National Youth Conference. In Dallas, I actually met people with HIV and met people who were involved in prevention. I caught on to their energy and the excitement of fighting HIV and educating people. It just got into my blood and it hooked me. I was a different person. I didn't feel alone.

"In Dallas I met people who had been living with HIV for more than twenty-five years, and it made me feel a little bit better. It made me feel like, 'Okay, I still have time. I can do this.' I met a woman from New York with her daughter who was eighteen and was living with it. I was just like 'Wow! Look at these people! They're healthy! They're laughing! They're enjoying life.' It was just like 'Okay, I'm not alone and I'm not just going to have to die from this. I'm going to live *with* it rather than die *from* it.'"

At the conference Paige learned that more than 800,000 other Americans were HIV positive, and many were angry about their condition, not ashamed. Convinced that other young people should not suffer her fate, she went public about her HIV status when she returned to Billings and began to volunteer for YAP. "I started getting involved in speaking to schools, youth detention facilities, and colleges. Wherever they'll let me in, I'm in there talking about it, trying to raise awareness." Paige was recently offered a job outside the Billings area modeling for an HIV drug manufacturer, but she feels that she can have more of an impact in her own hometown because young people know she is local and can identify with her.

She started working for YAP in the summer of 2004, when the group's client advocate quit. "At first it was kind of a glorified party planner, but I've molded the job into my own thing. I try to be there and make sure that other people who are living positive are living healthy lives. I try to ensure that they're taking care of themselves, educate them, make sure that they're getting the proper treatments, make referrals, assist them with medical bills, getting jobs, and stuff like that," she said.

"You become friends with these people and it just becomes that much more real. It gets to you. It kind of lights a fire under you," Paige said. She joined the April 2005 AIDS Watch march on Washington to lobby against funding cuts for AIDS treatment and housing. Each of the 8,500 marchers from all over the United States carried a shoe to represent a person somewhere in the world who had died from AIDS over the past year. Paige was featured in press stories on the event.

She still continues to encounter some discrimination. "Some people won't say it to my face, but they'll say it around other people. They told my boyfriend 'she's dirty.' A lot of people would hate on it." On the whole, the responses from her hometown are good. People respect Paige for her courage and her unselfish willingness to teach.

"I take people by surprise just because I don't look sick. I'm vibrant, exciting. I have a sense of humor." She laughs. "I always figured someone with AIDS was going to be homely looking, the hunchback with stuff all over your face, hair falling out, sick, sunken in, bloodshot eyes. That's how I always figured it, and that's how a lot of people out here look at it. They think, 'You'll be able to tell because they'll look sick.'"

Her biological father, Gordon Grant, says, "One of the most profound things I saw ever since I've known PJ—that's my pet name for Paige—was on her twenty-third birthday. I went up to spend the day with her, and she did a speech before a high school. When she took the stage, everyone thought she was going to introduce this withered away, crack-ridden girl that was HIV positive.

"Then they realized that this beautiful, tanned, gorgeous girl was not the introducer but the girl that was carrying it. They didn't know I was her father. I was sitting in the back and I could hear all the guys say 'wow' . . . and . . . anyway, needless to say it was moving. When she opened the floor to questions, no one said anything. Everyone was completely dumbfounded. So I just stood up and applauded and said "Happy Birthday."

Paige contacted Gordon, a deputy sheriff in Houston, after she learned her HIV status. He told her that three years before, her grandfather had died of AIDS. "It was a shock to everybody because nobody knew he even had it," Paige said. "He was in his sixties or seventies. It was kind of like 'Wow! How crazy is that?' But it showed me that it can happen to anybody." Gordon describes his father as "a severe womanizer. He loved women, literally. He never believed in HIV. He just thought it was society's way of trying to control one's activities. He was very stubborn man."

THE CHANGING AIDS DEMOGRAPHIC

"When I found out I was positive," Paige said, "I thought my life was over and the world was going to end, that there's not a God. But it's become something that's made me look at things so much differently that it's changed me in a good way. Somebody had to have decided that this is what was meant for me, to use me to educate people because I'm not the stereotype. I'm not the typical person. I can wake up people who are like me who don't know they are infected. I'm sick of being ignored because we don't fit a certain demographic."

Paige is not the typical AIDS "demographic" in Montana, where most of the 300 HIV/AIDS cases reported in 2003 were homosexuals or drug users. She is not the typical demographic of AIDS in the United States, either, but the AIDS epidemic is rapidly catching up with her. It also caught up with her grandfather. Both are examples of the emerging demographic of HIV/AIDS in the United States as it expands into two widely divergent generations: teens and their grandparents.

When HIV first hit the United States, its victims were members of what was sardonically called the "4-H club": homosexuals, heroin users, Haitians, and hemophiliacs. Most lived in major cities. By the mid-1990s HIV's aggressive "migration" into minority groups through sex workers, bisexuals, and injecting drug users had transformed AIDS into the major killer of men and women ages eighteen to thirty-four.

In the 1990s, AIDS changed color and gender. In 1990 it was largely a disease of white men, but by the end of the decade it was primarily infecting blacks. The HIV rate among women, who constitute 26 percent of people living with AIDS in the United States, continues to accelerate. AIDS is also spreading from cities into rural areas, so that many of the states with the highest new infections levels are in the South, especially South Carolina, Florida, and Louisiana. And AIDS also aged. Between 1991 and 1996, infection in people over age fifty were increasing more than twice as fast as infections among young adults. Now more than one in ten Americans with AIDS are over age fifty, and experts fear that their number will continue to grow.

After 1996, however, another trend began. Many more young Americans were becoming infected through drug use and sexual activity. Now half of all new infections are in people under twenty-five, and one-quarter are in people twenty-one or younger. The reasons why HIV is spreading rapidly, however, is similar for all Americans no matter what their age, sex, or gender. They simply do not believe they are at risk of getting it, so they are having unprotected sex (sex without a condom), and they are using drugs.

The responsibility for profiling AIDS in America falls on the U.S. Centers for Disease Control in Atlanta. The CDC, as it is commonly called, collects and compiles data on all diseases in the United States, including AIDS, from state health departments. It's not an easy job to get a clear picture of how any disease affects people in different age, sex, and racial categories, but experts are now beginning to admit that it's an especially difficult task for sexually transmitted diseases like AIDS.

Biologically, sexually transmitted diseases (STDs) don't behave the way many other infectious diseases do. People with an STD don't like to admit it, or may not know they have them. HIV, for example, can live in a person's body for a decade or longer without causing any symptoms. Only thirty-two states report AIDS cases to the CDC, and even those reports are not complete because not all hospitals, health centers, clinics, and physicians are included. So it's easy for the CDC to vastly underestimate how many Americans have HIV.

Dr. Carlos del Rio of Atlanta's Emory University thinks that the CDC's report card is worse than it is saying. Although the CDC says that the number of new infections has remained constant at 40,000 per year for the past five years, del Rio believes that the number of new infections is probably much higher, as many as 60,000 new cases per year. He is not alone among the experts who think that the CDC's methods for tracking new infections are falling far behind the epidemic curve in the United States.

A professor of infectious disease, del Rio is also chief of medical services at Grady Memorial Hospital and sees the epidemic's impact firsthand on Atlanta's inner city, which he says looks just like Africa because few people with HIV are getting treatment or care. He says that our prevention efforts have been "woefully inadequate. And we're paying. We're paying with the number of new infections. We already are in a big-time epidemic. The U.S. has the most severe HIV epidemic of any developed country, and I think that's something that we shouldn't be proud of."

Sixty percent of Americans polled in 2000 said they were concerned about contracting STDs, but thirty percent took no protective measures. While most said they blamed people with HIV/AIDS for getting it, they did not know how the disease is actually transmitted. Despite the change in the "demographics" of AIDS, most Americans still think the disease affects only gay men. In this case, ignorance is definitely not bliss. This false sense of security affects educated and uneducated alike. In late 2003, early 2004, and again in 2005, the CDC announced outbreaks of AIDS in two populations previously thought to be at extremely low risk: college students in North Carolina and Florida.

Americans are not alone in their fatal ignorance about AIDS. As the disease spreads, experience in country after country has shown that scientists and politicians who thought that HIV could be confined to "high risk" groups (sex workers, men who have sex with men, injecting drug users, and soldiers) were wrong. As AIDS epidemics have become increasingly heterosexual all over the world, "ordinary" people network with "high risk" individuals, who also interact with one another.

Studies prompted by the growth of the AIDS epidemic all over the world show that many closeted bisexual men are having sex with spouses and other male and female partners. Debbie Hendrick, community health services director for the Montana State Health Department, tells me about a Montana senior who learned after the death of her husband of almost fifty years that he had been leading a double life. His parting gift to her was HIV. "I think we're going to see a steady increase of HIV, especially in the population that is on the down low." Men on the down low identify themselves as heterosexual, but have sex with men on the side. Down low sex is also called "sneaky sex," because the men have sex with unsuspecting female partners, or "prison sex," because some men became accustomed to sex with men while they were incarcerated.

In a national survey of 15- to 44-year-old Americans released by the Center for Disease Control's National Center for Health Statistics in September 2005, 1 percent of the males interviewed reported having both same and opposite sex partners in the last twelve months. This means that over 600,000 men ages 15 to 44 across the country are on the down low; if men in older age groups are taken into account, this number probably exceeds 1 million. Perhaps even more startling because it has not received the same media attention is the survey's finding that 3 percent of the women in that age range, or about 114,000 women, report partners of both sexes.

Injecting drug users also have sex partners and spouses. In her role as an AIDS counselor, Paige says "It just kills me, some of the stories I hear. One gal found out she was positive after giving birth to her daughter and donating her cord blood for stem cell research. She was infected by her husband. She thinks he was shooting up drugs. Her baby is negative. She's only a couple of years older than me so when she first found out, she was referred to me. I had told people that if anyone was newly infected, they could talk to me because I know that scary part about not having anyone to talk to. It's nothing that anyone should have to go through by themselves.

"I think a lot of us choose to pull the blinders over our eyes and kind of go through life that way and think 'what happens, happens,'" she continues. "But we all have an opportunity to make changes and make choices, and if we have the education to do it properly, then why not?" Paige says it's important for people to realize that "it really probably could happen to me if I was at a vulnerable point in my life.

"That's how a lot of older people who are just recently divorced and getting back into the dating scene get infected. They didn't have to think about those types of things when they were younger, and they've been out of it for twenty-some years. They think that everyone's honest and end up dating somebody who isn't. If you're at a vulnerable point, that's when you need to be the most aware for yourself."

Sarah, who asked that her real name not be used in this book, is an affluent sixty-something divorcee who divides her time between her home in Newport, Rhode Island and her apartment in Venice, Florida. She shyly admits that after she mourned her husband's death several years ago, she found that she wanted the companionship of a second husband. Personal ads placed in a local newspaper resulted in several unpromising dates. While in Venice last winter, she visited an internet café to check on the results of what she described as a carefully screened on-line dating service.

An attractive sixty-something man sitting next to her at the café struck up a conversation. He told her that he was from California and was checking on e-mails from his family. "We hit it off instantly," she recalled, and she enjoyed several dates with him. "I loved going out to eat and he danced beautifully, but he was very aggressive afterward." Sarah gently fended off his sexual advances. "I told him that I wanted to wait until I got to know him better."

After she refused him twice, "he dropped me like a hot potato. I still saw him at the internet café, but he ignored me. I was

shocked when I found out later that he regularly used the internet to link up with casual sexual partners in Venice. When my
friend and I shared notes some months later, we realized she
had dated the same man. He wined and dined her just like me,
and she gave in. After a few times, he dropped her too." She
giggled self-consciously. "What my friend said was really rude,
but she was still angry about the whole thing. She actually
caught a disease from him, but fortunately her doctor could
treat it. She told me, 'if you're an older man and you can walk,
why date any woman more than a few times?' I don't think all
men are really like that, so I'm still dating, but it's made me
more careful than ever."

Most people over fifty do not think they're at any risk of HIV
infection, despite the fact that older Americans routinely engage
in sexual activity. A 1994 University of Chicago study found that
60 percent of men and 37 percent of women ages fifty to fifty-
nine reported having sex at least a few times month. A 2004 survey by the American Association of Retired Persons (AARP)
reported even higher rates extending into older age categories,
thanks to Viagra and similar drugs. Half of the men and women
surveyed by the AARP with regular sex partners had sex at least
once a week. Eight percent of the men and 4 percent of the
women said they had extramarital affairs.

Older adults know less about HIV than young people and
are less likely to use a condom. Only 13 percent of women fifty
years and older surveyed by Emory University in 2005 knew that
HIV transmission could be prevented by using condoms, half
thought they could not be infected by a man with a vasectomy,
and 63 percent thought HIV was transmitted by kissing. Many
women still believe that taking birth control pills protects them
from infection.

There is also a hidden epidemic of drug addiction and injecting drug use in older Americans. A 2003 federal drug survey
found that about 1.25 million people over fifty-five used illegal
drugs. Stephan Arndt, a University of Iowa psychiatry professor, calls this "the leading edge of the wave," anticipating even
more addicts as baby boomers age. By 2004, 4.4 million Ameri-

cans over age fifty will have drug and alcohol problems, according to the U.S. Substance Abuse and Mental Health Services Administration.

Late onset of drug and alcohol abuse grows out of early, more casual use, precipitated by a traumatic or life-changing event or even a mild midlife crisis. "People don't think of drug addicts being my age," says Jon Roberts, a father and grandfather now in his sixties. He "was a 'functioning' addict," and kept his job as a building manager until his habit forced him over the legal line and into a treatment program for senior addicts. Clean now, he works as a counselor.

Older people are also not getting tested for HIV. Twice as many young people as older adults have had a test. In addition, people over fifty have more illnesses, ailments, and symptoms of aging that mask HIV symptoms. AIDS-related dementia can be attributed to Alzheimer's; fatigue and weight loss can be dismissed as part of the "normal" aging process. HIV prevention education campaigns never show older faces, making adults over fifty "an invisible at-risk population" for AIDS, says the CDC.

At least one-quarter of HIV-positive Americans of any age do not know that they carry the disease, increasing the possibility for transmitting it. Most new HIV infections are transmitted by people who do not know they carry the virus. Despite widespread testing and rapid test kits that provide results in minutes, a third of those who test positive at CDC-sponsored sites around the country do not come back to learn their results. And little wonder.

Getting tested for HIV, as anyone who's done it can tell you, can be a nerve-racking experience, whether you have to wait two weeks or twenty minutes for the results. I was tested twice in the 1990s, once after a car accident in Africa and once to get a job clearance in order to work for the U.S. Agency for International Development. Back then, it took a week to get the results, more than enough time for me to consider every horrible hypothetical and wonder what I would do if I was positive.

After talking with people who were HIV positive for this book, I decided to get another HIV test because I'd recently had a blood transfusion while recovering from a burst appendix. This time I had to wait only twenty minutes for the results, but it was still plenty of time to review my sins. Getting to that point was even more trying. Even in a state as sophisticated as New York, with 15 percent of the country's AIDS cases, the medical system seemed remarkably indifferent to my right to privacy and callous to my need for information and comfort.

The nurse at my family doctor's office, purportedly an experienced HIV counselor, asked if I had "concerns" (meaning risk factors), but made no effort to find out what they were or counsel me about them. She told me nothing about HIV, except that it was "not so bad anymore," and that "people are living a much longer time." Then she cut straight to the chase.

"What would you do if you were HIV positive?" she asked, unsmiling. "Would you consider committing suicide? A lot of people feel that way when they are first diagnosed. But I want you to know that if you're considering suicide, you can't get your test done here." My mouth dropped open. "It would just be too much of a liability for the doctor," she explained. "So if you're considering committing suicide, you'll have to get tested at the Board of Health."

With the issue of suicide taken care of, we moved on to more important matters. She told me it would take two to four weeks to get the results (not true). They did not offer rapid testing. She had no idea what the test would cost, and told me that HIV and other STD tests were not covered by insurance (also not true for all insurance companies).

"But to be honest with you," she continued, "I wouldn't have my test done here if I were you. If we do it here, the results go straight in your chart. Not that we would ever tell anyone, you understand, but insurance companies audit our records about twice a year, and you never know what might happen with the results. I would never have it done here. If you really don't want anyone to know, like your husband or your friends, I would go to a public health clinic in another county." By this point, I could read the handwriting on the wall pretty clearly, and slunk out the door.

The 800 number I found in the white pages under "HIV/ AIDS Hotline for Free Anonymous Counseling & Testing" took me to an indifferent voice almost 300 miles away, who managed, after some prodding, to find the 800 number for my part of the state. When I dialed it, a man answered, "Ralph." Ralph represented the state's health department's HIV office, but after telling me to call my county STD clinic, he became noticeably impatient and turned the phone over to an HIV counselor named Joyce.

She explained that I could get a rapid test at my county's STD clinic on Tuesday nights. If I didn't want to be seen at an STD clinic, I could try the state health department clinic at a Planned Parenthood office a half hour drive to the south, where free testing was available twice a month. They were booked for the next three weeks. Joyce explained that both types of test, slow and rapid, are free and anonymous at either of the clinics. The rapid test takes twenty minutes, the slow test takes a week, and both are highly accurate after the three month infection "window," ninety days or more after you "have a risk, have sex or something like that."

My husband agreed to be my worried partner, and we went to the public health clinic the following Tuesday evening. The place was bustling. An AIDS education video was playing on a small TV and the nurses scurried around, carrying boxes and equipment in from their cars. We sat on folding metal chairs in the hallway across from a trim middle-aged man in shorts and a T-shirt, and leafed through STD brochures while we watched the video. It wasn't your average soap. A young doctor wearing his baseball cap backward was telling his college audience that he didn't have the heart to tell his friend that he was getting the last-ditch AIDS treatment before death.

When the nurses had everything organized upstairs and down, one of them approached the man who was waiting with us and asked him if he wanted his HIV test now. I looked at my husband and he rolled his eyes. Another ten minutes passed before a young blond woman named Lauralee led me into one of the back rooms. I thought we would be counseled as a couple, but my husband has seen too many *ER*s and knew that couples are always split up so they can spill their guts. For HIV testing, couples were counseled individually so counselors could gauge the potential for domestic violence if one partner turns up positive. If they sensed any likelihood of violence, they would refuse to do the test.

I faced Lauralee across the corner of an old table draped with a large gauze pad and covered with a tumble of soft aluminum packages marked OraQuick, along with a digital timer and some files. She separated little gauze pads and put a narrow two-inch test tube in a small plastic stand while she talked. After pricking my middle finger, she scooped two drops of blood into the test tube with a "developer." Some public health clinics use the Ora-Sure saliva test for people who cannot stand the sight of blood, but it was not available in my town yet.

Then, Lauralee removed a plastic stick that that looked like something you would find in a pregnancy test kit from one of the aluminum pouches, and plunged the pad on the end of it into the test tube. Blood and developer were drawn up the stick, and it took about a minute for a small red line to form across the top where it was marked "C" for control. She explained that we had to wait twenty minutes to see if a matching line would form across the "T," or test position. If that happened, I would be HIV positive.

I stared at the stick like it was a cobra about to strike, so she turned it away so neither of us could watch. "For now," she said, "let's not think about that." As she moved quickly through a set of questions about why I was taking the test and what my risk exposures were, all I could think about was the stick. You never know when you'll get hit by a truck in the middle of the street of life, so I reached out and turned the test tube holder toward me. There was still only one line, but there were also twelve minutes left on the timer. I heaved a small sigh of relief with each minute that passed away. If another red line was going to form, I wanted to know the second it happened.

Since I decided to take the test anonymously rather than confidentially—which means my results are identified only by a number—we skipped all the identifying data in the questionnaire and went right for the sexual risk, domestic violence, and drug use questions. Lauralee told me how HIV is contracted through various sexual acts and drug-using behaviors. Anal sex, common among teenagers, is the most dangerous sexual act, as is sharing needles in intravenous drug use, although you can also get HIV by sharing coke straws (cocaine, that is, the kind of coke that is snorted through your nose).

The timer hit 0. The second red line had never formed. I wiped the sweat off my palms and went to sit in the waiting room. When my husband returned from his test, I could tell by the expression on his face that the second line never formed on his stick either. I was enormously relieved, but having been through the testing process, I can see how people could become discouraged, especially if they are young or fearful of another person finding out that they have tested. While Lauralee was a gem, she was a rare one.

Many insurance companies are not as "liberal" as mine and cover STD tests only if they are "medically necessary" or if patients are symptomatic. Since many patients are not—or show symptoms only when they are at an extremely advanced stage— many have to pay for the tests themselves or go to a public clinic. The Commonwealth Fund found that women with no insurance and those with Medicaid are more likely to discuss STDs with their doctors than women with private physicians. But some states underfund STD screening in public clinics, spending $1 in prevention for every $43 spent in treatment.

HIV is only one of the 15 million STDs diagnosed in the United States each year. They cost $8.4 billion a year to treat, and they are the tip of the iceberg. One quarter of all Americans will have at least one STD in their lifetimes, but many are never diagnosed. STDs are linked to dangerous systemic diseases, and also increase the risk of HIV transmission by a factor of seven. Despite their prevalence, neither my husband nor I have been counseled about the risk of STDs or offered an STD or HIV test by our family doctor, who has never broached the subject of sexual behavior or STDs with either of us. My gynecologist has never said a word about them either.

Our experience is typical. American physicians do a notoriously bad job of keeping their patients informed about STDs (including HIV) and detecting the diseases in their patients. Forty
percent of women are never asked about their sexual histories on
preexam questionnaires, and 84 percent of women (72 percent of
teens) have never discussed STDs with their doctors. Many
women think their annual exam includes tests for STDs, and
their doctors aren't telling them otherwise. Three quarters of
American men and almost as many women guess that only one in
ten Americans is at risk. "STDs are very hidden, secret, and mys-
terious," says one health expert.

Physicians themselves are often embarrassed and even less
likely to talk about STDs than their patients. "Some patients get
insulted if you ask about STDs," said Dr. Robert Hagler, who
chaired the Gynecological Practice Committee for the American
College of Obstetricians and Gynecologists. "You run the risk of
offending them, and this can make discussing STDs difficult."
Official guidelines from medical professional bodies and health
maintenance organizations (HMOs) vary, so doctors are left on
their own to make sense of the muddle. "That's helping these
germs replicate like crazy," Hagler said.

Some of the most common STDs, including chlamydia, herpes, and HIV, are asymptomatic and many others are asymptomatic in women. When symptoms like rashes or discharges
appear, most people shrug them off. Women's organizations rec-
ommend asking for a routine annual screening because the
"Don't ask, don't tell" approach leaves many women exposed to
long-term damage. "I had never been sexually active before my
ex-husband, so STDs were the furthest thing from my mind,"
said a thirty-seven year old policy analyst from Phoenix who now
has the strain of human papillomavirus that causes cervical cancer. "It never occurred to me that his past would come back to
haunt me."

Women are haunted not only by their partner's pasts, but by
their present behavior as well. The 2005 National Center for
Health Statistics study of American sexual behavior found that
while 63 percent of male heterosexuals ages 15 to 44 were in

monogamous, faithful relationships, 18 percent had two or more partners in the previous year.

Men also need to protect themselves. Sixty-eight percent of single women 15 to 44 years old are in an exclusive monogamous relationship, but 15 percent have had multiple partners in the past year. When an older male acquaintance of mine in Phoenix started dating again at the end of his twenty-nine year marriage, he ended a promising relationship with an attractive woman who refused to test before they became intimate. Although she'd had other partners, she relied on her crystals for advice on their suitability and health. "I'm sorry," he told her, "but at my age you have to do everything you can to preserve your health!" The typical male has as little information about STDs as his partner. The number one question in a recent national poll of men—ahead of "How can I avoid getting bald?" and "How can I make my penis larger?"—was "How can I tell if I have an STD?"

More than half of all U.S. adults do not know their HIV status. Although it is possible to get a free HIV test, 41 percent of people diagnosed with AIDS did not get tested until they became sick, either at the same time as their AIDS diagnosis or within the year before it. This means that they had at least seven years to infect their partners.

THE HOMOSEXUAL DEMOGRAPHIC

Tom Donahue's face looms over U.S. route 220 near Lock Haven, Pennsylvania from a large roadside billboard. "My name is Tom," the billboard reads. "I'm 25 years old. I'm HIV positive. And I live in your neighborhood, JUST LIKE HIV. Have you been tested recently?" Tom, the founder of Who's Positive, was infected four years ago in what he describes as "one moment of passion, of intimacy, of irresponsibility," a moment that "not only changed my life, but changed the lives of so many people" and one that "could take me to my grave."

Although the demographics of AIDS is changing quickly, the Americans still most at risk are young homosexuals and men on the down low, men who do not identify themselves as homosexuals but have sex with men. Tom is gay, was infected through a random online hookup, and learned he was HIV positive during a routine college physical. He is open about his homosexuality but knows many men on the down low who aren't. "A lot of jocks do this," Tom says. "They may come from a rural home or a rural community, and they come into a very diverse community such as Penn State. They may have a girlfriend back home. I think it's prevalent in all communities."

The religious right claims that homophobia is growing in the United States, but public polls show that attitudes toward homosexuality have loosened considerably over the past thirty years and that Americans have become better informed about sexual preference. In 1977, 43 percent of Americans agreed that homosexual relations between consenting adults should be legal. By 2001, when Gallup conducted the most recent national poll on the subject, that number had increased to 54 percent.

For the first time in 2001, as many Americans interviewed by Gallup said homosexuality is genetically determined as said it is environmentally determined. In 1977, four times as many people believed that environment was the main determinant. Why is that important? Simple. If you believe that homosexuality is environmentally determined, then you believe that it is a choice, a learned behavior, and that you can "cure" homosexuals with information and training. If you believe that sexual preference is genetically determined, then you believe it is innate from birth and that homosexuals have as much of a right to express their innate qualities as heterosexuals.

Tom says that he "knew I was gay from the age of thirteen, but never acted on it because I couldn't be gay living in a home with a father who was an Army sergeant major and a grandfather who was very old school. I never even thought of acting on it. In the rural town where I lived, there were no openly gay people or gay people my age. My father and my family were always very heterosexual, and you just never talked about anything gay. I always wondered why I felt differently when I was growing up. But I had pursued a heterosexual lifestyle until I had the opportunity to get away from the influences that prevented me from becoming who I was.

"When I started to come out, I'd been living in New Jersey for a while. Somebody I met said 'Oh, this is the gay bar where my friends hang out.' Before I tried it, I went online to see what it was like. I would go on with 'Bicurious' as my screen name and go into gay chat rooms or answer personal ads. One day I drove to that bar. I thought I would sit in the parking lot and then drive away, but I walked in. The bartender handed me a beer and said, 'Here you go, honey.' I was scared, wondering 'Do I belong here?' Then I walked around a corner—it was a bar for older gays—and there were a bunch of gay guys around a piano singing songs, and I'm like, 'Hmm, I kinda like this.' I went to a gay club every weekend and felt comfortable shooting pool. I started to get to know other gay people, and that's how it evolved."

Tom's mother, Cathy, believes that Tom made a choice to be gay, and hopes he will change "because it's not something a parent, especially a mother, wants for a child. I would have liked to have seen Tommy grow up, find a wonderful girl to marry, and have a bunch of kids so I could have grandchildren." Tom's father stopped speaking to him for a year when he learned Tom was gay. Although Cathy supports Tom strongly and has hosted Tom and his partner for dinner, she nurses the hope that he'll come around. "I'm not ashamed to say that I pray to the dear Lord every night that somehow he might change Tommy's life around. That maybe he would decide that this isn't what he really wanted.

"Discovering the fact that he was gay to begin with was hard enough for me to accept," Cathy said, "but when he told his father and I that he was HIV positive, it nearly destroyed me. Tommy called me and he told me that he had just come from the doctor, and the results weren't good. Then he just came out point blank and told me he was diagnosed HIV positive." Cathy went to see him two weeks later. "Tom cried, I cried. He screamed, I screamed. I did most of the screaming. One thing I'd always told both of my children was that 'if you're going to play, you need to protect yourself.'"

Tom's father is still a little distant, but Tom's mother and sister remain close to him, telephoning frequently to check on his CD-4 count. CD-4 cells (also called T-helper cells) are a type of white blood cell that fights infection, and their number declines as the HIV disease progresses. HIV positive people have periodic blood tests to count the number of these cells, an indicator used in combination with other tests to determine treatment needs. This is a different test from the one used to tell if you are HIV positive, which only detects antibodies to HIV in your blood.

Tom's mother researched HIV/AIDS online as a way to cope with her son's status. "I have been having a very difficult time trying to live with the fact that I could be losing my son at a very early age. I try not to think about it for my own sanity's sake, but I know that eventually it's going to happen, and when it does, I don't really know how I'm going to handle all of this. But like anything else in life, you play with what you're dealt and go on."

Tom frequently speaks to young people about HIV/AIDS. "I was only at one of his presentations," Cathy says. "Tommy knew I was there, but I pretended I was just another person. He said something to the effect of 'I see that some of you folks are older here, not students. How would you feel if your child were diagnosed with HIV?' I raised my hand and he said, 'Yes, ma'am.' I said, 'You want to know how I personally would feel?' He said, 'Yes, ma'am.' I said, 'Scared.' He said, 'What do you mean by scared?' And I said, 'Scared for the fact that I am going to have to bury my child at an early age.'

"I'll never forget the look on his face. He just stopped right in the middle of the auditorium. He looked at me and the tears started running down his face. He turned around to everybody in the auditorium and he said, 'This woman who just answered my question is my mother. This is the pain that I have put on my family by my stupidity and my ignorance.'"

Cathy's advice to parents of HIV-positive children is to "never give up and love them more than you ever did before, because you don't know how long you'll have them. Medicine is not an exact science. And you need to enjoy every moment that you still have in this world. This thing is so scary because you never think it would happen to you. I've thought to myself, 'Why did this happen to our family? Why did this happen to Tommy?' But I've always been a firm believer, I've grown up with the idea embedded in my mind that everything happens for a reason.

"There's been many, many times where I've sat here and cried, wondering to myself, 'Did I bring this on somehow? Should I have done things differently? Should I have watched the warning signs?'" Cathy was reassured "over and over and over again" by HIV counselors "that this was not my decision for Tommy and I shouldn't let it make me feel that it is. Yet, as a mother I can't help but somehow feel that way. We're not supposed to question why. But we are human, and we can't help but question why. There is a reason for everything that happens to us. We take those reasons and we try to put them in perspective, and we just go on with them. You usually learn why later on. They happen for good reasons."

Human sexuality expert Anne Fausto-Sterling says that "the presumption that most people are heterosexual and the idea that heterosexuality and homosexuality represent sharply distinct behaviors seem reasonable to most of us. But human behavior is far more complex than that." In the United States, new research is verifying much of what Alfred Kinsey discovered in his pioneering research in the 1940s. In 1948, Kinsey researchers discovered "a continuum of sexuality," on which hetero- and homosexual behavior could be placed. In their national survey, 37 percent of the men and 13 percent of the women reported overt homosexual experiences to orgasm. Most occurred during adolescence, but 10 percent of the males and 8 percent of females had "more than incidental homosexual experiences" for at least three years of their lives. Four percent of males and 3 percent of females remained exclusively homosexual after the onset of adolescence.

Anti-Kinsey lecturer Colonel Ronald Ray says that the United States "lost the most important war of the twentieth century" when it lost what he calls "the war against the sexual revolution." In a recent newsletter his abstinence education group Why KNOW? compared the publication of *The Kinsey Report* in 1948 to the 9/11 attacks, saying that it created cultural terrorism.

But blaming changes in sexual behavior in America over the past fifty years on Alfred Kinsey is blaming the messenger; differences in sexual preference and behavior already existed. Kinsey and his team documented them and brought them into public discussion. The newly released survey of American sexuality released by the National Center for Health Statistics in September 2005 shows that these figures have not changed much since Kinsey first measured them. In the latest survey, 6 percent of men and 11 percent of females ages 15 to 44 reported having at least one same-sex contact in their lifetime.

Kinsey found that Americans of the late 1940s were adventuresome in certain aspects of their sexuality but conservative in others. Some 70 percent of American couples he interviewed had never tried anything other than the "missionary position" for intercourse. In the same year, American anthropologist Clyde Kluckholm found that this position was customary or preferred in only 17 of the 131 societies for which he could find evidence. However, the Kinsey researchers also found that 8 percent of American males and 3.6 percent of females had sex with animals sometime in their lives, including half of all men living in rural areas. In the 1970s, the overall proportion had dropped to 5 percent as more farms disappeared, but proponents claim that interest is again on the rise in urban populations.

The Kinsey Report went through nine printings in the first year and a half after publication. While the public was hungry to know more about a taboo subject, their doctors felt differently. In 1954, the American Medical Association accused Kinsey of instigating "a wave of sex hysteria," and a conservative Congress accused him of causing "the depravity of a whole generation" and increasing juvenile delinquency. Pressured by the House committee that controlled tax-exempt status, the Rockefeller Foundation withdrew its support of Kinsey's work and he died in 1956, crushed by the vilification of his work.

In the early 1990s, Congress withdrew funding for the first national study of sexual behavior in the United States since Kinsey's, even though the National Research Council warned in 1989 that "we don't know enough to win the war against sexually transmitted diseases, including AIDS." It argued that we have to know more about behavior and the relationship between sex and drug and alcohol use, especially among teens. Its projects were just starting when funding was squelched.

The National Institute of Child Health and Development awarded a contract for a Kinsey update to Edward Laumann, dean of the Division of Social Sciences at the University of Chicago, who planned to study the influence of sexual networks on behavior. He argued that the information gained from the study would be instrumental in understanding the spread of sexually transmitted diseases in different age groups, but when U.S. Senator Jesse Helms, a notoriously conservative Republican from North Carolina, learned about it, funding was immediately withdrawn.

Helms also pulled funding from a survey of teens and their parents by the University of North Carolina's Population Center one year after it had been initiated so the money could be put into organizations that encouraged premarital celibacy. These surveys were canceled even though they were supported by a broad cross-section of the American scientific community. Detractors said they were part of a conspiracy by homosexuals in the Department of Health and Human Services who want to legitimize homosexuality. "As long as I stand on the floor of the U.S. Senate," Helms said, "I am never going to yield to that sort of thing because it is not just another lifestyle, it is sodomy."

Since the introduction of abstinence-only sex education in 1998, many American teens have begun practicing the very behavior Helms condemned out of fear, ignorance, and the desire to be "abstinent." Anal sex has become more common in the United States because of the concern for "abstinence" among teens of all sexual preferences. It is a common homo- and heterosexual practice in many cultures, including our own. The 2005 National Center for Health Statistics found that by age fifteen, 4.6 percent of males reported having anal sex with a female. The proportion jumped to 34 percent by age twenty-four. For females, the proportion who have had anal sex with a male increased from 2.4 percent at age fifteen to 32 percent by age twenty-four. By age 44, the percentages rise to 40 for men and 35 for women.

It is especially unfortunate that teens of all stripes are being pushed into this practice by their schools' and communities' single-minded dedication to abstinence-only education, because it is the most risky sexual behavior for transmitting HIV/AIDS. According to a 2005 Centers for Disease Control estimate, the probability of HIV infection for the receptive partner in a single act of anal sex is five times higher than vaginal sex and fifty times higher than oral sex.

Updated information on changing sexual practices allows us to become more practical about our approaches to HIV prevention.

Thanks to Kinsey, popular publications on sexuality, and frank talk about sex in the media, Americans' notoriously puritanical and hypocritical attitudes toward sex are slipping away and practices are changing quickly, especially among young people. Tolerance has led to a wider acceptance of gays in all walks of life. "Who they are as a person," said one student interviewed in a 2001 survey, "is more important than who they sleep with or love."

The majority of Americans do not oppose hiring gays and lesbians to work as clergy or elementary school teachers, and 80 percent think that equal opportunity protections in the workplace should be extended to homosexuals. In 2001, 53 percent of the Americans polled by Barna Research, an evangelical Christian polling company, said that they do not believe the Bible condemns all forms of homosexual behavior. Barna found that one-quarter of people describing themselves as born-again Christians think that homosexuality is acceptable, but that 95 percent of Christian fundamentalists firmly disagree.

While social acceptance of gays and lesbians continues to expand, cases of violent homophobia from the Christian Right still hit the airways from time to time. In 1998, Pat Robertson likened gays to Nazis. The aging preacher declared that gays want to "destroy" Christians and that "the acceptance of homosexuality is the last step in the decline of Gentile civilization." The Family Research Council claims that gays are pedophiles, Satan worshippers, hurt families and communities, and embrace a culture of death. The American Family Association has claimed that gays support pedophilia, incest, and bestiality, and give children AIDS.

Attacks like these are now prohibited by hate crime legislation in many parts of the country because they encourage the minority of Americans with homophobic tendencies to persecute gays. In 2001, Human Rights Watch, a highly-respected international advocacy group, interviewed 140 young people and 130 teachers in seven states (California, Georgia, Kansas, Massachusetts, New York, Texas, and Utah) and documented systematic violations of the rights of children with other than heterosexual identities.

While students who are openly gay incur harassment, abuse, and violence, teachers and school administrators ignore their requests for help, refuse to take reports of harassment or condemn it, and do not hold the aggressors responsible for their attacks. Worse, some school officials encourage or participate in attacks, taunt and condemn gay teens for not being "normal," and justify their inaction by arguing that students who "insist" on being gay must "get used to it."

Many gay students interviewed by Human Rights Watch thought that their fellow students were more accepting of their choices than the adult professionals who were supposed to be protecting them. Nine of ten high school seniors surveyed in 2001 by Zagby International and Hamilton College think homosexuals should be able to serve in the military, and 85 percent think that lesbians and gays should be accepted by society. Eighty percent supported same-sex marriage, although many said that it was opposed by their churches.

An increasing proportion of first-year college students (58 percent in 2001) support same sex-marriage. Mike Haley, gender and youth analyst at the fundamentalist Christian agency Focus on the Family complained that "the gays have used a 'tolerance' message to push this through, rather than a truthful message. The problem is, we have kids who are tolerant of everything."

Young people tend to be much more liberal in their opinions than their elders, possibly because they know more gays. The 2001 Human Rights Watch study found that "despite what some adults may want to believe, lesbian, gay, bisexual, and transgender youth are everywhere—growing up in rural communities, in small towns, in suburbs, in immigrant communities, in communities of color, in inner cities, in religious communities, and on the streets."

In 1996, the National Longitudinal Study of Adolescent Health found that 6 percent of all young people hold these sexual identities. The 2005 CDC/National Center for Health Statistics survey found that among 18 and 19 year olds, 3 percent of males and 8.3 percent of females identified themselves as homosexual or bisexual. As many as 2 million school-age children in the

United States "are dealing with issues related to their gender orientation," says Human Rights Watch. A 1996 study found that while both girls and boys begin to identify themselves as lesbian or gay by age sixteen, both are aware of same-sex attraction much earlier.

The association of homosexuality and AIDS is still remarkably strong among Americans even though the epidemic's "demographics" are changing rapidly. The Christian Right sustains the myth to promote hatred of gays, a position supported by U.S.-government funded abstinence-only sex education curricula. Homophobia has a number of negative effects. First, it increases fear of persecution among gays, drives them underground, and makes them suspicious of official pronouncements on any subject, including efforts to promote safe sex. Second, it sustains the link of HIV/AIDS with homosexuality, making other Americans feel complacent about their own risky behavior because they do not identify themselves as gay. Third, because gays are still stigmatized, men who have sex with men but do not identify themselves as homosexuals or bisexuals think the prevention messages are not for them.

The Christian Right's campaign to turn society against homosexuals sustained a major blow from the U.S. Supreme Court in 2003. On June 26, the Court ruled 6 to 3 in *Lawrence v. Texas* that the Fourteenth Amendment right to privacy protects consensual adult sexual intimacy in the home. The Court declared that the Texas "homosexual conduct" law was unconstitutional, overturning an earlier Supreme Court decision upholding state laws making homosexual sex a criminal offense.

John Lawrence and codefendant Tyron Garner argued that they deserved equal protection and that Texas law was unconstitutional because it prohibited sodomy for same-sex couples but not for heterosexual couples. The Court agreed and also noted that Texas's homosexual law "furthers no legitimate state interest which can justify its intrusion into the personal and private life of the individual." Jay Alan Sekulow of the American Center for Law and Justice wrote that the decision "was a drastic rewrite" that calls into question other legal limitations on homosexual rights. In deciding that homosexuals be given the same marriage rights as heterosexuals, for example, the Massachusetts Supreme Judicial Court cited *Lawrence v. Texas.*

Tom Donahue recognizes that homosexuals and heterosexuals who do not practice safe sex both face the risk of HIV transmission, although heterosexuals tend to be more complacent about the dangers. On his website, www.whospositive.org, he tells the story of how he was infected and how HIV has affected his family, and by sharing the real-life stories of other young people living with AIDS, he tries to "humanize HIV." In the short year and a half since he started Who's Positive, more than 100,000 people in more than thirty countries have contacted his website, and he's reached more than 35,000 people through speaking engagements at high schools, colleges, and universities. Tom urges everyone who comes to his website or attends his live educational programs to act responsibly in their sexual relationships.

"Beyond affecting anybody who hears or reads my story, HIV's affected my mom and my dad and my sister and my grandparents, and one day when my nieces and nephews are old enough to understand, it will affect their lives. It's impacted the lives of my roommates, the life of my partner at the time, and the lives of other partners I've been with. Imagine looking at your partner," Tom says, "somebody you love or who you are with, and saying 'Hey, honey, I'm about to tell you news that may change your life forever.' This person may be responsible for infecting you, or you could have infected them."

The story of Tom's organization and his HIV infection are closely intertwined. "When I found on October 13 of 2003 that I was HIV positive," he told me, "I started to tell the people I needed to tell, and it started to get out. I was working as an associate editor for a construction trades publication. Things were going well. I was very happy with my partner. Life for a while had finally started to simmer down just a little bit, and I felt very comfortable with my partner. We'd been together for several months. It was certainly a developing relationship, but it was a relationship that I had a lot of faith in.

"On World AIDS Day, 2003, which is December 1 each year, I went to an event at Penn State University where they had pieces of the AIDS Quilt lying on the floor. I walked around them and I thought about all the legacies and memories that people have left behind for others. Their families put this collage of pictures, stories, and poems together for somebody like me to read. That's part of humanizing HIV, and it's so powerful because you are thinking about the real person within that quilt who has either been infected or affected by HIV.

"As I stood there, I wondered, 'What is someone going to write on my piece of the quilt one day?' That's when I realized I had an opportunity to make a difference in people's lives. I went up to the facilitator and said, 'Look. I just found out a month and a half ago that I was HIV positive, and I would like to speak.' They put me on the program and when they called my name I sat on the edge of the stage.

"I just told my story. I said, 'My name is Tom Donahue and a month and a half ago I found out I'm HIV positive.' I popped down off the stage and I walked among the audience telling the story of what it was like that October day to find out I was positive, to tell my partner and tell my family. People were spreading the word, and everyone knew about it but nobody would come to me. So, if people already know about it, why not be open about it? At least I can correct a lot of the rumors that were already going around. After I was done, the response was amazing. People came up and gave me hugs and encouragement.

"That's what started Who's Positive. I sat among a group of students in the audience, and nobody knew or could tell that I was HIV positive until I stood up to say that I was." Tom's used that format in his educational programs ever since. "You don't know who is positive. I'm a little overweight, I'm young, and nobody would ever know I'm HIV positive. More importantly, I would never have known that I was HIV positive unless I'd gotten routine testing. I had just moved to State College and I had a full-time job that gave me the benefits I needed to get a routine physical."

Tom's program has been rated as highly effective in helping young people realize that they are at risk and should go for testing. "I'm not saying that the HIV was a good thing for Tommy," said Cathy, "but I'm proud of what he's doing to educate other people and make them aware of the fact that people need to protect themselves in any type of relationship, no matter whether it's physical or emotional. If it takes the HIV to make him do what he's doing, then that was God's purpose for it. I'm very surprised that he has accepted this the way he has, because if it was me I don't know how I would handle something like that. I am amazed that he has the fortitude to keep going with this thing when most people would just give up."

Who's Positive has IRS status as an educational charity, but struggles to find funding for its prevention campaigns because it is swimming against the tide of federal funding guidelines. For example, although Tom acknowledges that abstinence and discipline are important, he also speaks clearly about the importance of using condoms and not having unprotected sex. Since 1998, federal funding for programs that give equal time to condoms and protection has dried up. Tom may also be facing discrimination because of his sexual preference.

Tom's grandfather, eighty-one, strongly disapproves of Tom's homosexuality, although they visit and speak on the telephone. "I know that my father is somewhat afraid to be near Tommy because he's afraid he'll catch something," Cathy says. "Those myths are out there and people need to be educated. There's a lot of ignorance all over the world, and people need to understand that this isn't just a gay disease. Look at poor Ryan White. There was a twelve-year-old child who contracted HIV from a blood transfusion. I think that the world's population needs to be educated much, much more. People are afraid. They don't understand. For instance, you can't get HIV from hugging someone, or sitting on the same toilet seat they just sat on, or eating from a dish or a cup."

Tom says that most Americans do not realize that HIV can happen to them. "I was raised in a small rural town in central

Pennsylvania where the only thing I remembered about HIV and AIDS was seeing pictures of lesions on people, never somebody my own age battling with HIV." He also finds that many young people are not concerned because they think antiretrovirals can cure AIDS. "A lot of people say, 'Oh, I'll get it, that's okay'—but what about people around you that are going to find out that you have it and have to think about the consequences also?"

Writing for the *New Yorker*, Michael Specter says, "After years of living in constant fear of AIDS, many gay men have chosen to resume sexual practices that are almost guaranteed to make them sick." Gay men have accounted for most of the 400 percent rise in syphilis in New York City over the past five years, Specter says. "Perhaps for the first time since the beginning of the AIDS epidemic, the number of men who say they use condoms regularly is below 50 percent; after many years of decline, the number of new HIV diagnoses among gay men increased every year between 2000 and 2003."

"Look at the statistics closely," he continues, "and you will almost certainly find the drug"—crystal methamphetamine, and you will find the Internet. While Tom says that he's not part of the drug scene, he admits that "the online community is a very dangerous tool when it comes to sexually transmitted infections. People who have a need can go online and within twenty minutes be able to satisfy that need. Gay.com is the conduit through which I hooked up with the individual who infected me. Older people and straight people are also making use of the web to find new partners. There's hookup sites for escorting or websites intended for people who are traveling. Gay.com has a chat room for every city or state that you're in. There's a lot of AOL chat rooms where straight people can do the same thing," he added.

He says that he thinks it's probably true that young gay men see HIV as a badge of courage. "I think that a lot of people don't even get tested because they automatically assume that they're HIV positive and that it's not a big deal, but what they don't understand is that this is going to affect their health. Some people are very careful about it, but others say, 'Well, you know, I've already had bare-back sex, and I'm probably already positive, so it doesn't really matter.'

"People aren't getting tested and they don't know their status. People must understand the importance of knowing their status and letting other people know." Tom believes that many young people simply want the thrill of a sexual encounter, but for others, sex can mean "just having a person touch you, just having somebody there, to hold you. To pleasure somebody and have that person be pleasured. I think there's a certain level of humanness here. We all have our moments. In other cases there's something missing in relationships. People may be afraid of commitment, may be afraid of just having a relationship, or else they enjoy the lifestyle of being able to go out to a bar and hook up with somebody if they want."

Tom believes that no matter what our gender, age, or sexual preference is, each of us must take steps to protect ourselves. "A lot of people ask me if I'm mad at the person who infected me," Tom says. "I'm not, actually, because I think it's everyone's responsibility to protect themselves. He came up to me and I give him a lot of credit for it. He said that he didn't know he was infected at the time he infected me. How sad this was, because I didn't even remember who he was when he came up to me. I'm not mad at him. First of all, he's going through the exact same thing as I am. Second of all, it was my responsibility to protect myself. Could I be upset with him? Sure. But ultimately it's my responsibility to make my health my own priority."

When Tom speaks, he warns his audience that the moment of passion and irresponsibility could strike them too. "One of the stories I share is that my parents, who were married for twenty-nine years, got a divorce because my mom over several years had been cheating on my dad. So no matter how long a relationship you have been in, no matter if it's two minutes, two days, two years, or thirty years like my parents, if you're sexually active, you're at risk because you really don't know what your partner's doing when you're at work. You think that there's a certain level of trust, but you also have to keep in the back of your mind 'What if . . . ' I think there's always a certain level of need. For instance, my mom's need was that my dad was hardly ever home."

Cathy says that "Tommy knew probably for the last ten or fifteen years that the relationship between me and his father was going downhill. He knew it, and he would get very upset when his dad was away for weeks and months at a time. Tommy knew I was working a full time job, trying to take care of a big fourteen-room house, and trying to take care of both of the kids.

"I raised both him and his sister most of the time by myself. His father was on the road most of Tommy and his sister's life. My husband was an authoritarian. He was very strict with the kids. He wouldn't allow them to grow up just like normal teenagers would. He ran his home like he did his soldiers. I was married to him for twenty-nine and a half years, and that's basically why I just decided I had enough. I couldn't deal with it anymore."

Cathy met a man who was more attentive and eventually decided to divorce. "Although I don't agree with her actions," Tom said, "I don't think that it's fair to criticize her for the way she chose to live her life. In return, I expect the same respect, that she shouldn't criticize me for the way I live my life. I think it's important, especially since now that I found out I'm HIV positive, that I keep a close relationship with all of my family."

Neither Tom nor his mother ever mentioned a critical factor in the upsurge of HIV among gay men: the introduction of abstinence-only education in 1998. AIDS is growing fastest among young gay men under the age of twenty-four, who are the first cohort of teens denied comprehensive sex education in their schools. Tom is right that personal responsibility is important, but when schools fail to live up to their responsibility to provide comprehensive education to teens, it is no surprise that many more young homosexual men are practicing unprotected anal sex and becoming infected.

TEEN SEX AND ABSTINENCE

While Paige and Tom represent opposite poles of sexual choice in the United States, they are alike in a very important respect: they are members of the first generation of young people in our country to be subject to abstinence-only education in their high schools. Both learned that "safe sex" meant no sex at all, at least until marriage makes it okay. If Tom is the "poster boy" for the awful impact that abstinence-only education in the United States is having on young gay men, Paige is the poster girl for straight young women.

In the age of HIV/AIDS, abstinence-only education is not just a poorly conceived experiment in public policy, it is a disaster that is already having severe effects on teen health and safety. HIV infections are increasing fastest in 18- to 24-year-olds, and nearly 60 percent of these are sex-related. Since teens are not taught realistic information about how to protect themselves, the number of infections will continue to grow over the coming years unless we come to our senses and help our children learn how to protect themselves. The HIV rate for American teens is already five times that of German adolescents. We are now reaping what we sowed with this first generation of abstinence-only teens left ignorant by their school systems, and we are likely to reap what we've sown for many years to come.

Paige and Tom are but two of the millions of American children who were taught when they are at their youngest and most vulnerable that condoms are not effective against HIV. In fact, condoms are the only sure protection against all STDs for people who have sex. The people teens trust teach them nothing at all about the dangers they face in sexual experimentation, so they learn what they can from TV, the Internet, the library, and/or their friends.

U.S. Planned Parenthood argues that the Christian Right has been central to promoting the policy of abstinence-only education. Their white paper on adolescent sexuality says that "one of the most misguided and destructive messages that endangers adolescent health and life during this age of AIDS emanates from a vocal minority bent on suppressing or willfully ignoring the truth about sexual activity among adolescents in America. Under the guise of protecting our youth, they declare, inaccurately, that premarital sex among adolescents is a relatively new and corrupt social phenomenon.

"They are not content to teach that society should tolerate no sexual activity among adolescents," Planned Parenthood continues. "They say that if *any* sexuality education is to be offered at all in public schools, the only acceptable curriculum is one that not only endorses abstinence only and the postponing of sexual activity until marriage but also actively *withholds* information on how to prevent pregnancy and sexually transmitted infections."

Like so many other young people in the United States who are now becoming infected with HIV, Paige and Tom learned the hard way that sexually transmitted diseases play for keeps. Few realize that sexually transmitted diseases, including herpes, chlamydia, hepatitis, gonorrhea, trichomoniasis, and syphilis as well as HIV can be transmitted by oral and anal as well as vaginal intercourse, and that unprotected anal sex is especially dangerous.

New data from the National Center for Health Statistics shows that one in three boys and one in four girls in the United States have had oral sex by age 15, increasing to 70 percent by age 19 for both boys and girls. This should not surprise us, because the practice is very common in our culture. By age forty-four, 90 percent of men and 88 percent of women have given or received oral sex, a proportion that increased only slightly from when it was measured ten years earlier. Anal sex is being tried by more Americans, and whites are more likely to have had both experiences than either blacks or Hispanics.

The proportion of teens and young adults experimenting with oral and anal sex appear to have increased over prior surveys, although researchers say that the evidence is hard to interpret. What may be surprising to adults is that teens are adopting both practices at a very early age as a way of avoiding pregnancy and that girls are just as likely to get as to give oral sex.

Thanks to abstinence-only education, a whole generation of U.S. teens is threatened with HIV infection. In fact, research shows that the situation of "abstinent" teens is even worse than those who make no claims about their "purity." A 2004 study of 12,000 teens by Yale and Columbia Universities found that adolescents who pledged to remain virgins until marriage are four times more likely to take chances with anal sex than those who do not and are also less likely to use condoms.

The threat to our children can be easily contained. Study after study has shown that comprehensive sexual education has a positive effect on slowing teens' entry into the world of sex and ensuring that they take care of themselves when they do. The National Survey of Family Growth, which interviewed 1,280 teen girls between fifteen and nineteen, found that adolescents using birth control were no more sexually active than nonusers and were more likely to use protection when they had sex.

Perhaps the saddest footnote in the outrageous history of abstinence education in the United States is that the teen pregnancy rates and teen sexual activity were going down during the 1990s, thanks to comprehensive sexual education. Both pregnancy and reported sexual activity rates, used by public health officials as proxy indicators for safe sex behavior because STD rates are so hard to measure, were declining because teens were using condoms and were beginning to delay the start of their sexual lives.

Abstinence-only education began to have its effects in the late 1990s, when Paige was still in high school. Thanks to the misinformation handed out by these campaigns, a large number of the many American teens and young adults who have sex rarely protected themselves from pregnancy or infection. "When I was growing up," Paige said, "I had no idea about HIV/AIDS. I was just doing the same things everybody else does. You don't hear about it in Montana, you don't think about it. It only happens in the big cities, it only happens to minorities and gay men. I had a lot of ignorance about it."

Many teen coming-of-age behaviors put them at risk of HIV infection. More than 5 million U.S. teens—23 percent in a 2002 survey—said they had unprotected sex because of alcohol or drug abuse, cross-over behavior that contributes to rapid HIV spread. By the age of twenty-one, one in every five teens has received treatment for an STD. The direct medical costs of STDs for fifteen- to twenty-four-year-olds was $6.5 billion in 2000 alone.

More troubling, however, is that most teens go without treatment because they were never taught about STDs or their symptoms. Seven of ten sexually active teens has never been tested for any STD, although many are infected. Of the 12 million STD infections including HIV that occur each year in the United States, 8 million are in people under the age of 25. Almost half of sexually active teens say that neither they nor their partner used a condom during their last intercourse.

Young Americans are having sex at increasingly younger ages and have more partners by the time they reach twenty than their parents dreamed of in a lifetime. The University of Minnesota's Center for Adolescent Health and Development reports that 34 percent of ninth graders in the United States have had sexual intercourse. One in twelve had sex before they were thirteen years old. A national Centers for Disease Control (CDC) survey shows that almost half of all high school students had had sexual intercourse, and 16 percent had already had four or more partners before they got their diplomas. The average sixteen- to twenty-year-old has already had five partners, gaining ground quickly on twenty-five- to thirty-four-year-olds with eight partners and those over forty-five who report an average of nine.

Abstinence-only education tells teens not to have intercourse, but most do not think that oral or anal sex is intercourse. Teens believe that oral and anal sex are safer than vaginal intercourse, help them avoid pregnancy and STDs, and are more acceptable to their peers. A seventeen-year old girl who has had seven partners says that pregnancy is a more immediate concern than HIV, although "the anxiety [about AIDS] never leaves me. But I still have sex. And I know I can always get oral sex without getting too emotionally involved."

A report in the April 2005 issue of *Pediatrics* says that one in five ninth graders has had oral sex and one-third intend to try it in the next six months. To many young people, especially those from middle- and upper-income white families, oral sex is not as significant as it was to their parents' generation. Claire Brindis, a University of California-San Francisco pediatrics professor, says that to teens, "oral sex is far less intimate than intercourse. It's a different kind of relationship." Because more than half of American teen boys and girls have had the experience by age 19, it's become "a major social norm. It's part of kids' lives." Bill Albert of the National Campaign to Prevent Teen Pregnancy, says that "We used to talk about sex in terms of first base, second base, and so on. Oral sex maybe the dugout."

Paige's sister Lauren, who is fifteen, estimates that "of the kids my age, probably between 25 and 50 percent are having sex. Over 50 percent if you include oral sex because kids say 'I'm still a virgin.' I ask them why 'sex' is in the word 'oral sex' if that is true. Some say 'I'm a virgin still because I didn't orgasm.' Well, even people who have sex over and over, most of them don't. And they say, 'It only lasts five minutes.' It doesn't matter."

When I asked the counselor who administered my HIV test if the kids in my town were sexually active, she snorted with laughter. "Are you kidding? You got twelve- and thirteen-year olds doing oral and anal sex in the bathrooms, in the closets between periods at school. They don't think it's sex because you don't lose your virginity." My husband scoffed too. He said, "Just last week, when I was playing music in Saratoga and I came out on a break, there were two teenage girls going at it right in the parking lot. One had her hand up the other one's skirt, and they were going at it."

Lauren and many other teens around the country are campaigning for better sex education in schools. She told me that students who challenge false facts in abstinence-only curricula have been penalized and punished by their schools. A local teen who's working with Planned Parenthood as a peer education volunteer told me that her biology teacher let her teach the sex education unit to her class after she proved that many of the assertions in the federally funded abstinence-only curriculum were wrong.

Lauren says, "A lot of my friends come up to me privately and ask me for information. Young people really don't know anything about sex except the obvious. That's really the most sad thing. They go into it and think, 'It won't happen to me,' so they go and have sex because they want to be like everybody else or for their own personal reasons, like to make someone mad. I think that having personal reasons not to do it work better than a parent telling you, 'You shouldn't have sex or I'll get so mad at you.' That will make them want to go have sex.

"One of my personal reasons is that it happened to my sister. She went and had sex because she wasn't thinking and she said 'It's not going to happen to me,' and it did. She got pregnant when she was seventeen, so that also happened to her. She said that wasn't going to happen. It did. She got HIV. People don't know when they're young. People don't pay attention to it."

Without appropriate sex education, only 10 percent of the teens who have contracted HIV are tested. Paige was lucky to find out when she did. "I'd only been infected for three months before I found out," she told me. "I didn't know about partner notification, so I took it on myself to tell people. My previous boyfriend was negative, and the other people I had notified were too."

Paige says that her relationship with Damien (not his real name) was casual, "and after we split up he started dating one of my best friends. I told her and she went and got tested. He refused. He said he was tested a couple months before and he was fine. Her first test came back negative, but when she went back about six months later, outside of the window period, her test was positive." Her friend had had no other sexual partners in the interim. "So we found out who infected us," Paige says. "I believe Damien infected five or six other girls in town.

"I live in a fairly small town, so people like him stand out. He was the flashy guy. He looked healthy, he was good-looking. He was about six foot, nice build, a nice caramel color, clear complexion, really nice eyes, he had his hair shaved, he was always very well kept, no earrings, no flashy jewelry. He looked like a college type. He was black, and in Montana there aren't very many black men. I think he was from Arizona. He was seven years older than I am."

Paige's casual relationship with Damien is typical of the relationships of many young Americans. U.S. teens, like three-quarters of young women in all developed countries, become sexually active before they are twenty. But they are more likely to have sexual intercourse before age fifteen, and since they have shorter and more sporadic relationships than teens in Canada, France, Great Britain, and Sweden, they are more likely to have more than one partner in any given year.

U.S. teen pregnancy, childbearing, and abortion rates are higher than those in any other developed country because our teens have lower overall contraceptive access and use. Societies with lower levels of adolescent pregnancy and childbearing have greater societal acceptance of teen relationships. They provide balanced information about sexuality and clear expectations of commitment and responsibility for prevention of pregnancy and STDs.

While the Christian Right tries to portray teen sex as an aberrant, deviant, and very modern phenomenon, research shows that premarital intercourse was common among American young people well before World War II. As the age of puberty fell from 16.5 in 1840 to 12.8 in the early 1990s, sexual interest began at progressively earlier ages. As the age of marriage goes up—it is now twenty-five—the teen who wants to remain abstinent now has a much longer wait between puberty, at age twelve or thirteen, and marriage.

For teenagers, sex is more than a way to satisfy raging hormones. It is part of broader exploration of the world and a way to separate from their families and form new social bonds that may require rebellious and even destructive or copycat behavior. The teenage years should be a safe time to explore, but abstinence-only education, coupled with the increase of HIV/AIDS in the United States, is making it a very dangerous time to be young.

There are other undesirable outcomes of teen sex besides STDs. One-third of teen girls become pregnant before they reach age twenty. Despite a decade of decline, the United States still has the highest rate of teen pregnancy of any developed country—more than 900,000 per year. Canada's rate is half the U.S. rate and in Germany and France, it is one-quarter. More than three-quarters of teen pregnancies are unplanned, indicating high-risk behavior, coercion, and the potential of HIV infection.

Studies show that the future prospects of teens—male or female—involved in a pregnancy decline significantly. Two-thirds are females, and they are less likely to complete school or ever earn a high school diploma. Paige is atypical in this respect because she managed to earn a General Equivalency Diploma (GED) and is planning to start college. For most teens, pregnancy is closely linked to poverty and single parenthood, and in this case Paige is no exception. The growth in single-parent families is the single largest cause of increased poverty of U.S. children over the last twenty years.

The cycle is repeated. Children of teenagers often perform poorly in school, are less likely to complete high school, and have less adequate health care. Children of adolescent parents are more likely to be neglected and abused, and many receive less adequate parenting because their mothers are still maturing emotionally. All of these factors contribute to higher rates of risky behavior, including sex, drug use, and the possibility of contracting STDs, including HIV.

Paige's family is typical of the repeating cycle. As Paige's sister Lindsay told me, "My mom got pregnant with Paige at nineteen, Paige got pregnant at seventeen. I got pregnant at eighteen." At the time they got pregnant, both Paige and Lindsay had rejected Tamara's discipline and opted to live with their father because David, busy with his work, provided little supervision. Both Paige and Lindsay wish it had been otherwise. Lindsay says that Lauren is different. "My little sister Lauren is awesome. She's actually on the right track compared to me and Paige, which is good."

Paige and Lindsay hope that while their mistakes were costly, they may help Lauren make better decisions for herself. "I think we showed her a lot, what it does to the family when you do something bad. I had her stand in the room when I had my son." Lindsay giggles. "It wasn't a very pretty sight, but I had her watch. I was hoping that might knock something into her head. Lauren wants to go to college. She's a cheerleader and a dancer. She's on the right track, and I want to help her keep it that way."

The Christian Right has been able to convince parents and school boards that abstinence-only education is a good idea by arguing that comprehensive sex education *increases* sexual behavior in teens. They discredit research findings demonstrating that sex education counteracts impulsiveness and compulsiveness. Teens armed with the facts tend to be much more responsible about their choices, initiate sex later, and use protection when they do.

Keeping disease prevention information secret when pornographic materials and explicitly erotic sex in television and films abound is nothing short of hypocritical. Research shows that teens who view sexual content on television, even if it only involves characters talking about sex, are twice as likely to start intercourse within the year. Lacking accurate and specific information from parents and school, they take no steps to protect themselves. Research also shows that the most vulnerable young girls are preyed on by much older men, who manipulate their desire for affection and do not take the responsibility to use protection. Paige's experience is sadly typical.

Paige says that she was seduced by Damien, who is actually thirteen years her senior, when she "was at a vulnerable point in my life." When she met him, "I had just got out of a really bad relationship with my ex-boyfriend. I was at the mall doing some shopping and I noticed this guy was following me in a car," she says. "I pulled over to put gas in my car, and he pulled up and we had just started talking. Damien had all the right things to say. He was like, 'Can I take you out to dinner?' and that was something that I had never had before. I had always paid for dinner. He took me to this fancy restaurant and got a limo and everything, and this was our first date. So I'm thinking, 'Wow! This guy is pretty cool.'

"I remember he said, 'I couldn't help noticing you,' and we just started talking. 'Do you have any plans for tonight? I'd really love to get to know you and take you out to dinner.' He seemed very independent. I didn't see anything wrong with him. I think part of it might have just been that I didn't *want* to see anything wrong with him. I felt like I was being respected. He was footing the bill for dinner and taking me out to all the fanciest places, so I didn't want to see any of the bad stuff. His smile seemed genuine. It seemed like he was actually happy to see me.

"But that's just kind of how I remember those things. It's been so long, and it was such a short period of time that I spent with him. It pisses me off that I spent that little time with him, but now I spend every day thinking about him. He pops up in my thoughts regardless, and I'll just get these shivers up my back. That little amount of time. Was it really worth this? The sex really wasn't even that good. It wasn't worth it. It just blows my mind, and my friend says the same thing. She was like, 'Mr. Minute Man, and it just wasn't worth it!' Five minutes of pleasure for a lifetime of pain. And the five minutes wasn't even that pleasurable. It just ticks me off."

A California study showed that teen girls who are sexually exploited by older men have nearly three-fourths of all teen births, 70 percent out of wedlock. Nationally, the overall proportion is two-thirds, 700,000 pregnancies of the 900,000 total teen pregnancies every year. The younger the girl, the older her partner is likely to be, the more likely the sex was involuntary or unwanted, and the more likely her partner is to be HIV positive.

National studies show that three-fourths of young women who had intercourse before age fourteen and two-thirds who had sex before fifteen report that the sex was involuntarily. Two-thirds of teen mothers had their sexual debut at the hands of their fathers, stepfathers, or other relatives or guardians in violent abuse or rape. Men over twenty father five times more children among junior-high-school girls than do boys their own age. Many girls in these relationships are coerced into abortions. And many are exposed to HIV and other STDs.

"He seemed to have a good explanation for where all the money came from," Paige said. "He told me he was from Arizona, and his family owned a golf course and he was going to school, that he had just sold his car and he had had some previous legal problems but it was all okay. So I just automatically assumed, 'Oh, yeah, he's telling the truth.' He's a good-looking guy, he looked very clean cut. He wore glasses and turtleneck sweaters. I didn't think he was a thug. I thought he was a cool, standup guy, and so I ended up kind of liking him."

Damien was driving a red Ford Probe when he met Paige. "He said he was driving his friend's car because he just sold his. I found out later on it was another girl's car. I think later on down the line he ended up marrying her. I haven't heard what's going on with her, but I'm pretty sure she's been infected. He told me he was going to buy a fancy car but he didn't really like driving too much. That's why he would get limos most of the time. When a guy's driving you around in a limo with money to go in the clubs and you're twenty years old, just out of a bad relationship, you're young and vulnerable and think you know everything but you don't. It could happen to anyone, and whether you think about things or not, sometimes it will just sneak up on you.

"We were seeing each other, and I didn't really like him as much as I had thought I did. Then I started noticing little things. . . . I felt like I was put on the back burner a lot, I wasn't first priority. That just irked me. I'm pretty sure he had other women. As it turns out, he did. He was seeing all these other people, and doing all these other things, and wouldn't pick up my phone calls. I figured we were just kinda messing around anyway, so I just let go and got back with my ex-boyfriend. I was the top priority with him. He didn't like going out, and he wanted to be with me at all times. I had such abandonment issues, it just seemed like that was the right thing. He said he loved me and he said he cared about me, and I believed him.

"I had a lot of resentment and a lot of anger toward Damien because he did know," Paige says. "Now I just use my anger to educate other people. As far as I'm concerned, I don't think a letter of any word that Damien spoke was true. I don't trust anyone anymore. It's just kind of difficult."

While public policymakers assume that teens like Paige make their own decisions about sex, Joe McIlhaney, a physician STD expert, says that "a substantial proportion of teenage sexual activity is more a matter of manipulation, coercion or abuse than anything else." Girls are plied with gifts, alcohol, and drugs. Even when they are having sex with partners their own age, McIlhaney says, "teens are not having 'beautiful, consensual sex' as portrayed in films and TV. They are having horrible, manipulative sex that is saturated with drugs, alcohol, and loneliness."

A 2005 national study of 10,000 women and girls found that most girls date boys closer in age, with whom they are more likely to use contraception. But even when they dated boys their own age, one-quarter of the teen girls surveyed reported repeated verbal and sexual abuse from their partners, and more than one-third knew a friend who had been hit, punched, slapped, kicked, or otherwise physically hurt by a boyfriend. Girls who grow up with both biological parents in the home are less likely to have sex than those who grow up in single-parent homes or with stepfathers.

Besides the personal costs, the social costs of unwanted teen pregnancies and exposure to STDs are also high. The fastest-growing group of homeless families in the United States is headed by young mothers who dropped out of school and had their first child when they were still teens. The cost of delivering a low-birth-weight baby, typical for a teen mother, is more than $34,000. One condom costs $.90, and oral contraceptives cost $540 a year. People living with AIDS quit work early and have annual treatment costs of more than $10,000.

Teen pregnancy rates (and by inference the rates of STDs) dropped in the United States and all developed countries in the

1990s because more young people started using contraception (most often condoms) and reduced their sexual activity. Young people are now more motivated to seek higher education and interesting employment before they start marriage. While our rates are still the highest among developed nations, between 1991 and 2002 our teen birth rates fell 19 percent, thanks to a more than fourfold increase in the use of condoms and other contraceptives among teens, a trend that started in the mid-1980s.

Progress may be short-lived, however. In 1998, federal sex-education funds were restricted to states that teach only abstinence and who refuse to acknowledge birth control as a reliable means of preventing pregnancy. It was the culmination of a long lobbying effort in both state and federal legislatures by the Christian Right, which enjoyed its first triumph in 1981. In that year, Congress passed the Adolescent Family Life Act, also called the "chastity law," which funded programs promoting "self-discipline and prudent approaches" to sex and "chastity education."

The act funneled so much money into churches and religious organizations that the American Civil Liberties Union challenged it in court for pushing Christian Right values, especially their opposition to abortion, on public school children at public expense. They argued that the law violated the separation of church and state. When the Supreme Court finally ruled on the matter twelve years later, it held that funded programs must delete any reference to religion, including the suggestion of one program that students "take Christ along as a chaperon on their dates."

Dissatisfied because many states were not using abstinence-only programs, the Christian Right forced a 1998 ruling that refused any federal sex education money to states that allowed anything else. The Christian Right influenced many state legislatures to exceed federal proscriptions by adding explicit prior restraint provisions to the abstinence-only requirement. In New Jersey, teaching materials were reviewed and teachers were subject to close surveillance. Although Utah's governor vetoed such a bill, he directed state agencies to monitor sexuality education programs, removing inappropriate language and subject matter.

The curricula developed by Christian organizations with federal funds were never subject to review or evaluation. A 2004 Congressional study found that the abstinence-only curricula used by more than two-thirds of public schools, health departments, hospitals and religious groups getting federal money contained "false, misleading, or distorted information about reproductive health." The curricula taught that condoms do not protect against STDs, that there are male and female sperm, that humans have 48 chromosomes, and that confining sex to the wedded bedroom eliminated jealousy, poverty, substance abuse, and suicide. The curricula also taught that "you can get AIDS through sweat and tears," and that "you have to perform 10 different steps to put on a condom." Not surprisingly, students educated according to these curricula were less likely to use contraception when they did have sex and less likely to seek STD testing.

The Congressional study also found that the curricula scrambled Center for Disease Control information about HIV in gay teens, telling students that half of all gay male teens are HIV positive. All the CDC actually says is that half of all male teens with HIV had sex with other men, but that half became infected in other ways. The Christian Right curricula are rampant with sexual stereotyping as well. One course teaches young people that women feel successful if they have good relationships, while men gauge their success by accomplishments outside of the home. Another says that men need admiration and sexual fulfillment, while women need conversation and financial support, adding that men are always ready for sex, while women need hours of emotional and physical preparation.

In 2004 the Bush administration widened its campaign of providing erroneous and sexist information by establishing a website called 4parents.gov, which it says "is a guide to help you and your pre-teen or mid-teen discuss important, yet difficult issues about healthy choices, abstinence, sex and relationships." According to the national Sexuality Information and Education Council (SIECUS), human rights and health groups reviewing the site were so appalled at what they found that 150 organizations asked that the U.S. Department of Health and Human Services (DHHS) immediately take it off the Internet. As a consequence, the site was modified to discuss a broader range of options for teens and to reduce the objectionable implication that only two-parent families could raise normal children. The National Organization of Women said that "site development was driven by ideology and not a commitment of government officials to ensure that the posted information is reliable."

Human Rights Watch (HRW) said that "the DHHS website censors and distorts lifesaving information about sexual health and HIV prevention. It also violates parents' and children's fundamental rights to information and health, and puts youth at risk of HIV infection and premature death." HRW said that the site claimed condoms provide only "moderate protection" from HIV and other STDs, although they are better than 90 percent effective when used correctly and the only effective means of prevention for people who have sex. The site also erroneously claimed that it is easier to prevent teens from having sex than to help them increase their contraceptive use, that the only safe sex is with a heterosexual partner in marriage, and that the effectiveness of antiretroviral drugs in prolonging the lives of people living with HIV is questionable.

"Young people have a right to know about all effective methods of HIV prevention" under international human rights guidelines, Human Rights Watch says, and have a "right to information without bias or discrimination. The government, in turn, has an obligation to refrain from censoring, withholding or intentionally misrepresenting health-related information."

Highly respected federal agencies that we trust to be scientific and objective about matters relating to our health are bending to pressure from the Bush administration. The National Institute of Health (NIH) and CDC removed information about condom and sex education effectiveness from a list of "Programs that Work" on their websites, and National Cancer Institute findings that abortion did not increase a woman's risk of breast cancer were removed from the NIH website. In a letter to Tommy Thompson, then DHHS Secretary, twelve Democratic

House members protested DHHS actions, concerned that "scientific decision making is being subverted by ideology."

A White House–appointed committee of experts sent to see what worked against HIV/AIDS in the African country of Uganda quit after the U.S. administration attempted to bribe them to say condoms did not work when their findings showed just the opposite. Bush Food and Drug Administration advisory committee appointee Dr. David Hager is an obstetrician-gynecologist who opposes abortion rights and condemns oral contraceptives as a "convenient way for young people to be sexually active outside of marriage."

Sex Respect and Teen-Aid, two of the biggest federal abstinence-only grant recipients, turned their curricula into large for-profit businesses with the backing and protection of Christian fundamentalist groups. Since 1998, more than $1 billion has gone into funding abstinence-only programs. Declaring that "I've got the will of the people at my back," Bush ignored the congressional report on the shoddiness of abstinence-only curricula and asked for another $38 million for the programs in early 2005, while at the same time cutting funding for Medicaid and HIV housing and care.

Despite the Supreme Court's ruling prohibiting use of federal money to promote religion, much of the federal funding for abstinence-only programs is being used in ways that blur the line between church and state and is being given to programs that teach patently religious material in public schools. In school-sponsored chastity rallies held on school property in California, Alabama, Pennsylvania, and other states, students are required to pledge "to God" that they will remain abstinent until they marry.

Textbooks are also being censored. Texas is now buying health textbooks that provide information on abstinence only. Three chapters were literally sliced out of a ninth-grade health textbook at the order of the school board in Franklin County, North Carolina. The chapters covered AIDS and STDs, marriage and partnering, and contraception. In Lynchburg, Virginia, the school board ordered that an illustration of a vagina be covered or cut out of a high school anatomy and physiology textbook, even though a committee of parents, teachers, and students approved the books.

Some states that have documented the ineffectiveness of abstinence-only education programs are resisting Christian Right pressure. In 2004, the Minnesota Department of Health found that these programs were contributing to an increase in sexual activity in junior high school students and doubling the number who said they planned to have sex in high school. In Ohio, three agencies called for immediate suspension of the abstinence-only programs in mid-2005. "It is more harmful for our children to go through an abstinence-only-until-marriage program than to do nothing," said Earl Pike, executive director of the AIDS Task Force of Greater Cleveland.

Parents want their children to delay sexual activity, but they also want them to know how to use birth control and practice safe sex. The Kaiser Family Foundation's national survey in 2000 found that the vast majority of American parents want broader sex education in their children's schools. Seven out of ten parents also say that students should be taught how to get tested for HIV/AIDS and other STDs, how to talk to a partner about birth control and use condoms, and how and where to get a variety of birth control devices.

The Kaiser study found that nine in ten teachers think that students should be taught about contraception, and half think it should be taught in grade seven or earlier, but that one in four cannot legally teach the subject. The vast majority think that students should be taught where to go for birth control, where to get information about abortion, the correct way to use condoms, and about sexual orientation. One in four teachers do not think they are meeting student's needs for information or that schools are doing enough to prepare students for puberty or how to deal with the pressures surrounding decisions about sexual activity.

Students want more information too. The Kaiser survey found that students wanted to know what to do in the event of a rape or sexual assault; how to get tested for HIV and other STDs; how to talk with a partner about STDs, birth control, and condoms; where to get birth control; and how to handle pressure to have sex.

Totally safe sex, as Paige's biological father, Gordon, points out, is only two things: abstinence or masturbation. He says that abstinence is "a hard row to hoe," even for a man in his forties. When I ask Tamara about abstinence-only education, she says, "I think it's a great idea, but it's unrealistic. Even as adults we know—*especially* as adults we know—the realities of sexual attraction. It's there and can be overwhelming. Someone who is mature has a challenge dealing with that. Someone who's immature, they have no clue. I think it's better to teach them prevention, let them know their options, and also give them condoms. Paige is bringing a new reality to the people in Montana, because everybody here is clueless, including myself. AIDS? HIV? What's that? That's not here! We're in Montana, for God's sake!"

There is a good reason why so many Montana residents are unaware of the threat of HIV. Anthropologist Kimber McKay, who teaches human sexuality at the University of Montana in Missoula, wanted to expose her students to abstinence-only education firsthand. She invited speakers from Sexual Abstinence and Family Education (SAFE), an organization that gets the bulk of federal money in the state for school sex education programs, to address her class. The SAFE presentation outraged and confused McKay and her students. "They say condoms aren't effective against STDs and explicitly predict that those who have premarital sex have unhappy marriages because people feel insecure when their partners have had previous experiences," McKay said.

SAFE claims that it has been responsible for the 20 percent drop in teen pregnancy rates in Montana over the past twenty years (1982 to 2002), although it has been operating for only the last five years (2000 to 2005). Stacey Anderson, the state's teen pregnancy prevention coordinator, says that the drop is in fact largely due to wider use of condoms by teens, and that "just one approach is not adequate to meet the needs of all our teens. Communities, schools, and public health programs should continue providing comprehensive, interdisciplinary programs that teach responsible decision-making, delaying sexual activity, and contraceptive use."

Raquel Castellanos, executive director of the Missoula Mountain Clinic, says that abstinence-only education has caused STD rates to soar among Montana's teens since 2000. "Although we do not have scientific research which links the sharp rise in chlamydia to education that dismisses the effectiveness of condoms, I believe it's no coincidence that we are seeing this exponential growth of chlamydia among youth." SIECUS's communications director Adrienne Verrilli says that teens are being told by abstinence-only programs to forego medical visits and to adopt "secondary virginity as a solution, pretending the sex they already had didn't happen. A lot of women get massive infections." Other evidence shows that southern states, which adopted abstinence-only education programs earliest, have seen the highest rates of HIV increase.

McKay said she tried to do "damage control" for her class after SAFE's presentation by bringing in speakers from the campus health center and local women's clinic, but she worried that some of her students were having trouble deciphering what they had heard. Castellanos said that high school teachers around the state are telling students that condoms are only 50 to 60 percent effective and do not work on teenagers. "The abstinence people are so well funded that they can travel all over the state. We have nothing to counter the kind of federal money that is pouring in."

In his 2004 presidential campaign, President Bush promised to "elevate abstinence-only education from an afterthought to an urgent priority." To do this, he has overridden objections to federal funding for religious groups, many with no prior experience in health or sex education. Verrilli says that federal grants are flowing into explicitly anti-abortion pregnancy crisis groups, churches, and Christian megachurches.

"Bush is funding his base and creating an industry and advocates to do recruitment. It's part of a broad strategy to start moving federal dollars into the evangelical community. It's a neoconservative's dream come true," says Verrilli. Planned Parenthood calls the funding of abstinence-only programs "one of the religious right's greatest victories."

Julie Sternberg of the ACLU's Reproductive Freedom Project says that while the Supreme Court has approved provision of federal money to religious organizations, the monies must be used exclusively for secular purposes. "Taxpayer dollars may not go to the promotion of religion," she says. "If a group is using taxpayer dollars, those dollars may not be used to advance religion in any way." Christian Right abstinence-only education programs routinely violate this rule.

In 2002, violations of the rule were tested in Las Cruces, New Mexico, with ACLU help. New Mexico's Community Abstinence Network had gone into a seventh-grade classroom with a video that included extensive references to God. Parents protested to the Department of Health and superintendent of schools, and the video was removed. A teacher who had told students that abortion was murder was also forced to clarify that, under the law, abortion is a legal procedure. The ACLU also pursued a case in Louisiana, where federal money had been used to transport public school kids to anti-abortion protests, as well as to purchase Bibles and to stage religious plays.

These are small victories compared to the number of routine violations occurring every day, says the ACLU. Lawyers say that it is difficult to sue federally funded organizations for violating the separation of church and state because a paper trail connecting government dollars to overtly religious activity must be established. The ACLU is investigating the many reports it receives, "putting out brush fires," and trying to determine if funding "pervasively sectarian religious groups" is a violation of the law.

The ACLU also says that the U.S. Department of Health and Human Services is responsible for preventing religious groups from preaching or proselytizing. The DHHS warns faith-based groups receiving direct government funds that they "should take steps to separate, in time and location, their inherently religious activities from the government funded services they offer." Failure to comply can lead to the cessation of funding, but monitoring is virtually nonexistent, the ACLU says.

SIECUS's Verrilli believes that "the federal government has every intention of defying federal law and continuing to use taxpayer dollars to fund programs that are overtly religious—Christian—in nature. Not only do these programs make reference to Christianity, they include anti-abortion messages, gender biases, particularly as they relate to controlling young women's behaviors, and completely exclude lesbian, gay, bisexual, and transgender-oriented youth."

Politicians are bowing so readily to the demands of a small minority of Americans—only 20 million Americans are fundamentalist, right-wing Christians—that their sincerity is becoming increasingly suspect. The Alan Guttmacher Institute says that the growing body of research on abstinence-only education shows that there is a serious and worrying "disconnect" between what teachers, parents, and students want and what their politicians are giving them. One can only conclude that politicians are not as interested in their own constituents' wishes as they are in the campaign donations and support they are receiving from the Christian Right.

SIECUS thinks that the Bush administration is getting away with violating both young Americans' right to essential health information and the legal principle of separation of church and state for two reasons: parents are not paying attention, and it is difficult and expensive to undertake a lawsuit. Lisa Stone, executive director of the Northwest Women's Law Center, says that in order to sue, you have to identify a harm that has been done. "If a kid is taught that condoms don't work and she gets an STD or becomes pregnant, who do you sue? Is it the entity that gave the money to the community-based organization or the group that taught the class, or both?"

In the 2004 election, 40 percent of President Bush's vote came from white evangelical Christians, and it should not be lost on us that on the second day of his second administration, he re-instituted the 1981 "Mexico City rule" that prohibits federal support for institutions that provide abortion, discuss it with their clients, or refer them to abortion counseling services. Bush also pulled the plug on U.S. funding for the UN Population Fund, which provides condoms, voluntary family planning, nutrition, and AIDS prevention education to millions of young women living in poverty around the world. Venerable institutions invaluable in the war on AIDS, such as the International Planned Parenthood Federation and Marie Stopes International, stood up to Bush and were rewarded with crippling funding cuts that forced them to shut down vital reproductive health services for women in the most vulnerable areas of the world.

Other organizations that have resisted Bush's anti-science approach to HIV prevention have also suffered grievously. In May 2004 the Bush administration cut funds for the Global Health Council's work, which focuses on sex, health, and young people, and also reduced support for the fifteenth international conference on AIDS, the biennial meeting where policymakers and scientists from around the world learn about the latest advances in AIDS control. The Council and the Conference are both vocal about the importance of condoms and comprehensive education for young people.

A 2001 audit of San Francisco's STOP AIDS Project by the Department of Health and Human Services concluded that two of the organization's workshops were obscene and encouraged sexual activity because they included condom demonstrations. SIECUS was audited soon after it began opposing federal funding of abstinence-only education and has been audited two other times since 2002; no misconduct has been found. Members of Congress are getting in on the act, demanding that federal funding be cut for any organizations that protested then-DHHS Secretary Thompson's speech at the International AIDS Conference in Barcelona in 2002. The Gay Men's Health Crisis in New York City said that audits by conservative congressmen have "created a chilling effect" on the group's HIV prevention activities.

It appears that even Miss America can be bought or intimidated. Katie (not her real name) was a seventh grader when the reigning Miss America, Heather Whitestone, spoke to her junior high school. "She stood on a platform in a gymnasium full of seventh and eighth graders, holding a tennis racket, and asked for a volunteer," Katie wrote. "She handed the young boy who came on stage a fistful of BBs, then instructed him to throw them to her as she tried to hit them back with a tennis racket. 'This,' she told the youth, 'is how condoms work.' A couple of months later the first girl got pregnant. The second girl got pregnant a few weeks later. . . . There didn't seem to be any point in going through the humiliation of buying condoms. We'd been told again and again that they didn't work."

"I'm afraid we are going to raise a generation of kids who have little understanding of sex and sexuality," says Verrilli. Planned Parenthood staffers are collecting anecdotes attesting to the spread of ignorance: a male student in California asked his teacher where his cervix was; a female wondered if she could become pregnant from oral sex.

"It's so dangerous," Verrilli continues. "Rights are so hard to get and so easy to take away."

WOMEN AT RISK

In its drive to return America to some idyllic biblical state, the nation's Christian Right has not confined itself to attacking homosexuals, banning comprehensive sex education, and threatening the separation of church and state. It is also chipping steadily away at the rights of American women. The Bush administration continues to lead a three decade-long presidential and congressional attack on women's reproductive rights and their rights to equal education, employment, and compensation.

This administration has accelerated conservative initiatives to "right size" American women, returning them to their more submissive "Christian" roles of mother and homemaker. This assault is an affront to America's men as well as to its women. It ignores the progress women have made in education, their significant economic contributions to their families as household heads, working partners, *and* mothers, and their basic rights as human beings and members of a modern society.

It also has a critical bearing on the rapidly accelerating spread of HIV/AIDS in the United States. Respecting women's reproductive rights, affirming their ability to refuse sexual advances, and protecting them from male violence is crucial to stopping epidemic spread. AIDS in the United States is "taking on a female face," to use the words of Dr. Frances Priddy, a physician at Atlanta's Grady Memorial Hospital. Priddy says that "more than half [of their] AIDS patients are women," noting that Centers for Disease Control statistics show that AIDS is now growing fifteen times faster in American women than in men. By reducing women's rights and increasing the chance of a wholesale AIDS epidemic, the Bush administration seems more than willing to sacrifice human lives to achieve its retrogressive program of social control.

Guarantee of women's basic rights and equality under U.S. law is relatively recent. American women got the right to vote in 1920, far later than in other developed countries, and women's equality is still not guaranteed in the U.S. Constitution. In the 1970s and 1980s, women made piecemeal advances by winning equal rights to education and employment and to control of their own reproductive choices. Unfortunately, the moment women made gains in any arena of American social or economic life, religiously motivated conservatives worked doggedly to take them away.

The area of reproductive rights is a good example of the pernicious effects of persistent conservative attacks on women's ability to maintain their basic freedoms. In 1973, the U.S. Supreme Court's decision in *Roe v. Wade* struck down a Texas law criminalizing abortion. The Court ruled that the decision to bear a child is a fundamental right guaranteed by the U.S. Constitution and any restrictions on abortion would be subject to the highest degree of scrutiny and protection by the courts. The conservative backlash has not abated since. President Reagan's Justice Department asked the Court to overturn its judgment, and both Reagan and President George Bush appointed judges who did not support the strict-scrutiny provision of the ruling.

In 1992 the Court ruled that abortion restrictions can be mandated in state and federal law unless they constitute an "undue burden," leading to a growing number of restrictions on abortion. When Congress approved a ban on partial birth abortions in 2003, Christian right-winger Ken Connor, president of the Family Research Council, hailed it as a victory in their efforts to "dismantle, brick by brick, the deadly edifice created by *Roe v. Wade*." The bill was so vague it did not even define what "partial birth abortion" is or in what month of pregnancy it occurs. It also contained no exceptions for the health of the mother, similar to a

Nebraska law found unconstitutional by the Supreme Court in 2000.

In abortion, as in abstinence-only education, there is a growing "disconnect" between public policy and public opinion. Abortion rights are gradually disappearing even though a majority of Americans have supported a woman's right to a legal abortion for a decade. Gallup Poll trends data showed that in 2004, 52 percent of Americans were pro-choice and had been since 1996. A 2005 ABC News/Washington Post poll found that 56 percent of Americans favored keeping abortion legal in almost all cases, compared to 27 percent who wanted some restrictions and 14 percent who thought it should be illegal no matter what the circumstance. A recent survey by The Mellman Group found that 62 percent of respondents did not want the government to interfere with a woman's right to abortion and only 33 percent thought the government should be involved. Sixty percent felt that Bush nominees to the Supreme Court should support *Roe v. Wade.* In this as in so many other matters, Washington does not seem to be listening.

Women's rights to birth control and control of their reproductive health are being whittled away by other less dramatic and visible actions. The Federal Drug Administration (FDA) has delayed introduction of the "morning-after pill" in this country for two years, despite the fact that emergency contraception has been used freely in Europe since its introduction. American Medical Association studies demonstrate that emergency contraception does not increase unprotected sex or cause women to forgo regular contraception and is used predominantly by women who are raped or coerced into sex. The FDA is still seeking to limit use of the emergency pill by women under sixteen, the very age when these types of encounters occur most often. The American Academy of Pediatrics strongly supports emergency contraception and has formally stated that minors should have access to this form of birth control. It also clearly opposes abstinence-only education for teens.

Although medical professionals publicly support emergency contraception, politicians of all stripes have bowed to the religious right's bullying. In 2005, when the New York State legislature passed a bill to make emergency contraception available to women of all ages, Governor George Pataki, courting the Republican nomination for president in 2008, vetoed it. Massachusetts governor, Willard "Mitt" Romney, also vetoed the Bay State's newly passed legislation allowing emergency contraception because he also has aspirations for the 2008 Republican nomination.

Anticipating further incursions by the Congress and state legislatures on women's access to any form of birth control, the National Organization of Women is seeking passage of a law to guarantee it. This need stems from a decision by the American Pharmacists Association in 1998 to create a "conscience clause," which says that pharmacists can ethically refuse to fill a prescription if it conflicts with their personal beliefs. Women seeking birth control have been humiliated by pharmacists exercising this "right" of conscience, and some pharmacists even refused to return the woman's prescription so it could be filled elsewhere. "Today they might not fill a prescription for birth control pills," said one of the bill's congressional sponsors. "Tomorrow it could be painkillers for a cancer patient. Next year it could be medicine that prolongs the life of a person with AIDS."

Because their genital tracts are more biologically vulnerable to HIV infection, women run a higher risk of HIV infection than men with each sexual encounter. Despite this fact, no female-controlled form of HIV prevention has yet been developed or widely distributed. The female condom, which came on the scene in the early 1990s, has never been taken as seriously as it should. Ninety-five percent of men and women who have tried it say it is "user friendly," and scientifically, it is also more effective than male condoms in preventing HIV infection (97 percent compared to 90 percent). Microbicides—gels, creams, films, sponges, or suppositories inserted in the vagina or rectum before sex, which can be used without the partner's knowledge—prevent HIV transmission by killing or inactivating the virus. After almost two decades, no one has invested enough money to develop one that will not damage women's vaginal tissue.

Annie Laurie Gaylor, who heads the Freedom from Religion Foundation, argues that "we are in the midst of a religious war not just against abortion rights, but against women's rights in general." Gaylor points out that "the foot soldiers of the religious right" are just as willing to use violence and force in limiting women's access to abortion in the United States as the Islamic Taliban. In their campaign to curtail women's rights, conservative Christians are backed by the Catholic church, whose newest pope was instrumental in threatening excommunication for Catholic congressmen who upheld a woman's right to choose. Some analysts believe that the threat of excommunication against John Kerry's Catholic supporters was even more important than the Christian Right in turning the 2004 election in Bush's favor.

"Whether declared or undeclared," Gaylor says, "there is nothing new in this religious war against women. After the organized women's movement was officially launched in 1848, Elizabeth Cady Stanton said the 'Bible was hurled at us on every side.' In the 1970s and 1980s, it was the churches—Catholic, fundamentalist Protestant, and Mormon—which marshaled political forces to defeat the Equal Rights Amendment."

Conservative churches are even willing to unite with old enemies across borders and sects if the cause is curtailment of women's rights. In 2005, the Bush administration supported the Iraqi constitution's clauses that impose Islamic restrictions on women's rights in areas of marriage, divorce, custody, and inheritance. By adopting Sharia or fundamentalist Islamic law, the new Iraqi constitution takes away many of the rights women had under Sadam Hussein. Reuel Marc Gerecht of the American Enterprise Institute, a conservative think tank in Washington, D.C., told Meet the Press that "I think it's important to remember that in the year 1900, in the United States—it was a democracy then—women did not have the right to vote. If Iraqis could develop a democracy that resembled America in the 1900s, I think we'd all be thrilled. I mean, women's social rights are not critical to the evolution of democracy."

Efforts by the conservative right to roll back women's progress have been a theme of Republican presidents for more than thirty years. The Reagan administration played so fast and loose with Title IX that it gutted the 1972 law's guarantees against sex discrimination in education, forcing Congress to pass the Civil Rights Restoration Act of 1987 over the president's veto. During the first George W. Bush administration, the Supreme Court was asked to interpret Title VII, the federal law prohibiting sex discrimination against working women, in such a way that employers could deny jobs they believed could be harmful to fetuses to fully qualified women of childbearing age, even if a woman was not pregnant. The Bush administration also urged the Supreme Court to prohibit victims of sex discrimination under Title IX from obtaining monetary damages. Analyses by the American Association of Retired People and other organizations demonstrate that Bush's proposed Social Security changes would imperil women's retirement incomes far more than they would those of men.

The conservative campaign to turn back the clock on women's rights to reproductive health and other basic civil rights ignores the fact that "women are at very high risk" of HIV infection, Paige says. "Women have always been so oppressed, told what to do, and believe that it's the man's job to have the condoms. But the man's not going to protect you. In the long run, it's up to us to protect ourselves." Paige said that "empowering women, empowering children to make the right decisions and have the education to make an informed decision when it comes down to the moment" has become a critical part of her mission. What the Center for Disease Control calls "high-risk heterosexual contact" (commonly called "partners with a past," or sex with people who have had multiple partners, sex with bisexual men, or have used injecting drugs) now accounts for more new HIV cases than injecting drug use.

Pittsburgh AIDS activist Susan Howe says, "Women who have been infected by their partners have been betrayed. She's loved someone who was not faithful, and he did not tell her and she's been betrayed. Sometimes it's not a long-term marriage thing, but they're still betrayed because the guy didn't tell." Susan says that while the door of betrayal swings both ways and many women are also not using protection, "the chances of a man getting it from a woman are so slight that it's not the same injury. It's not the same level of crime."

Women's risk of HIV transmission through heterosexual intercourse is much greater than that of men for other reasons. The United States has one of the highest rates of rape in the world. Susan was the victim of a rapist who intentionally infected her. "The doctor told me that the things the rapist did to me he did on purpose," she said. "He knew exactly what he was doing. I had had a breast operation to remove some kind of mass. The rapist came up behind me and he felt that tape and gauze and he ripped that open, so there was a lot of blood. He tried to do it from behind and that wasn't working, so he turned me over and he was kneeling on me and he came in that wound and rubbed it in me. This rape was not about sex. It was about power. He was going to make sure that other people had HIV too. As far as I was concerned, he was a murderer. He made sure I got this. He wasn't just a rapist."

Susan was raped eleven years ago, "right after the death of my brother-in-law and just before the death of my son from brain cancer. It was a very, very painful, extremely painful time, and I didn't think it could get any worse. I certainly didn't think that God would allow any more to happen. They told me that I might have been infected, but said that I had to take an HIV test after six months. My gynecologist was one of the people that told me 'Oh, no, no, no. God's not going to let this happen to you. You're going to be fine.'

"But after my son died, I started really getting nervous. I didn't trust life so much anymore, and I wasn't sure that this was going to turn out right." When her doctor learned that she was HIV positive, he called her into the office after sending all his staff home and asking his wife to come in for moral support. "They told me together, and we all cried," Susan said. "We didn't have the medications then. When I was diagnosed, this was a death sentence. They told me I had seven years to live and if I was really lucky, I might have nine. The longest-living people were living up to nine years."

In addition to coping with HIV, Susan had posttraumatic stress disorder from the rape. "The rape had a great effect on me. It happened at my home. It's been ten years since I have been willing to go out on my back porch. I can't take public transportation. I'm very frightened in the street. I cannot go out at night. When I take the garbage out, it better be daytime. I can't take that last bit out at night."

The rapist attacked Susan on her back porch after he followed her and learned her routines. She even bought him a cup of coffee and a doughnut at the shop where she met a woman friend each night after work. "The reason I was at the doughnut shop was my brother-in-law was dying, my son was dying, and I was messed up over it. No matter what I went through all day, every night I would meet my friend at the doughnut shop around seven o'clock. These goofy men would come in there every night. They would laugh and carry on, and we would sit there and listen and laugh. They were just ridiculously funny. It was my levity for the day. I loved to have a break from all the pain and all the sorrow.

"I would go home and I would cry some more, but every night I met her and we would eat doughnuts. It was wonderful eating cream-filled doughnuts. I thought it was my fault that I was raped because I thought that I was weak. I was weak! I know now I was coping, but back then I thought, 'If I just hadn't been weak enough that I had to go to a place every night and have a schedule that somebody could figure out and follow me home and know when to wait at the side of the back porch. I shouldn't have been so weak that I went to a doughnut shop every night.' It wasn't a bar! I'm not going to a bar, I'm just eating doughnuts! I'm not hurting anybody! But I blamed myself. 'Look what happened. It's your fault! You should have been stronger. You shouldn't have been overwhelmed!'

"The rapist came in one night and said that he was hungry. Nobody else in there offered him a thing. I felt sorry for him. I offered him a sandwich, but he said 'No, I'll just take a doughnut and coffee.' The rape counselors said he was testing to see who he felt stronger than, and I just signed right up. I just signed right up! I said, 'Oh, yeah. I'll buy you a sandwich.' I thought I did the Christian thing. My father was a minister. Somebody's hungry? Okay, I have an extra couple bucks. I'll buy you a sandwich. Then when I saw how it turned out, I kept going around saying 'I bought the rapist a cup of coffee. I bought the rapist a cup of coffee. It must be my fault.'"

Like Susan, women all over the United States have been fed debilitating messages about their responsibility for negative male behavior, and the Christian Right, in abstinence-only education programs, is reinforcing these messages. Teens are being told that men have natural sexual urges that they cannot control, and young women are being told that they must submit to their husbands' will. An entire new generation is being brainwashed to believe, like Susan, that they are responsible for their own rapes or for the threat of domestic violence in their homes. Most of the violence against women is called "partner" or "domestic" violence, committed by the men with whom women live.

A third of all women in Canada and a fifth in the United States have been beaten by their husbands, the most common form of violence against women in every country. The CDC estimates that the health-related costs of rape, physical assault, stalking, and homicide by intimate partners exceeds $5.8 billion each year in the United States alone. The ultimate costs are even higher because many women and children do not seek medical assistance. Former DHHS secretary Thompson said that "violence against women harms more than its direct victim. It also harms the children, the abuser and the health of all our families and communities."

Women with HIV are much more likely to have a physically violent partner, and almost half said they could not deny their husbands sex after a beating or if they feared HIV infection. "Women especially at risk are those in a heterosexual marriage or long-term union in a society where men commonly engage in sex outside the union and women confront abuse if they demand condom use," says Human Rights Watch.

The return to passé gender norms being fostered by the Christian Right limits what "good" women are supposed to know about sex and sexuality, reducing their ability to accurately determine their risk and learn how to protect themselves from HIV infection. They must rely on their husbands, many of whom are just as ignorant as their wives or more so. They also rely on their husbands to be honest about sexual relations outside the union. Gender myths about sexuality that encourage men's promiscuity and lack of marital fidelity not only threaten women's health in marriages and partnerships, but also sustain the burgeoning sex industry in the United States.

Social systems also control women's ability to speak out, either within their family or in a public setting. The fact that such a large portion of rape and domestic violence goes unreported in the United States shows the impact of social control. Social norms also determine whether women can own property and build up economic security on their own without relying on a man. Many women my age remember the difficulty of getting loans, mortgages, and credit cards as single women in the 1970s. These curbs on freedom of women to own and accumulate wealth and property force them to enter and stay in partnerships with men in order to access basic economic rights, even if the men are violent, unfaithful, or infect them with STDs or HIV.

Organized religions are an important source of beliefs about women's essential nature and the essential nature of the universe in which they reside. As organized religion gains increasing control over our country's power structures, they can reinforce damaging cultural stereotypes and social structures by changing laws and restricting women's rights. Communities and families also help children learn cultural stereotypes, often teaching women to be their own best enemies.

A society's gender system encompasses ideas of what women can and cannot do. It is a useful tool in keeping more than half the population in line and preventing them from complaining about injustice, even when it means death. Women, who now outnumber men in the U.S. population, accept beatings, sexual assault, and coercion and remain silent, thinking, like Susan, that it is their fault. Women are caught in a social trap that promotes vulnerability to HIV/AIDS and other negative outcomes of sexual intimacy, such as unwanted pregnancy. When their own government turns its back on their need for protection, they have few other places to go for help.

In a July 2005 decision that National Organization of Women (NOW) president Kim Gandy characterized as "truly outrageous," the Supreme Court exempted police officers from legal action, even if their refusal to act results in death. The woman whose case was overturned by the Supreme Court had won a suit against police officers in Castle Rock, Colorado, after they repeatedly failed to enforce the restraining order she had obtained against her husband, who kidnapped and later killed their three daughters.

As a result of the Supreme Court's action, "Abusers may feel they have the green light to ignore restraining orders, and police departments could see domestic violence as a 'no penalty' area to cut resources," Gandy told the press. Archconservative Supreme Court justice Antonin Scalia claimed that Colorado's law does not entitle people who receive protective orders to police enforcement. If the police do not enforce restraining orders, who will?

In August 2005 the women of America suffered another setback when Wade Horn, assistant DHHS secretary for children and families, refused to accept a report on violence against women prepared by NOW. The report found that welfare case workers were not informing women of essential provisions in the federal law that could help them escape domestic violence. Almost two-thirds of women on welfare have been subject to domestic violence at some point in their lives and are forced to return to violent situations because they have no financial independence. Since these women are the most likely to be exposed to HIV infection by their partners, Horn's indifference has serious implications for the AIDS epidemic in this country.

"Marriage promotion is not the solution to helping women off welfare," said NOW's vice president Olga Vives. "Marriage for money instead of love sends the message that women are not valued as people, but as possessions. It also tells women they are only worth the government's time if they are on the arm of a man." Women who must rely on men for economic support have little negotiating power if their partner is violent (one third of American women in all income brackets), or engages in sexual or drug-using behavior that threatens them with HIV infection.

Since 1996, the Christian Right has pushed the White House, Congress, and state legislatures to "protect" monogamous, heterosexual marriage and "promote" marriage among poor women. In 2001, President Bush told the Fourth National Summit on Fatherhood that "fatherlessness has emerged as one of our greatest social problems," calling for $315 million to promote two-parent families. He declared October 12 to 18, 2003 as "Marriage Protection Week," and in January 2004 asked for $1.5 billion to promote marriage through social marketing and education for low-income individuals.

Policies such as these assume that single motherhood is an aberrant and idiosyncratic behavior, although the imprisonment of increasing numbers of black men leaves more and more women without husbands. The matriarchal family predominant in many inner cities because of high rates of imprisonment is seen as a root cause of African American disadvantage. Many experts agree with Adolph Reed, an expert on U.S. race and class relations, when he questions the administration's "misty-eyed" support for marriage and two-parent families, saying that poor communities need education, health care, employment, and safe neighborhoods.

The Supreme Court decision that American police are not obliged to respect court restraining orders against violent men is a serious threat to women's safety. When Susan Howe finally spotted the man who had raped her and gave her HIV, she got no help from the police. "I didn't know him, but I had seen him at this doughnut shop. My girlfriend and I went down to there and we would wait every night, but he never came back. I saw him a long, long time later. He came to a McDonald's near there. I called the police, but they would not come.

"I think all women should be a little more cautious," Susan said, to protect themselves both from violent attack and from infection by the men they trust. "I know a lot of HIV-positive women now who are younger," she says, who were infected by their partners. "I can't imagine being young and having this diagnosis. Can you even imagine? Having your life ripped out from under you by this diagnosis?"

In August 2005 the U.S. Congress was considering reauthorization of the 1994 Violence Against Women Act, which provides funding for rape crisis centers, domestic violence shelters, and law enforcement agency training to prevent violence and protect women and children affected by violence. Partisanship and funding for the Iraq war threatened to halve funding for these basic protections for women, despite the fact that many more women are threatened in the course of their daily lives in the United States than American soldiers are threatened in war. One-third to one-half of all women in New York City are likely to be raped or brutalized at least once in their lives.

Most violence against women is slower and more systemic than sudden attacks in the night, taking the form of the grinding daily humiliation and danger imposed by living in poverty. Women in the United States are 40 percent more likely to be poor than men. One in every eight women is poor, compared to one in eleven men. The gender-poverty gap declined slightly over the past five years, but the United States still has the highest poverty rate and the highest ratio of women's to men's poverty of any modern nation. Many American women are aware of how systematically disadvantaged they are compared to women in other developed countries.

Growing poverty in the United States threatens all lower- and middle-class citizens without regard to gender. The most recent Census Bureau report on poverty in the United States shows that more people fell into poverty in the United States in 2004, even though the economy was growing. Increasing income disparities between the country's richest and poorest citizens mean that middle-class and poor people are falling even further behind because income is becoming more concentrated in the hands of the wealthy. In the face of the devastation caused by Hurricane Katrina, Congress temporarily delayed estate tax cuts that would have benefited the top 2 percent of the population, concentrating income even further and throwing the country further into debt.

The Census Bureau's poverty report had other negative implications for women. More Americans have shifted from private to public health insurance programs as their employers cut benefits or they lost their jobs. Since more women live in poverty and rely on public insurance, more women than men will be left uninsured by government cuts in public health insurance coverage made to fund tax breaks for the wealthy. In the United States, HIV-positive women are much less likely to receive treatment than HIV-positive men, a reflection of the current gender gap in access to health care that will only grow worse as cuts in public insurance coverage deepen.

Women's precarious income position in the United States is reinforced by persistent wage inequality for working women, who still make 73 percent of male wages in comparable jobs. One in fifteen working women is poor compared to one in twenty-six men. Financial independence is key to women's ability to resist abusive partners, insist on their rights in their homes and in their society, and support their children if they are single moms. But our government works with employers to hold employment costs down and maximize profits by not enforcing equal wages for women or other vital safety nets like health insurance.

Walmart, one of the country's largest employers, is now facing a class action suit from 1.6 million current and former female employees, who allege that they have been subject to years of systematic discrimination in pay rates, benefits, work hours, and promotions. Begun by six women in different parts of the country, the suit became the biggest civil rights court case in history when it was approved as a class action case in 2004. The case has symbolic importance as well, because of Walmart's multinational status. Its annual sales of more than $250 billion are greater than the output of many countries. Decisions in this case will affect workers worldwide and will also affect the image of "these good ol' southern boys who have become Masters of the Universe," remarked BBC business editor Jeff Randall.

Governments in every country in the world, including the United States, are controlled by men, who ensure that women's access to power is low. Only in Nordic countries do women approach fair representation, averaging 40 percent of parliamentary seats, and it is in those countries that women's rights are best protected and their social safety nets are strongest. American women are fourteen years away from celebrating the hundredth anniversary of obtaining the vote, yet only 8 women currently serve as governors; women hold only 14 of 100 U.S. Senate seats and 48 of 435 seats in the House of Representatives. Only 29 women have ever held cabinet positions in the country's history.

International collusion supports perpetuation of national systems of gender inequality and the disinclination to change them. U.S. support for a new Iraqi constitution that reverses women's rights in that country is one example. Our failure to provide leadership on adoption of UN human rights conventions on women and children is another. For more than twenty years, the United States has failed to ratify the Convention on the Elimination of All Forms of Discrimination Against Women (CEDAW). UN Secretary General Kofi Annan says that "this 'Women's Bill of Rights' is a milestone because it reflects the principle of universal and indivisible rights sacred to all nations, foreign to no culture and common to both genders." The treaty has helped reduce sexual slavery, increase women's education, and improve health, and the U.S. refusal to support it has undermined its enforcement everywhere.

As of January 2004, 175 countries had ratified or acceded to the treaty, including every other industrialized country, but the United States has elected to keep company with Afghanistan, Iran, Syria, and Somalia in refusing to endorse it. Our failure to join the rest of the developed world in ratifying the convention signals our government's disdain for women's rights both at home and abroad, and makes it difficult for the UN to enforce measures to improve women's human rights in other countries. The convention could serve as a vital wedge to improve women's economic conditions and reduce their sexual exploitation and exposure to HIV, but it is weakened as an international instrument by our lack of support.

The United States also supports a foreign policy that actively tries to prevent condom use, even in countries where 20 to 30 percent of adults are HIV positive, funding abstinence-only education for the prevention of HIV/AIDS instead. In 2003 the first "Global Women's Scorecard" gave the current U.S. administration a high mark for rhetoric on global AIDS policies, but failing grades on policies to protect the rights of women and vulnerable groups from infection and for restricting family planning services worldwide by cutting back on condom distribution.

Although the administration promotes itself as compassionate, its actions have been exceptionally damaging to human rights and the effort to prevent the spread of HIV/AIDS around the world. In Uganda, the first heavily hit African country to control its huge AIDS epidemic, U.S. pressure on the government has created a condom shortage, and the epidemic is beginning to rise again. Preaching abstinence-only is cynical "for the majority of women and girls in many cultures and situations," says Noerine Kaleeba, founder of The AIDS Support Organization in Uganda, one of the first home care programs on the continent.

UNAIDS says that 62 percent of all new HIV infections around the world are among women, a trend that is just emerging in the United States among 15- to 24-year-olds. Women without rights have little say in the decision to remain abstinent. "The typical woman who gets infected with HIV has only one partner—her husband or steady boyfriend," said Oscar-winning actress Emma Thompson who serves as an international ambassador for ActionAid International. "Regardless of their relationship status women desperately need new HIV prevention tools that they can control."

Women are often perceived as the "bearers" of HIV. When a woman becomes infected, gender myths lead to stigmatization by the community. HIV-positive women whose status is known are more likely than men to be abused, abandoned, or even killed. Even if they caught HIV from their husbands, it is assumed that they are "bad" women who sought sex outside of marriage. The statistics on the fate of "bad girls" are mind-numbing. At least four million are sold into sexual slavery every year in the world, including many in the United States.

Women who are systematically marginalized and devalued by their societies can easily be exploited for sex work, a huge and growing business everywhere, even in America. As sex work becomes increasingly profitable for American corporate interests, they have more incentive to limit and take away women's rights. For the sex sector to thrive, the political system it calls home must support it, either explicitly or tacitly. The U.S. government accomplishes this by refusing to endorse CEDAW—thereby evading international human rights agreements—and by turning the clock back on women's rights in law and policy every chance it gets.

In spite of the threats the AIDS epidemic poses to American women's health, safety, and lives, politicians at federal and state levels have shown themselves consistently willing to shortchange them. Rather than risk losing the support of the Christian Right (or the Catholic church, and their conservative backers), American politicians of all stripes are willing to sacrifice women's human rights and equal treatment before the law as American citizens.

It seems that men in power simply have too much to gain to concern themselves with the health and rights of their better half. The sword, however, has two edges, and men are cut as well. The majority of traditional American households rely on the wages earned by both husband and wife. Many men will see that their domestic standard of living is threatened by attacks on the education and earning potential of their wives. And they will grieve as more of their children become HIV positive because they cannot cope with the increasing stress on their families and their young lives.

MARRIAGE, FAMILY, AND THE COURTS

All over the United States, people are trying to cope with the demands of the complex social and economic changes that have occurred in our country over the past half century. The changes in American sexual behavior and family life that are behind Paige's story started well before she was a gleam in her parents' eyes.

As Paige's life shows us, pressures on families can create difficulties for children and teens that can lead to risky sexual behavior and HIV infection. Trends in marriage and family formation also create changes in adult sexual behavior that can contribute to HIV infection later in life. When these changes are discussed openly and honestly, they can be appreciated for what they are: adaptations to broader economic and social trends. Cloaked in religious distortion and exploited for political gain, they are vulnerabilities that contribute to the growing AIDS epidemic in America.

Although these changes are not often acknowledged in discussions of family values, American society and family have been radically transformed since the 1950s and even before. Social statistics show that the traditional family of mom, dad, and two or three children central to the Christian Right's agenda has probably been the minority form of family throughout our history. Families take many shapes in every society. The reason? No one form of family ever meets everyone's needs, and family forms change in response to the economic and social demands of society.

In proposing a constitutional amendment to outlaw gay marriage in America in February 2004, George W. Bush told the press that such a serious measure had to be taken because "the preservation of marriage rises to this level of national importance. The union of man and women is the most enduring human institution, honored and encouraged in all cultures and religious faiths.

"Marriage cannot be severed from its cultural, religious and natural roots without weakening the good in society," he said. Although this may be true, perusal of Christian Right propaganda shows that those roots are in their theology, not in history or human cultural experience. The Christian Right website Citizen Link states that "anthropologists tell us marriage, a permanent linking of men and women, is found in every civilized society throughout human history," but it does not say how many women and men have been linked or how permanent "permanent" actually is. It also does not mention that anthropologists know that "marriage" takes many different forms in different places, and some of its forms would not be recognizable to us.

As in other areas, the Christian Right's rhetoric on social proprieties is way off the mark, clearly out of line not only with American but with international history. Only 16 percent of human societies even claim to be monogamous; the other 84 percent actually call themselves polygamous. This statistic, however, is somewhat misleading, as anthropologists who have spent untold numbers of hours classifying marriage systems know. In most polygamous societies, only the richest males, about 10 percent, can actually afford more than one wife at a time. The rest content themselves with "serial monogamy," marrying (or mating with) one person at a time but more than one partner in a lifetime. This pattern is paralleled by high divorce and remarriage rates in our own society.

Concerns about the demise of the traditional family and appropriate sexual expression are common in every period of radical social change. As far back as the early 1800s, the Industrial

Revolution brought about a dramatic change in the "traditional" family form of agrarian societies: the extended family and transitory farm hands who lived, worked, ate, played, and prayed together. The Victorian era was a time of enormous social and technological change that included advances in the natural sciences, public health, microbiology, and world conquest. It was also a time of enormous change in social attitudes toward sexuality and the family. Nowhere in the Victorian world were attitudes universal. Our notion of the Victorian era as overwhelmingly prudish is largely the result of careful selective editing.

Historian Matthew Sweet says that many of the manuals, books, playing cards, devices for sexual titillation, and advertisements for sexual pleasures that might have demonstrated the extent of Victorian appetites have long been purged by official repositories and anxious homeowners who did not want the neighbors to know what Uncle Harry did on his nights out. Victorians produced "bisexual pornography in which the two heroes indulge in guiltless sex with each other before climbing into bed with the two heroines; the children's adventure starring a cross-dressing teenage boy; the advertisements that wooed people like you and me into meetings with personalities like Julia Pastrana the Baboon Lady, Miss Atkinson the Pig Woman, and the Bipenis Boy," says Sweet.

Although Victorians purportedly dressed their piano legs in knickers so they would be less lascivious, in London's swank Burlington Shopping Arcade, "sex and shopping were pursued with equal enthusiasm—and transvestite boys were its specialty," Sweet says. During England's early Victorian era, religious and social moralizing tried to repress sexuality through a drive for self-mastery and through social control over excess and "irregular" pre- and extramarital sex, culminating in a concern about prostitution that reached panic levels in the 1850s and early 1860s. While prostitutes were detained for medical examination to protect soldiers and sailors (and non-uniformed men) from debilitating STDs, the 1860s also witnessed a resurgence of sexual freedom for men. This was encouraged over the next two decades by the idea that men had natural sexual urges and drives that had to be satisfied, a sentiment that arose in part from Charles Darwin's demonstration of human links to other species.

The curtain came down on this freedom for men in the early 1880s, when Social Purity Campaigns decried the double standard and demanded male continence outside of marriage. Men were expected to control themselves, an idea that early suffragettes turned into a political slogan in England, "Votes for Women, Chastity for Men." Syphilis had been an important disease in Europe since the 1500s, but it was not until sexual permissiveness brought the disease home—when the virginal bride and her innocent offspring were infected with syphilis by a sexually experienced husband—that gender inequities were seen as threatening family life in England. Similar movements were afoot on the European continent and in the United States, but there were still cross-currents of disagreement.

Many Victorians argued that sex was a natural force beneficial to the humans who pursued it. Far from being of one mind about repression of sexuality, the Victorian era was, until the late 1890s, a battlefield of opposing views about appropriate sexual expression. In much the same way as it is today, this battlefield was a highly politicized exercise of legislating private behavior and social norms in the service of other interests.

With the coming of the postindustrial age in all developed countries, not just the United States, sex, marriage, and family have again been subject to radical upheaval and political debate. Since the 1960s, our ideas about the goals of family and marriage have shifted from rearing children, taking care of members in sickness and health, and continuing the family line.

Now the happiness of the individual couple and their children and personal fulfillment are the central missions of family life, pushing traditional obligations to the periphery. Although some believe this outlook is a result of increased selfishness and irresponsibility, it actually corresponds to wider changes in the social fabric and social institutions that support it. In both industrial and postindustrial countries, the state has taken over many of the functions the family had in older societies, including education, work, play, and care for the sick and elderly.

As marriage became a place to achieve private happiness and as more women became less dependent on it psychologically and economically, the age of marriage increased (from 20 years in 1950 to 25.3 in 2003). Divorce became more widely accepted as an appropriate safety valve in an unhappy marriage than an immature choice or a sin, partly because it is so common in the United States. Our divorce rates more than doubled between 1950 and 1981, when they peaked and began to stabilize. Since then, marriage and divorce rates have both declined slightly as more young couples try consensual unions that may or may not lead to marriage.

Young people have learned from their parents' difficulties and are trying partnerships before they make a commitment to marriage. The proportion of couples who are unmarried has risen from 2.5 percent of the total in 1970, when the experiment first began, to more than 15 percent. As one of the early experimenters with this form of "trial marriage," as it was known in the early 1970s, I can attest to how shocking it was to my family and friends. By the mid-1990s, when almost half of all twenty-five to forty-four year olds had cohabited at some time in their life and 5 million nonmarried couples were sharing quarters at any one time, this form of partnership had become a social expectation, a sensible adjustment to social change. I was an early pioneer, but social transformation has turned me into a dinosaur in less than one generation.

By the 1970s, changes in sexual lifestyles and marital patterns—and the public debate about family—were already in high gear. A cover of *Ms. Magazine* graphically depicts the changes in family form that had already occurred by 1977, when mom, dad, and the kids accounted for only 34.5 percent of all American families reported by the U.S. Census Bureau. In that year, single parents with children already accounted for 12.8 percent of all U.S. families. In 2000, thanks to the increased divorce rate, that proportion was 33 percent.

Studies of divorce have shown that loss of the partner in itself does not significantly increase psychological distress, but loss of income and increased economic hardship in single-parent families does. Divorced people are also forced to realign their social relationships and supports, which also contributes to stress. Because of divorce, more than half of all children in this country will live with only one of their parents at some time in their life. However, more than two-thirds of all divorced adults remarry, which means that the majority of these children will also live with a stepfamily. The experiences of Paige, Lindsay, Lauren, and Tom are not a deviation. They are a social norm.

The advent of modern birth control helped women finish their educations and stay in the workforce. A majority of women are now in the workforce, unable or unwilling to stay at home to raise their children from infancy to adulthood. The real American family must change and adapt to economic and social changes. A husband's unexpected loss of employment, for example, means that his wife must work outside the home; a woman subject to abuse by her husband now no longer feels the need to stick with the marriage. As the American family changes, roles and decision making shift as well.

Although the notion of the "traditional" family of mom, pop, and two or three kids popularized in the 1950s was never the predominant family form, it has been used by the Christian Right to terrorize us ever since. So, too, have traditional notions of appropriate sexual behavior. Disapproval of sex before marriage, prevalent in the 1950s—accompanied by a double standard of virginity for women and premarital sowing of wild oats by men—has also long disappeared. In the 1960s, less than 25 percent of Americans approved of premarital sex, but by the 1980s almost 60 percent approved. The preference for a female's virginity before marriage, which grew out of feudal land claims, has now taken on a symbolic cast, and is conveniently reinterpreted by imaginative teens.

In every society, what people say about sex and what they actually do are two very different things. International surveys show that men and women all over the world are adulterous. In 73 percent of cultures worldwide, married men and women report that they have had other partners while married. In the 1970s, women in the United States began catching up with men on this measure, although in most cultures, more men take on new partners than women. In every society, men report that they want four times as many sex partners as women do, have more sexual fantasies, and let less time elapse before seeking sex with a new partner. Men are also more willing to have sex with a total stranger.

Human mating may be somewhat universal in its patterns, but human marriage systems vary a great deal in the importance they give to the male-female bond and in the living arrangements of men and women. Where economic conditions allow and modernization encourages, men and women who marry generally try to establish their own households as soon as possible. In African and Asian societies, the male-female marriage bond is weak because marriage patterns are still agrarian and traditional. Women and men remain more closely tied to their own families than to their marriage partners.

The conflicting messages Americans hear about social norms aggravate the innate tension between sexuality and familism. Americans think that their sexuality should be an expression of their highly prized rights to individualism, freedom, and the quest for happiness. However, the other widely touted American value of familism emphasizes commitment, monogamy, fidelity, and sacrifice. Balancing these conflicting urges within a monogamous relationship takes a maturity and sense of timing that our media and education fail to inculcate.

An estimated 2.5 million couples in the United States try to balance these competing urges by swinging, or having recreational sex with others on a regular basis, according to the North American Swing Clubs Association. More than 8 million (1 to 2 percent) of all Americans have tried it and an estimated 3 million practice it on a regular basis. Initially popular in the 1970s, John Woestendiek of the Knight-Ridder News Services says that "swinging never died, not even with the onset of AIDS. It just lay low, riding America's seesaw of morality, never becoming acceptable, never disappearing." It enjoyed resurgence in the 1990s, thanks to a boost from the Internet. There are magazines, websites, travel agents, vacations, tours, getaways, and conventions for practitioners devoted to "The Lifestyle."

Popular culture, as well as the Christian Right, continues to promote the Victorian idea that men have urges and good women guard the hearth; men are from Mars, women from Venus. The June 2005 *O Magazine* includes a thirty-page spread on men, including advice on "What Men Wish You Knew About Them" and "How to Get Through to a Man." The May *Esquire* promises us the results of "The First-Ever Women of the World Sex Survey: 15 Countries, 11,000 Women. Totally Scientific."

As the majority of Americans who have been married or co-habited more than once in their life can attest, finding the right partner is not easy, no matter what your cultural background. The process can be dangerous, resulting in unprotected sex and exposure to HIV infection. As I thumbed through the May 2005 *Ebony* while waiting for my doctor, my eye was caught by the re-lationship advice in "Sisters Beware! Are You Really 'The One' or Just One of Many?'"

Author Zondra Hughes tells her readers that "the typical Brother is an intuitive cast director who knows what role, if any, that you will play in his life long before you do . . . a major part of the Brother's plan is making sure that you don't know what he knows, especially if his intentions are not on the up-and-up." But *Ebony* readers are encouraged to keep trying. In April, Zondra clued readers into the "5 Mistakes that May Be Keeping You From the Altar," while Nikitta Foston provided "10 Ways to Tell if He's the One."

A 2004 study found that couples who stayed happily married were able to handle conflict well, treating one another with re-spect even as they tackled difficult relationship issues. Partners who are unhappy, on the other hand, will brutalize one another and their children. A quarter of American women report being raped or physically assaulted by a current or former spouse, co-habiting partner, or date sometime in their lives. Although child abuse rates declined slightly by 2000, they rose dramatically through most of the 1990s. Experts estimate that 30 to 40 per-cent of girls and 13 percent of boys are sexually abused. Boys who brutalize girls in their families and high school are just as likely to do so in college and later in their marriages.

When a society is changing, adults and children alike suffer because consensus about appropriate conduct is lacking. Real people live real lives that are often very far from the Christian Right's ideal. Tamara and Paige both agree that Paige's problems stemmed from the lack of a father in her life. "When I was married," Tamara says, "Paige was adopted by my husband, and they clashed from an early age. She was about five when David adopted her. He wasn't there for her—pretty much for the rest of us either. He was a good guy, but his work was his priority. Paige felt second fiddle, and when she did get attention from him it was always discipline. She just never felt loved, and I think that's what Paige still strives for, to feel loved by a man."

Paige, reflecting on her experience with men, says, "I want to grow and expand my insights and take a good honest look at myself. I'm realizing that some of this stuff isn't about me, and some people are just screwed up and you just can't change them. You just need to do what you can for yourself instead of worrying about everything else. So now my thing is 'You can't change a man unless he's in diapers.'" She laughs.

Tamara says that Paige's HIV is "almost like a blessing in a way, because this has brought a whole new awareness to her. I see a lot of growth, and it's actually revealed to her some of her own strengths. She's blossomed. She's found that she can do things and she's found things that she's good at. She's enjoying life and she's put so many more things in perspective, and figured out what's important."

Family and social changes can take a toll on teenagers. Suicide has tripled among U.S. teens since the 1970s and is now the third leading cause of death in that age group, often linked with depression and substance abuse. Female teens are more likely to report suicidal thoughts, as are children of single-parent families. While all of these problems are more prevalent in single-parent homes, social change creates distractions and pressures that can also make two-parent homes less than ideal.

With higher rates of divorce and changing social aspirations, more women enter the workforce when their children are young, placing them at risk of abuse by paid caregivers. Paige was molested in day care before she even entered kindergarten. "One of the day care provider's husbands would come in when all the other kids were out on the swings, and I'd be sitting there watching the monkeys on Nickelodeon. He would come in and touch me and start tongue-kissing me and putting his hands down my pants and feeling around. I thought it was my fault because my babysitter, the day care owner, actually came in and caught him one time and put me in the corner and said I was bad and that it was my fault.

"I never said anything until I was fifteen," Paige says. "I had fought that back for so many years and then I finally said something to my mom. She said, 'I should have listened to you when you said you didn't like that day care center.' I just told her, 'You didn't know and I didn't know,' so it's nothing that I can blame myself or blame her for. That day care center fed us tomato soup every day, and I still cannot eat tomato soup. I will not do it."

Tamara says that Paige "inherited a lot of the men problems from me." She laughs. "I never seem to have been real successful in that arena." Tamara's relationship with Gordon was brief and stormy. She returned to Montana when she was nineteen, and a year after she gave birth to Paige, she married Lindsay's dad, who "got into drugs and women after we were married and I was pregnant, so that marriage lasted a short time, about a year," Tamara said. "That's when I met David. We were together for thirteen years."

Of the Swanberg women, only Lauren, the youngest, seems to have escaped the emotional rollercoaster of Tamara's relationships. Lindsay, now twenty-one, left home to be with her biological father in Las Vegas when she was seventeen. Paige describes her as "a little bit more on the wild side. She is kind of out there. She's works at a strip club and she doesn't really pay attention to a lot of stuff and it really scares me. We communicate quite a bit, but she is just a strange girl."

Tamara describes Lauren as outgoing and happy-go-lucky on the exterior, but says that "she's going through a rough time herself right now. She's challenged with issues with men as well. Fortunately, she has seen a lot of the choices that her sisters have made, and has also lived through some of the consequences and she's making better choices."

Paige says the fact that her adoptive dad has not spoken to her since she told him she was HIV positive "kind of breaks my heart." Her biological father, Gordon, has been very supportive, although she "still has issues in the relationship with him." Paige is proud of the fact that Gordon had done the AIDS walk in Houston. Gordon says he's actually done it twice, and he's also run a marathon, but he did not tell her because he was afraid it would alienate her. Their new relationship is still developing.

Paige contacted him two years after she learned that she was HIV positive. Gordon describes himself as "five-seven, with a shaved head, and heavily tattooed—yet I'm conservative," and laughs. He says, "Paige sent a letter to my ex-wife, which was the last known address that her mom had. I was excited to get it. Everybody said, 'Leave it alone, man, just don't go there. Nothing good can come of it.' I didn't agree at all. I was glad that she wanted to seek me out." She told him she was HIV positive "almost immediately. I felt shocked. I thought, 'Oh my God! She's dying and that's why she's getting in touch with me.' I didn't know that much about it. I always thought that it was a disease that gay people get. I was kind of ignorant in that regard.

"I got married a year after Paige was born and had a family, three boys with another woman. I'm divorced from her now for four years, but I was married to her twenty-one years. PJ contacted me just after my divorce was final," Gordon says. "The timing for me was perfect. She filled a necessary void in my life, but I felt really guilty because I hadn't filled the void that she had needed for so long. Not knowing who your real father is has gotta be difficult. You want to know 'Why wasn't he here for me? What happened?' Sometimes the truth can be ugly and painful, so I didn't think it would be respectful to her mother to tell Paige exactly what kind of relationship we had. We were both loose cannons, you know, rebels without a cause, and neither one of us really needed to bring a child into the world at that particular time, but it happened. That was '81. I'm fifty-two now. I was twenty-eight then."

Gordon says that Paige is just like her mom. "I think the most important thing I can say is that if you don't lead by example, your kids will emulate what they see. If you ever get a chance," he tells me, "watch PJ and her mom walk side by side; they have the same walk. You can see the same thing when young boys walk with their dads. If their dad has a strange gait to his walk, the boys have that same gait. Why? Because they see Dad do it. If Dad's smoking dope on the weekends, don't tell the kids when they get older 'you shouldn't be doing this. It's bad for you.' It doesn't hold water, and they'll lose respect for you because they'll think that you're a hypocrite. Even when parents are there, kids don't get direction, or parents will say one thing and do another. If you don't lead by example, your kids will emulate what they see.

"My dad's situation was much like my situation with my daughter," Gordon admits. "He took off when I was a kid and didn't resurface until I was an adult, and he made the mistake of trying to tell me how I should live my life. I made no bones about telling him exactly what I figured my daughter would tell me. 'Where were you when I was formulating my personality? Don't come and critique it now! Here I am. You're welcome to take part in my life, or you can sit on the fence. But don't preach to me on how I should live my life!' Especially when I found out exactly what kind of man he was.

"I've got three boys. The oldest one is married. He's in the army. But the other two are nineteen and seventeen and they're virgins. They don't fool with any of that stuff. Why? Because I've been divorced for four years and I haven't even been dating until just recently, over the last few months. If you don't practice it, don't bother with preaching it. If you can't live it, then don't tell them this is the way it should be. I've told all the boys and my other daughter that sex outside of marriage is wrong. Some people would say that's unrealistic, but I've tried to practice it these last four years.

"If you don't have a role model, it's tough. I don't want to be rude to PJ's mom, but she's had a lot of men in her life, and when you see that as a young girl, that's what you emulate. I told her mother that. I wasn't rude. I said, 'You know, how can you possibly tell her that what she did was immoral or wrong or dangerous, when you did the same thing?' You practice what you see.

"PJ simply being born shows what can happen through irresponsible self-centeredness. You just drop your pants at some testosterone burst, and devil may care. What happens, happens. It doesn't work like that. It leads to abortion, it leads to single-parent homes, it leads to all kinds of social diseases. Nothing good comes from that. And what's it last for? A few minutes, maybe an hour? But it's certainly all about self-centeredness and not about anything that matters."

Gordon is a born-again Christian who's thought a lot about the impact of his actions on Paige's HIV infection and about male-female relationships. "In a committed relationship, you can have everything that you can have on the other side and more if you've got an emotional tie. Back in the late '70s—this was before HIV and AIDS were even on the scene—I figured that if the woman doesn't take care of the birth control issue, it's not my fault. Typical male self-centeredness. The woman should be taking a pill or doing something. It's not my concern. If I end up with something, I just go to the doctor and I get a shot of penicillin or something like that and it goes away. That was the attitude back then, and for four years, I just ran footloose and fancy free. The rest of my life, I've been really staunchly conservative.

"I can understand that PJ would think that I was a hypocrite. Except for the four years between my first marriage and my second marriage I've lived this, and people who know me know that. I don't know if she'll ever believe it, but that's just the way it is. She didn't benefit from that at all. She is part of the reason why I believe the way I believe. I wouldn't want that to happen to anyone. It happened to her. There's nothing I can do to undo it. Her situation is like so many people that I know that have had a rough go of it, and I'm as guilty as anyone because I wasn't there for her when she needed me to be."

Parents like Tamara and Gordon have to face the emotional fallout of their earlier experimentation, and many try to make amends to the children who were hurt. Gordon says his relationship with Paige "is pretty good, considering the circumstances. I'd like to do more, but what can I do? I wrote her a poem. She said she was into hip-hop and rap. I said, 'Ah, that's a lot of noise.' She said, 'Well, I like poetry.' I said, 'If you like poetry, I'll show you what poetry is.' I sat down and it took me an hour to compose a poem about the life her and I could have had, and should have had, and didn't have, and the way I feel about it now. It says the whole thing, the whole story about what might have been, what might still be and the fact that I'm going to be there for her now regardless. All she has to do is pick up the phone or open her arms and I'll be there.

"But what can you tell somebody who was twenty-two-years old when you first met them? She certainly doesn't want to hear 'I love you.' I made the mistake of telling her that one time and she wasn't ready to hear it. She made no qualms about it. It was a big mistake. I try to be there for all her big events. I went there for her birthday. I've invited her to come down and stay with me. She can even move down here if she wanted to, but she's a grown woman now. She's got her own life. I'm just trying to let her know that I truly am there for her now.

"I telephone her, but most of the time I end up talking to her answering machine. She knows that I do call. I call once or twice a week, all special occasions. I sent her common-law husband a birthday card last year and this year. In spite of the fact that her mother and he don't get along very well, I've tried to show him that I accept him. Whoever she accepts I accept. It's certainly not my place to tell her anything about who she should choose or what her decisions should be. I just back her in anything unless it's obviously detrimental to her well-being.

"I guess if you have a chance to put this in your book, tell Paige that I truly do love her. I wish I could change what was. I'm very proud of the woman she's become in spite of the fact that I've had nothing to do with it."

The human inclination to mate with more than one partner, coupled with weak partner bonds and high mobility, make it especially easy for any STD to spread quickly in contemporary America. But this was also true of earlier periods in our history. After World War II, syphilis was officially reported as the number 10 cause of death in the United States. Like AIDS, syphilis was responsible for a larger proportion of deaths than those actually recorded. Many of its victims officially succumbed to heart disease or other medical problems brought on by syphilis. "Is it justifiable," a U.S. scientist asked in 1947, "to assume that syphilis actually ranks first, instead of its apparent tenth, among killing infections?"

While some would like to alleviate the suffering that comes from adjustment to change by returning to nostalgic bygone times, the clock of social change cannot be set back by fiat. Going back to the patriarchal model of family, which was never America's dominant family form anyhow, is just wishful thinking. It hardly conforms to the needs of modern social interaction and the economic realities of the working family.

There are other ways of addressing family problems than stuffing people back in an imaginary box invented by patriarchal theologians. Fortunately, wider awareness of the limits of the *Father Knows Best* model of family has created a greater tolerance of the huge variety of marital and family forms in the United States. Acceptance of change leads to normalization and wider acceptance of the children of change, easing their burden as widespread social shifts take place.

Recognizing that these changes are neither good nor bad but part and parcel of the postindustrial world, most developed countries have normalized them by providing supports to single-parent households and other people left vulnerable by change. When the U.S. government decides to stop providing this type of social support—something no other developed country is doing—many of society's weaker members are left at risk.

The Swanberg children are all too typical of the fallout of changing family forms in the United States, and of the resulting opportunities and adversities to which we are still trying to adjust. Society is shifting and our cultural institutions must continue to adjust to prevent children from falling through the cracks. Rather than adjust, however, our government leaders are blithely willing to play "let's pretend" with our "family values," abandoning vulnerable children to their fates.

The Bush administration is also busy undercutting single-parent homes. The administration's 4parents.gov website, clearly says that the only healthy form of family is mom, dad, and the kids. Conservative Christian Citizen's Link tells us that "family is the fundamental building block of all civilizations. Marriage is the glue that holds it together. The health of our culture, its citizens and their children is intimately linked to the health and well-being of marriage."

The Christian Right's message for independent moms? Get back to the altar, and fast! The message to troubled wives? Submit! On the conservative Christian site, Family.org, writer Stormie Omartian mentions that some women may face problems because a husband might use submission as a weapon, or has "not made the choice in his heart to be fully submitted to God" and treats his wife badly. Omartian writes: "A wife has a hard time giving her husband the reins to her life if she doesn't believe she can trust him to have her best interests at heart as he steers the course of their lives together. She has trouble going along with his decisions when he refuses to consider her thoughts. And if she has submitted to a male in the past and her trust was violated in some way, it is even more difficult for her to trust now."

All that said, Omartian apologizes for recognizing that the reality of submission may not be so sweet. "Okay, okay!" she acknowledges. "I know that God did not say that a wife needs to submit to her husband only if he proves to be worthy. Submission is a matter of trusting God more than trusting in man." All this seems like an awfully good deal for a male, which is what the Christian Right likes. According to Christian fundamentalists (like Islamic fundamentalists), a woman is like a child and can only know the will of God through a man. Let's just trust he doesn't have HIV, Stormie! In another of the site's articles, written by Mario Schlesky, a woman grieves because she has been struck by the "infertility monster": "I felt like a baby-making machine that didn't work," Mario says.

Following President Bush's speech on the importance of a constitutional amendment defining marriage, the House approved a Marriage Protection Act in July 2004 that defined the institution as strictly a male-female affair, simultaneously stripping the courts of all jurisdictions over same-sex marriage cases. Republican sponsors said it would prevent federal courts from ordering state courts to recognize same-sex marriages permitted by other states, namely Massachusetts. The bill faced strong opposition in the Senate and was never passed. U.S. Representative Jim McGovern of Massachusetts cut to the quick when he remarked that "this bill is mean-spirited, unconstitutional, a dangerous distraction. Instead of addressing the real concerns facing American families, the leadership of this house has decided to throw its political base some red meat."

Disgruntled because their push for a constitutional amendment defining marriage did not succeed in 2004, congressional conservatives introduced a new version of the amendment in the House and Senate in March 2005. It not only limited marriage to a male-female duo, but again stripped courts of their constitutional rights of review because more and more states had defied the 1996 federal ban on same-sex marriage. The legislative proposal would not only degrade the Constitution by amending it to *require* discrimination for the first time in history, but also seeks to reduce the power of the courts by subverting checks and balances established in the Constitution.

"When legislators rail that 'unelected judges' are finding legislative acts unconstitutional, they are attacking the very structure of our democracy," said Professor Chai Feldblum of Georgetown University Law Center. "The last time Congress passed a law stripping the Supreme Court of authority to hear a constitutional challenge was in 1868, when it feared the court might invalidate the military reconstruction of the South after the Civil War."

This drive to reduce—or, if possible, eliminate—the role of the Supreme Court and other courts is a key part of the Christian Right's platform because it would remove all barriers to government control of individuals and violation of their civil rights. The Christian Right website Citizen Link explains that in creating the judiciary, America's founding fathers "created a dangerously unaccountable branch that would usurp power and ultimately grant itself more power than the legislative branch." Citizen Link demands that "everyone who loves the Founding Fathers understand why it is essential to destroy a key tenet of our government," and reduce the power of the courts.

Although the Supreme Court has been stacked with more and more Christian Right-friendly conservative judges since the Reagan administration, state courts can also be meddlesome in achieving its agenda. For example, it was the Massachusetts high court that forced the legislature to give same-sex couples the same rights as opposite-sex couples in 2003, ruling that the state "has failed to identify any constitutionally adequate reason for denying civil marriage to same-sex couples." In March 2005, a San Francisco County Superior Court judge overturned California's legislative ban on gay marriage.

The drive to eliminate the protection our courts provide is useful to organizations that wish to deny civil rights and invade the privacy of citizens in their homes. In addition to patent disregard for women's civil rights and the rights of blacks exhibited in his past opinions, Bush's new Supreme Court justice, John Roberts, mocks the idea that Americans have a fundamental right to privacy, referring to it as our "so-called right to privacy." Like other members of the Christian Right, he was rankled by earlier Supreme Court decisions protecting adult male homosexuals' rights to consensual sex (*Lawrence v. Texas*), women's rights to reproductive choice (*Roe v. Wade*), and couples' rights to purchase contraception (*Griswold v. Connecticut*).

More than 80 percent of Americans feel that states should be prohibited from interfering with the rights of adults to engage in private, consensual sex, but the Christian Right does not. Christian Right archconservative Ron Santorum, Senate Majority whip, agrees with Roberts, saying that the right to privacy "undermine[s] the family" and that "this right to privacy that doesn't exist in my opinion in the United States Constitution, this right was created . . . in *Griswold*." If the Christian Right's attack on marital privacy for all couples is successful, we will be closer to a Christian police state where homes could be inspected for presence of unauthorized birth control and the state's approved version of the Bible.

Gay marriage is only the first type of marriage that defies the Christian Right's efforts to preserve caste and class in America. Mixed-race marriages are undoubtedly next on the Christian Right's agenda. In U.S. history, marriage has frequently been the arena where hidden racist and sexist agendas are carried out. In 1998, while voters in South Carolina finally removed the provision in their state constitution banning interracial marriages, voters in Hawaii and Alaska *added* provisions against same-sex marriages to their constitution.

Peter Wallenstein, a historian who has studied the rise and demise of interracial marriage bans, points out that such bans proliferated in the years between the Civil War, when slavery was abolished, and during the Civil Rights Movement in the 1960s. By interfering in individual marriages and families, the government has routinely tried to limit benefits of citizenship and entitlements to social programs, to control behavior, and to exercise unconstrained political power.

Ralph Neas, who heads the People for the American Way Foundation, hopes that "Americans are growing increasingly wary of the radical right's bid for absolute power. We saw it in the bid to eliminate checks and balances in the Senate. We saw it in the efforts by politicians to order federal courts to interfere with wrenching family decisions in the Terry Schiavo case." Now that Bush is trying to fill retiring Supreme Court Justice Sandra Day O'Connor's vacancy with a man whose Christian Right beliefs are starkly plain, Neas thinks "we will see far-right demands for justices [to] eliminate the right to privacy and other legal protections Americans cherish."

The Christian Right's attacks on the courts will help them continue their attack on the separation of church and state, furthering their interest in turning the United States into an officially "Christian" (read Christian Right) country. The connection of this administration to Dominionists, radical Christian fundamentalists who advocate that this country be run strictly according to the Bible's simple prescriptions for society, is well known. Too few of us take these threats to our civil rights seriously or understand how much ground has already been lost. Although we may be slow to see what is going on, others are not. By allowing our loss of civil liberties and the growth of the Christian Right's influence on our politics, we have become the brunt of jokes worldwide.

What does this progressive loss of our civil rights have to do with spreading AIDS? Several important things. First, abstinence-only education is already increasing HIV and STD rates in young people. Second, gradual restriction of the civil rights of homosexuals opens the doors to an outright attack by the government not only on their behavior, but on the intimate sexual behavior of us all. Third, the Christian Right is furthering its program against condom use in favor of abstinence for adults as well as teens by restricting access to other forms of birth control. Fourth, the Christian Right is tightening its grip on women's behavior, making them more submissive to men by stripping them of all of their civil rights. Fifth, loss of privacy in the home will mean that our behavior can be monitored and judged in all spheres of action.

Although it has plenty to say about restricting the rights of individuals in their homes and shaping our sexuality, our government is doing little to address the real drivers of the HIV/AIDS epidemic: prisons, the sex business, lack of health insurance, and poverty. According to Chris Anders of the American Civil Liberties Union, "It's time for the Republican leadership to stop messing around with the Constitution and get back to addressing the real problems that face Americans."

Everyone loses in a country that confines its vision of the good to the ideals of a very small minority whose agenda is pushed by a president, congress, and state legislators obsessed with pleasing that minority to reap political gains. But the real losers are young people who are trying to change but are not having the same luck as Paige or Tom in finding the social support they need to do it. Paige's sister Lindsay is now balanced perilously on a knife edge created by our society's exploitation of young women in the sex trade.

THE SEX TRADE

Lindsay Swanberg's voice sounds like it's been slept in. It is late in the afternoon when I call, and I do not expect a good reception. Paige has characterized her as wild and strange, and Tamara is tentative. "I had quite the experience with Lindsay," she says. "She's been my most challenging child." Only Lauren seems to have no biases against Lindsay because she's accepted that much of what her sisters have done were for deeper reasons. So I'm surprised that Lindsay is friendly, understands what I am doing, and only wants to help. We talk for almost an hour, and I am continually distracted by her voice, which is tinny. It is thinner, strained, and chopped, unlike those of her mother and sisters. But her laugh has the full rich giggle that is the hallmark of the Swanberg women.

Lindsay has accepted central casting's decision that she play the family role of black sheep. It starts with her appearance: "I look nothing like my family. Paige has brown hair, brown eyes, real tan. My mom's the same way. My little sister Lauren has naturally red hair. I'm the blond-haired, blue-eyed person of the family. I do not tan. I'm in Las Vegas, and I do not tan. I have no color in my skin whatsoever." Now and again during our conversation, she repeats that she was "the real bad one out of the family. I was the bad one."

Lindsay tells me that she started young. "I was a bad little girl," she tells me. "I ran away all the time. Everything my mom told me not to do I did." Tamara says that when "Lindsay tried to live with her adoptive dad, David, that's kind of when the bottom fell out. She had written a note that was sexual in nature, and he went through her purse and found it, and called her bad names. When those names come out from your father and he said he never wanted anything to do with her again, it seemed like life kind of turned around for her. She was fifteen when this thing happened, and he chose to step back. Lindsay started hanging around with some bad people here in Montana."

Tamara says that Lindsay tried many things to get their attention. "She stole two of my cars three times within a twenty-four-hour period and ran off. On her sixteenth birthday, she was arrested. She shows no remorse. Anybody that's tried to help her, she's just run them over. She's very angry. I can't understand it at all. She's lived with my parents. When she was arrested she went to jail for three months, then we sent her to a wilderness camp—Lindsay calls it boot camp—where she lived out in the country. She ended up having to stay there longer, so she was there for six months." Then she went to Job Corps in Utah, where Lindsay says she "did a lot of meth."

When I ask Lindsay why she felt so rebellious, she tries to dodge the question. "I have no idea why I was the way I was. Honestly, I have no idea." But then it starts to come out. "I didn't have a dad. Me and Paige were adopted when we were real young, when I was about five or six, by Lauren's dad. He raised us, but at the same time he was a workaholic. You never saw him. I have no idea if that has anything to do with it, not having a father figure in my life. I also thought that . . . maybe it runs in the family genetic-wise. My mom, from what I hear, wasn't that great. My [birth] dad was really not that great. He was a coke dealer. I don't know if that has anything to do with it."

Like Lindsay, kids all over the country are struggling with significant risks that other generations of teens never faced, risks that increase their likelihood of contracting HIV. Teens who have difficulty coping with stress are more likely to try drugs and abuse alcohol, have sexual relationships that result in pregnancy, commit crimes, or even try to kill themselves. Teens who drink and take drugs are much more likely to have unprotected sex and incur the risk of getting a sexually transmitted disease.

Few troubled teens get sufficient help, and many who manage to reform themselves cannot get a second chance. My friend Sarah's son Christopher (not their real names) was a hardworking kid throughout his teens, and had plans to use the money he had saved working as a short order cook after school and during the summer to finance a bachelor's degree in hotel management. These plans all came to an end when, one night after work, Chris and his friends were caught with a small amount of cocaine.

Adolescent experimentation? Longtime use? Who knows? Chris ended up spending six months in a "boot camp" facility somewhere in the center of the state. He did his time and, with characteristic discipline, became drug-free. What happened? As a consequence of his conviction, Chris found it very difficult to get a job, even at the low end of the restaurant hierarchy. All his savings disappeared in lawyer's fees and fines. His conclusion? "I might as well have committed a real crime, and I might be forced to do it in order to support myself."

In his 2004 book, *The Road to Whatever: Middle-Class Culture and the Crisis of Adolescence*, criminologist Elliot Currie says that "it is increasingly clear that being middle class and white does not provide reliable protection against even the worst perils of adolescence. They are more likely to kill themselves or die in traffic accidents than blacks or Hispanics; they use most illegal drugs at a higher rate than any racial or ethnic group except Native Americans; and their rates of binge drinking, smoking and prescription-drug use are the highest of all."

Currie suggests that we are demonizing troubled young people, who make headlines by gunning down their classmates, by focusing on problems of the minority underclass and exaggerating the difference between poor adolescents and those more fortunate. By doing this, we have lost touch with the fact that "alienation, desperation, and violence" is pervasive among the young people of our society. "These troubles tell us much about ourselves as a society and a culture." Our explanations of deviance, Currie says, focus on the "dark-skinned poor" so much that we miss the facts that deviance is widespread among our young people as a whole.

According to Currie, "The United States had long been a country distinctive in the advanced industrial world for the harshness of its policies toward children and youth, and especially toward adolescent deviance." We allowed corporal punishment of young people and upheld it in the courts for much longer that any other advanced nation, and we were the only country—the others are Iran and Nigeria—to allow execution of people for crimes committed when they were juveniles.

"We were also the industrial nation with the weakest and least reliable social supports for the young," Currie says. "We had no system of family allowances, no universal health care system, no paid parental leaves from work to care for children, no national apprenticeship system to link school with stable and rewarding work." With a growing conservatism in the 1980s and 1990s, the gaps between our policies and those of other advanced countries have widened. "We had increasingly become," Currie says, "the land of the 'non-helping hand.'"

The increasing violence and alienation of our young people are sustained as they grow into adulthood. Americans are the only citizens of advanced countries where a substantial minority of adults agree that violence is an appropriate way to settle a disagreement, says Canadian pollster Michael Adams in his book, *Fire and Ice.* Our values, which stem from our traditional belief in rugged individualism and our embrace of Social Darwinism more than a century and a half ago, are becoming more and more dysfunctional for the nation as a whole.

Currie says that the United States "is a world that is remarkably hard on its young—a world shaped by a careless, self-serving individualism in which real support from parents, teachers, or other adults is rare and punishment and self-righteous exclusion are routine." We have created a world "that places high expectations for performance on adolescents but does remarkably little to help them do well, a world in which teenagers' emotional problems are too often met with rejection—or medication— rather than attentive and respectful engagement." For children who fail to fit into "an increasingly competitive and unsupportive social order, these are hard times indeed." Currie holds that we have made adolescence "unduly harsh," and our children are retaliating against us when they are harmed and not helped by our "unhelping hand."

The National Runaway Switchboard (NRS) says that at least 1.3 million teens under the age of eighteen live on the streets. Some stay for a night, but others are "throwaways," kids who are thrown out of their homes because their problems exceed their parents' coping skills, or kids whose parents or guardians are addicts, incapacitated for other reasons, or in jail. About 70 percent of these young people engage in prostitution to meet their everyday needs. Forty-nine percent of teen prostitutes are girls and 51 percent are boys, says the NRS. On the streets, their risks increase even more.

When Lindsay left the Job Corps at seventeen, she avoided the streets by moving to Las Vegas to live with her biological father. He proved to be the worst port in the storm, a drug dealer who ended up living off his daughter. Hooked on crack, her weight dropped to 85 pounds. "I'm about five-seven," she says. "I'm already skinny as it is. I weigh 120 now, and I got down to 85 pounds. I just had to quit, because I looked so disgusting. I couldn't be around it." Lindsay managed to quit the addiction on her own and got a job detailing cars. "It's like cleaning them, getting them ready for shows. A car that I detailed was in the *Low Rider Magazine*. I don't want to do that anymore. The pay's not that great. I do it to my cars. I take very good care of my cars."

Lindsay was just coming off her coke habit when she learned she was pregnant with her son Jaden. She says, "That turned my life around a complete 180. When I got pregnant I had to get my shit together. I wasn't going to give him up for adoption. I wasn't going to get an abortion. It was a blood thing. I thought it would help me and my family get a lot closer, and it made me realize what's really important. It was a big change, especially when I had him. It was the greatest thing. It was the best time of my life, I think."

Jaden lives with Tamara in Billings, but Lindsay's "getting everything situated so I can bring him back down here. I'm getting this house and everything like that. Hopefully that will work out, but he should be back down with me within a month, I would say. Right now I'm living with my friend in a condo out here in Henderson, but I'm looking for a house out in Summerlin. I'm trying to do that so I can have everything good."

She tried to go back to Montana to get her cosmetology license, but found herself in with the same old crowd. "The reason I came back to Las Vegas is to stay away from everybody I hung out with in Montana. When I went back there, I'd go to one of the clubs, and nobody liked me because of the people I hung out with. It was more of a jealousy thing because of these guys. Everybody wants to hang out with these guys. They respect me. They're friends with me. I'm not one of their bitches, and girls don't like me because of that."

Lindsay has realized that, in the language of the Swanberg women, she can make better choices for herself. "I don't talk to those guys anymore. Since I moved back out here, I haven't talked to them. I don't want to talk with them. I don't want anything to do with them. I've been friends with them ever since I was young, but they're the hustlers, drug dealers, pimps. It's chaotic. Lot of drama. Lot of baby-momma drama. Lot of drama that I don't need and I don't want.

"It's hard in such a small city like that. Things are all packed together and you're going to run into them. You can't get away. I'd go to the mall and see them all over the place. All these guys come to Montana. My old friend Marco, for example, he's been in Montana for almost a year and a half and has four kids. Yeah, they're like male hos. They're whores out there. My other friend's got eleven kids."

In the United States today, there is a huge but hidden population of "lost" teens, says Jonathan Franzen in a 2005 *New Yorker* article, "some of them good students, some of them roughnecks, some of them just misfits, all of them undernourished by the values of their parents." Physical and sexual abuse of children—or neglect and family conflict—sends millions of children running away from home. They are finding work in or at the periphery of the adult sex industry, and most will struggle and lose in their addiction to alcohol, drugs, or sex. Since they have had abstinence-only education and form a pool for the recruitment of young prostitutes, they are likely to fail in the struggle to avoid HIV and other STDs.

Las Vegas, America's sin city, is a magnet for young people drawn by the promise of high-paying jobs in the sex and entertainment industry. More than 35 million tourists visit the city every year, which is home to fourteen of the world's fifteen biggest hotels. Tourists spend in excess of $25 billion a year, including $8 billion in wagers. Las Vegas vies with its next-door neighbor, Henderson, where Lindsay lives, as the fastest-growing city in the country.

"I'm a cocktail waitress at a strip club, the Sapphire, behind the Stardust. It's the world's largest gentlemen's club. Good money for a cocktail waitress, very good money. Cocktailing is not bad at all. The environment's not bad. People that work there are actually very nice. The girls are very nice. There's a lot of girls, though. It's humongous. It used to be a gymnasium up until three years ago, so it's huge. Friday and Saturday nights they have male dancers, but otherwise it's all females. It's mainly 95 percent males that come in.

"It's just dancing—they have very strict rules—just entertaining. Lap dancers, the VIP room, sky boxes. I just serve them drinks. Big bachelor parties come in and usually they get a bottle, and then I get a good tip off that. Bottles run $250. People actually pay that for a $10 bottle of booze. I just walk around. They don't pay you to work. You're like self-employed. You bring in your own money. Somebody orders a drink, you go get the drink with your money, and then you go get their money and whatever they want to tip you. So you work off your own money. That's actually pretty good. Now, I make awesome money. In one night I can make what somebody makes in a week in Montana, in two weeks in Montana. It's getting me up there. Even though the cost of living is a little bit higher than it is in Montana, if I work my ass off for one night I could make my rent."

Strip clubs like the Sapphire have proliferated across the United States. The *Exotic Dancer Bulletin* estimates that the number of clubs has jumped 30 percent in the last decade to 2,500, with at least 250,000 dancers. With an average audience size of 200, this leads to an estimate of over half a million customers a night across the country. New Jersey has more strip clubs (called go-go or juice bars) than any other state, over 300 in urban areas, some said to be under control of Russian "businessmen." In 1996, the *Boston Globe* estimated that the country's 2,200 strip clubs yielded annual revenues of $3 billion. A recent survey in Chicago found 25 clubs with exotic dancers or stripping and 27 that had occasional "special events."

Organized crime controls, finances, or backs most of the clubs, researchers say, but Lindsay tells me that "the mob doesn't run Las Vegas anymore. It's all corporate." Over the past ten years, more and more of the sex industry is coming under corporate ownership, according to *Insight on the News* reporter James Harcher. He says that "Fortune 500 companies are swooping down from their financial kingdoms to compete in the pornography industry for a market flush with profits, growth potential and increased public tolerance." This may also go a long way in explaining why we never hear President Bush or the Christian Right lambasting the sex trade or trying to invade the privacy of these giants.

The porn movie business alone produces 4,000 movies a year with sales topping $13 billon. Harcher says the "market is so lucrative that even blue-chip companies such as General Motors Corporation and AT&T have jumped into the dirty game." Brian Pryor, managing editor of *Adult Video News Online*, says, "It's more distribution for the industry, so it's all to the good." GM, the largest company in the world, markets through Hughes Electronics and DirecTV, its satellite-TV company, offering news, sports, movies, and porn to 9 million homes in America. AT&T offers a full array of adult erotica through AT&T broadband.

Paul Fishbein, the founder and president of the industry's trade publication, *Adult Video News*, says that more than 800 million adult videos and DVDs are rented each year from the country's video stores. "And I don't think that it's 800 guys renting a million tapes each." Bill Lyon, a former defense industry lobbyist who runs a trade organization representing 900 companies in the porn business, says that the industry employs 12,000 people in California and pays over $36 million in taxes each year in that state alone.

Harcher says that $56 billion is "up for grabs in the international porn industry," and even respectable hotel chains like Hilton and Marriott reap the profits of X-rated in-room entertainment. Only Omni Hotels decided to stop selling porn. "As a father of two sons, I was uncomfortable with the late-night entertainment available," said Omni's owner and chairman, Bob Rowling. "We didn't want to generate revenue on pornography." Omni faced a challenge, however, finding cable companies that were willing to exclude porn because of the loss of profits. When Omni increased family movie offerings to compensate, its profit from movie rentals increased.

Thanks to the competition of explicit sexual material on the Internet and television, and even from home videos, strip clubs have changed a lot over the past fifty years. When I was a kid, my mom and dad would head into downtown Baltimore from time to time to see Belle Starr. She was a dancer, and at her most risqué, she stripped to an outfit of silver pasties with bottoms more modest than you would see on a typical beach nowadays. Her long white ostrich feather boa spent most of its time covering her vital parts. I had no idea what strip clubs had become until I started researching this book, but I guess I am not alone. Researcher Jody Raphael says that "the public has not caught on to the transformation of the business."

While "gentlemen's clubs" say they allow only dancing, researcher Melissa Farley says that "physical contact has now escalated. Now you can buy a table or lap dance. This is socially normalizing prostitution." Kelly Holsopple, who survived thirteen years in the adult entertainment industry, says, "Stripping usually involves prostitution, and always involves sexual harassment and abuse. Women are expected to climb on small tables or couches and display their genitals, often within inches of a customer's face. At more and more clubs, women are expected to straddle a man's penis during a lap dance until he cums in his pants.

"Women are continuously called *cunt, whore, pussy, slut*, and *bitch* by customers and management alike. Customers spit on women, spray bear, flick cigarettes, and shoot water guns at them. Performers are pelted with ice, coins, and trash, hit with cans and bottles thrown from the audience. Customers pull women's hair, yank them by their arm or ankle, and grab their breasts, buttocks, and genitals. Women are commonly pinched, bitten, slapped, punched, and kicked. Men often expose their penises and try to stick their fingers, money, or bottles into women's vaginas."

In upscale and downscale reviews alike, women perform by taking showers and playing with sex toys in front of men. In some clubs' private viewing rooms, women perform erotic acts on request, shielded from customer assault by a sheet of safety glass. Private or back rooms are often the site for private violence, where dancers are paid extra by men who burn them with cigarettes, grab, beat, and choke them, or try to pull the hair out of their heads. One former prostitute says, "I don't believe that it was the acts of sex that their wives wouldn't do. I believe it was whatever in life they have been through, they wanted some way to act it out or give it back."

As one dancer characterized it, stripping is now a "contact sport," lap dancing is having sex with clothes on, and the Pretty Woman is a long-gone icon except at the very top of a multi-billion dollar-sex industry that earns more than sporting events, television, and movies combined. Few dancers end up married to major league baseball players like Anna Benson, wife of Mets Pitcher Kris Benson. Anna says, "I was a lonely latchkey kid." She dropped out of school in the tenth grade and left home when she was sixteen. "I was a dancer at the Atlanta strip clubs, the Mardi Gras and the Cheetah. I had a baby and then a husband when I was seventeen." Kris met her at the Mardi Gras when he was playing on a triple-A club and married her a few years later.

"It's not dangerous for the cocktail waitresses," Lindsay assures me. "They're very security conscious at the Sapphire. They're very strict. A lot of girls stay across the street at the Budget Suites. It's a weekly hotel. They actually walk them or drive them to the rooms. You can't leave with customers. They're very strict. If you're getting picked up, you have to be picked up by the same person that dropped you off. They check up on you a lot. The Vice [squad] comes in and they try to trick the girls, the girls that are prostitutes in there. They'll try to pull something on the dancers. Like, 'I'll pay you $3,000 if you come to my room tonight.' If they get a hookup like that, or if the girl does some thing in the VIP room or off the floor, they'll take them away to jail just like that."

Prostitution is illegal within the city limits of Las Vegas, but Lindsay tells me that "they have a couple of whorehouses on the outskirts northwest of Vegas, in Summerlin. When the mob ran Vegas, they thought if they made it illegal they would make more money. It's been illegal for fifty years. But it doesn't stop anybody. If I went into a casino right now, I could point out every single prostitute. I've been here for almost five years altogether, and I could point out every single prostitute. Most of them are very, very young, and a good majority of them have pimps. Anywhere from eighteen and up. There's a seventy-year-old prostitute. It scares me. I don't see how they could do it. Every day on the news, the first half hour of it is about death and all the stuff that happens to prostitutes. Vegas is getting real bad. They mentioned on the news a few weeks ago that there's over 300 gangs here. A little small city."

The safety of prostitutes generally declines with age, as most are forced to migrate from clubs and bordellos to street prostitution. Few nonwhite prostitutes have the opportunity to start higher on the food chain, so women of color are over-represented in street prostitution. A U.S. Department of Justice manual for law enforcement officers says that the "typical street prostitute," the lowest rung on the sex worker ladder, "works six to eight hours a day, five to six days a week, and has three to five clients a night. Street prostitutes' lives are organized principally around prostitution itself, and around maneuvering through the legal system. It is a cycle of engaging in prostitution, getting arrested, going to jail, paying fines, and returning to the streets."

"It's just crazy." Lindsay's voice drifts up nervously. "There's a lot of crazy people that actually come into the club. Just cocktailing, I had to punch a guy one time. He actually bit my ass. It was a big bachelor party, and I was bending to pour the drinks because I was serving them all the drinks out of the bottle, and he bit my ass. It made me mad. There's some nasty guys that come in there, very nasty guys. Any rich guy here has somebody on the side whether or not they're married. They'll take them out to dinner or take them shopping, like a Sugar Daddy. They'll just do anything for a girl if she treats them right."

Serious researchers know that the popular memoirs of prostitutes are far from the gritty truth for most women in the business. The illusion that prostitution provides economic upward mobility and a glamorous lifestyle is compelling for poor or homeless girls. Recruitment flyers are distributed for exotic dancers and escort services in every major downtown, promising $2,000 to $4,000 per week, room and board, and transportation expenses. Adolescent innocence is deliberately exploited to lure girls into the business. Pimps target girls who seem naive, lonely, homeless, and rebellious, and seduce them individually with false affection and gifts.

In testimony to the Michigan House of Representatives in 2000, David Sherman, who managed sex clubs in Detroit, testified that girls are lured first into waitressing, like Lindsay. Then, as they become accustomed to and desensitized by life in the clubs, they are asked to dance occasionally as a favor to management. They are gradually socialized into what he calls the basic dancer attitude, "when a dancer thinks that no matter what friends, children, husbands and families think about her, it doesn't matter. They can all be replaced because all of the patrons around her find her attractive, beautiful, and she is idolized."

Management and her fellow workers act as best friends. The young dancers, separated from the outside world, "exist alone in this dark subculture of sex, drugs, alcohol, and prostitution," and "perverse living" becomes a normal lifestyle, Sherman said. Strip clubs usually operate legally, while prostitution goes on in private rooms and "VIP" lounges.

The industry includes street prostitution, massage brothels, escort services, outcall services, strip clubs, lap dancing, phone sex, adult and child pornography, video and Internet pornography, live Internet performances, and sex tourism. Its billion-dollar annual revenues do not include many of these activities (only those resulting documented sales), nor do they include the casual sale of a child or family member's sexual services to another person, which is often the prelude to full-time sex work at a later age. They do not include being pimped by one's boyfriend or working on the side in high school or college to pay for extras or for college tuition.

The average age of entry into prostitution is thirteen years, and most young prostitutes are recruited or coerced into the trade, a large majority by a "boyfriend." Estimates of the prevalence of incest among prostitutes range from 65 to 90 percent. The correlation between child abuse and risky sexual behavior, including prostitution, is well documented.

Twenty recent studies have found that the experience of child abuse among prostitutes ranges from 30 to 84 percent, with a prevalence three to five times the estimated national average. As the level and intensity of child sexual abuse increase, the likelihood of later involvement in prostitution does too. Because many sexual abuse victims end up in trouble with the law, girls are frequently recruited through juvenile detention facilities; having sexual relations with staff members is an easy way for girls to get preferential treatment and small rewards, like sodas.

Women in the trade typically have been betrayed by most of the men in their lives, who view them as objects for their own gratification or profit. Some researchers say that early abuse causes a separation between emotions and sexual activity. Debasing a young female's self-concept facilitates her self-identification as a prostitute. Entry into formal prostitution is usually preceded by running away from home to escape violence, and having to support herself at an early age. Interpersonal contact with a sex worker or the coercion of a "boyfriend" then leads to involvement in the business.

For poor women, prostitution may be a coping or survival strategy. Debate continues about whether most prostitutes become drug addicts before or after they enter the trade, but it is clear that the need to support a drug habit often plays a role in keeping a woman working. Women and men involved in prostitution are three times more likely to use alcohol and illegal drugs because substance-abuse helps keep them desensitized to what they must do for a living.

Each year, federal statistics show that more than 34,000 men and 53,000 women are arrested for prostitution and commercialized vice. It is not possible to know how many of these were customers. A survey of more than 61,000 people in 9,000 jurisdictions found that 58 percent of those arrested for prostitution were white and about 40 percent were African American.

The U.S. Department of Justice police manual says that 10 to 20 percent of men admit they have paid for sex, but only about 1 percent pay for it regularly. Other national studies estimate the proportion of regular users of prostitutes at about 8 percent of all men. In a National Health and Social Life Survey in 1992, 16 percent of men said they had visited a sex worker at least once in their lives, but less than 1 percent said they paid for sex every year. Men who came of age in the 1990s paid for sex far less frequently than men who came of age in the 1950s. In 1996, a large national survey of adult U.S. sexuality found that 1.2 million adults between eighteen and fifty-nine years old had participated in prostitution over the last twelve months.

Few girls enter prostitution voluntarily. More than half report that their "johns" (customers) and pimps used pornography to show them what to do or desensitize them to the degradation of the trade. Sociologist Diana Russell argues that pornography encourages men to rape women because it is a major source of male sex role socialization. Exposure to pornography can encourage men to have forced rape fantasies and undermines the inhibitions of those with an existing desire to rape.

Russell says that pornography contributes to abnormal sexual behavior and leads to sexual addiction, sex with prostitutes, divorce, loss of family, and problems with the law. An investigator with the Los Angeles Police Department says that "the higher their education, the more prone these people are to becoming addicted" and that like all addictions, the addict graduates to successively harder-core porn to get his kick, to more deviant and kinky material.

After a while addicts become desensitized, so that even the most objectionable and degrading material becomes legitimized. Porn watchers feel more and more pressure to act out what they see in videos, including having sex with children and inflicting pain on partners. Paying to act out outrageous behavior in sex clubs is one way to "legally" do that. Being married or with a willing sexual partner made no difference. Researchers have found that pornography is a contributing factor in one-quarter of all violent sexual offenses. Pornography itself is sometimes made under conditions of near slavery, against the will of the performer.

Researchers think that the power differentials are part of what men seek out in sex clubs, where "the most vulnerable women are made available for constant sexual access," says Melissa Farley. Some surmise that the social distance between client and worker allows men to exploit women in ways that they would never exploit their mothers, wives, or sisters. In some clubs, the dancers act out the fantasy of being hunted beasts while the men play hunters, zoo keepers, or animal tamers.

Of his experiences in a "gentlemen's club," one man interviewed for a 1999 study said, "this is the part of me that can still go hunting." The sex industry employs primarily young and poor women to service the illicit demands of middle- and upper-class men, so they feel less inhibited in expressing socially unacceptable feelings. Often black prostitutes claim that their most sadistic customers are white men acting out fantasies of racial hatred and abuse.

With the exception of its supermodels and porn stars, America pays its women an income that averages less than three-quarters of that earned by men doing the same job. Fear Us, an antipornography organization, says that because money talks, "women have become socialized to view themselves as sexual objects. Supermodels and porn 'stars' have become role models for our young girls." The relationship between sexual violence in the media and increasingly callous attitudes toward women is stronger than the association between smoking and cancer.

This unhealthy imbalance of power is nurtured when men such as the president of Harvard muse that women are less gifted at math and science than men, despite numerous studies that prove him wrong. And when men as powerful as the President of the United States nominate Supreme Court hopefuls who are clearly and patently hostile to women's rights, the message to women is even stronger.

The high incidence of rape and involuntary sex in this country also signal severe power imbalances between men and women and is a precursor to female subordination in the adult entertainment industry and in prostitution. Many argue that since pornography encourages men to see women as sexual objects to be exploited, it contributes heavily to sustaining skewed sexual beliefs.

Although formal education—at least until the abstinence-only curriculum arrived in 1998—taught that male dominance and violence is unacceptable, children and adults are taught through violent television and movies and pornographic materials to accept it. In a recent poll of high school students, 39 percent of the boys and 12 percent of the girls said rape was okay if a male had spent a lot of money on a female or if she had turned the guy on and "he couldn't stop." The proportion of boys who said forced sex was all right increased to over half if the girl got him excited and changed her mind, "led him on," or they had dated for a long time.

In the United States, the myth of uncontained male sexual appetite and willing female submission is just that: a myth that has stronger roots in Christian theology than in the realities of male-female characteristics. According to anthropologist Lawrence Hammar, "Most Christian and customary doctrines and practices regarding land, money, reproduction, and sex assume that males have God-given rights to control the sexual and reproductive health of and regulate male sexual access to females more or less unhindered."

The male condom was invented in the sixteenth century; hundreds of years later, in the early 1990s, the female condom was invented. Viagra came on the scene in the mid-1990s, while "pink" Viagra still awaits development, as does a female-controlled vaginal microbicide that women can use to protect themselves from HIV. Medicare and insurance companies pay for Viagra while they refuse to pay for birth control pills; the U.S. military could foot the bill for their troop's Viagra but could not find money to armor vehicles in Iraq. The total market for male arousal drugs is $2.7 billion per year and rising fast. When the "little blue pill" broke sales records for drug manufacturer Pfizer, Eli Lilly and GlaxoSmithKline quickly brought copycat drugs to market. In the meantime, studies show that 43 percent of women are dissatisfied with sex compared to 31 percent of men.

Although private interests profit from the U.S. sex industry, the taxpayer foots the bill for the high public costs it creates. In 1994 San Francisco estimated that the cost of policing prostitution was $7.6 million. A more recent study of New York City street prostitutes found that sex work costs the city about $46,000 per year in jail time alone for each working prostitute. Prostitutes are very mobile, moving to avoid arrest or find customers, and their places of work are transitional neighborhoods, areas where other businesses profit, like hotels and bars, and where clients can readily buy drugs.

The City of Seattle Department of Housing and Human Services says that women in the sex industry were one of the three populations most in need of specialized services, primarily as a result of the violence inflicted on them in their work. Prostitutes are routinely raped, beaten, and emotionally assaulted by their pimps, their customers, and police. Many suffer from posttraumatic stress disorder, experiencing extreme anxiety, depression, insomnia, flashbacks, irritability, emotional numbing, or extreme physical and mental alertness. Counselors who work with recovering prostitutes say it is like working with torture victims. These women often have cumulative brain injuries from being beaten up and knocked out. Many prostitutes alternate between rage, grief, self-hatred, fear, alienation, and loneliness, leading to emotionally unstable and unpredictable behavior.

One survivor, whose experience is typical of even low-paid beginners, said "For a great part of 1992, I lived in a beautiful apartment on Capitol Hill. I drove an expensive car. I bought lovely clothes and traveled extensively out of the country. For the first time in my life as an adult woman, I paid my own way. I felt invincible." But the price was high. "I was miserable to the core. I hated myself because I hated my life. All the things I came to possess meant nothing. I could not face myself in the mirror. Working in prostitution, I had lost my soul." Many women in street prostitution—as many as 63 percent of them—try to hurt themselves because of their intense feelings of self-hatred and degradation. Eighty percent of participants in prostitution support groups report that they have made a serious suicide attempt.

Sex Industry Survivors, which provides support for former prostitutes trying to change their lives, says, "We believe it doesn't matter how long you did it, how you earned it, how much you got paid, or how long you have been out of it. We believe that the sex industry violates basic human rights: the right to be treated with dignity and respect. We do not believe it is a victimless crime." Human rights experts say that the sex industry violates all human rights guaranteed under international conventions, including the right to security, the right to be free of torture and cruel and degrading treatment, the right to privacy, protection of property, the right to liberty, and the right to life.

Paige's biological father, Gordon, says "There's a lot of organized prostitution in Houston. Any twenty-four-hour bookstore has advertisements on the door for escort services, massage parlors. Everyone knows that they're prostitution rings. I don't know what my department does about it. I'm sure it happens in every major city. What amazes me is that it's allowed to go on. There's politics involved there, I'm sure. There's so much money in it, but it's not helping the tax roles, it's not helping anyone. If we're going to let it go on, let's make it legal and take some of the money and dump it into the problem. Instead, none of it's going to the problem."

As a deputy sheriff, Gordon says, "People in my line of work bust young women all the time. A lot of them are much like my daughter. Dad's not around, Mom doesn't know what's going on. They'll go turn tricks on a weekend, and then go back home and go to school. No one knows anything about it. It's cash money. I'll come up on a scene, and there'll be people parking in a parking garage or a shopping mall. They're going at it and there's no protection going on at all. It's spontaneous. They're high on drugs or they've been drinking, and it's just something that happens, spur of the moment. 'Oh well, let's take a chance.' I see a lot of that.

"I don't think it's romance at all, I think it's lust. I think sex is everywhere. I think if there was more romance involved, you'd have more monogamous relationships because that's what romance is all about. There's nothing romantic about looking at a woman across the room and winking and blinking and then the next minute you're in the closet going at it like monkeys. That's not romance. That's lust. And you see it on all the billboards, you see it in all the magazines, you see it in commercials, it's everywhere. It's all about lust. And it sells."

Globally and in the United States, demand is increasing for prostitutes of younger and younger ages because they are more likely to be submissive and less likely to carry STDs or AIDS—or demand condom use. While upscale call girl and sex advisor Tracy Quan, who wrote *Diary of a Manhattan Call Girl*, may think that the AIDS epidemic has substantially changed the behavior of "johns," women lower on the ladder say that they often skip the condom because clients will pay more without it, threaten violence, or go to another sex worker.

Demand is so high that 50,000 women are trafficked from other countries and sold into U.S. brothels each year, according to U.S. Department of Justice estimates. On January 14, 2004, federal agents raided four suspected brothels in San Francisco's Sunset District and busted an international prostitution ring that smuggled Asian women into the United States. The women were forced to work off a $40,000 debt to the traffickers in a modern-day version of slavery. After drug dealing and arms trafficking, human trafficking is the third biggest criminal industry in the world today and the fastest growing. Some experts say that more women and children are trafficked today than Africans were sold into slavery in the 1800s.

The sex business accounts for an estimated one-third of all Internet activity. Child porn enthusiasts and pedophiles can find "hot young teens" with a click of the mouse. The typical online pedophile is a white male between twenty-five and forty years old with no prior convictions. In 1999, an American named Sandler added a live bondage show to his website. Operated out of his Cambodian "Rape Camp," men blindfolded, bound, and gagged women and used them in sex acts. The site even included a pay-for-view feature so customers could request their favorite acts of torture.

Now that these activities have been made prosecutable, some computer services offer "confidential" computer cleanups for people who do not want their online activities traced or do not know the history of their used personal computers. "I bought a used computer and because of the fact that I was afraid of the history of the computer, I had a buddy of mine clean it out," Gordon says. "Ever since I bought it, I know for a fact none of my boys would dare get involved in that crap, and I certainly don't need it. Why put that in your face? It's like any other vice. If you open the door, what goes in, comes out. I don't go there. I don't look at that stuff. I'm as normal as the next guy. I just don't crucify myself with it."

The federal government issued stricter regulations effective June 23, 2005 which require that all sites with explicit adult content must keep records to prove their models are eighteen or older, even if the postings are not made by the website owners themselves. After the new federal regulations came out, Gay.com took down all personal listings that it thought were underage, although PlanetOut Inc., Gay.com's parent company, protested the infringement of individual civil liberties.

Craigslist.com, labeled the "hottest si[t]
magazine *The Advocate*, has a "casual enc[o]
straight pleasure seekers where men outnum[
to 1. Internet sites offer immediate, home-deliv[
ity in every major city. The traveling enthusia[s]
vance bookings from the sites Gay.com, [
worldsexguide.org, and others, which provide he[   ] [l]ks to
travel reservations, airlines, government tourist information, and
city sites. Inexperienced readers contemplating a visit to these
sites should prepare for a shock. Advertisements are explicit,
using very young-looking models and hard-core language in
their descriptions of sexual services in every country in the world.
Patrons of the worldsexguide.com post reviews giving other customers up-to-date information on cost and availability of sex at
various clubs around the country and pointers on how to get
cheap lap dances or more for their money from adult entertainment venues.

In mid-2004 Los Angeles' pornographic movie industry was
shut down by an outbreak of HIV. It was not the first time. In
1998 a male actor infected five women, and in 1999, another
male actor tested HIV positive. In 2004 Darren James, who believes he was infected while filming in Brazil, failed to wait long
enough before he had an HIV test. He infected teenage Canadian porn star Lara Roxx while he was still in the window period.
She had been in the industry for only three months. All sixty-five
performers who may have been infected by James and three other
HIV-positive film stars were tested, but results were never reported by the media.

When Lindsay learned that Paige was HIV positive, she said
she "freaked out. I went for a drive, and that calmed me down. I
went over to my friend Janie's house, and she helped me out a
lot." Janie (not her real name) was a sex worker who befriended
Lindsay when she first moved to Vegas. "That night I found out
Janie had AIDS for ten years. She died three years ago. Her
daughter's father had it, and she found out when she went into
labor with her daughter. But her daughter doesn't have it, which
is good. Janie was at the point where she didn't want to live. She

as tired of it. She actually tried to kill herself. She would drink every day, all day long. She just wanted it to be over with. That's why I'm so proud of Paige. She takes really good care of herself. She's open about it. She doesn't try to hide it."

At the time, Lindsay says, "I was kind of promiscuous. That's how I got pregnant. Now I have boxes of condoms. I get tested twice a year just to make sure. I'm very cautious now. I don't sleep with anybody right away. With my boyfriend, I still use protection. He's been tested, and I go get tested. We all get tested. Everyone I know, I'm like 'Go get tested!' I've talked to a lot of people already, people I've run into, my friends and my roommate. Her little brother is sixteen, and we talk to him all the time. We tell him, 'If you have sex, use protection!'

"I know a lot of people in Vegas who also know somebody who's positive. My friend Renée [not her real name], her parents died of it. She's a dancer at the place I work. She's originally from Chicago, but was raised here. She's been on her own since she was sixteen because her parents died of AIDS. She's only twenty-two, but she had a daughter, bought a house, a car, dances, goes to school, and is going to open up her own business. She has her mind set. Last year she actually got signed by *Hustler* to do pictures. She was doing that for a while, but she couldn't travel that much with her daughter."

Researchers have found that sex is good for us in many ways. It is a response to a natural urge, it can open up communication between partners, and it can be a joyous experience. Sex also provides other important benefits to the body. Sexual arousal in the vaginal wall reduces the pain threshold 50 percent, while orgasm reduces it by 100 percent. Rutgers psychologist Dr. Barry Komisaruk says that lingering back pain can be alleviated for a full day with a few minutes of sexual stimulation, and says "orgasm is probably incredibly good for the brain. The entire brain is being oxygenated." Other researchers have found that orgasm increases immune system function. Interestingly enough, Komisaruk says, magnetic resonance images or MRIs of the female brain during arousal look just like the aroused male brain.

In the various sexual "revolutions" that took place during the 1960s to the 1990s, hippies, free lovers, gays, young singles, and teens challenged existing social norms of family and sexual behavior. These norms were already changing radically, and the challenges had positive benefits, encouraging more open discussion of sexuality and the double standard for men and women, and broadening the basis of sexual morality. The absolute rules of the 1950s—even the mere idea that there should be absolute rules—have given way to a morality of personal choice. However, while as a society we became more "permissive" and more open to diversity than our parents, this is not the same as an anything-goes policy. Sex should still include mutual consent, affection, and respect—when it does not, the consequences in terms of HIV transmission, violence, and physical and emotional harm are extraordinary and long lasting.

The sex industry violates most of our beliefs about good sex for the purpose of making a profit. Afraid of the violence and tired of the degradation of her work, Lindsay wants out. "I'm looking for a nine-to-five. I'm looking for something in an office, law firm, mortgage firm, banking. Just something not associated with a strip club." She laughs. "It's hard to change, to an extent. I don't do drugs anymore. I just turned twenty-one. I don't even drink that much. I've done all that when I was a kid.

"I'm planning on moving again. Not to Montana—I can't stand Montana. I hate Montana, and I won't go to California either. I've been traveling and checking out places, seeing what I like. My boyfriend wants me to move to Miami with him. I hear so many good things about Miami. My boyfriend is thirty. He's very nice. He has everything together. He wants a lot of things. He's one of the very few guys I really truly find that don't have a side hustle. He doesn't sell drugs. He's not a pimp. It's very hard to find somebody that's good, that has their shit together. He's a chef."

The exploitation of sex for profit or power over other human beings always leads to severe consequences. Just as her sister Paige had no trouble finding work in a Billings casino, Lindsay's good looks have given her an advantage in finding high-paying work in Las Vegas' adult entertainment business. Gradually Lindsay is becoming desensitized to club work, describing it like a walk in the park. When I go to the Sapphire Club's website, I learn that she is working topless, and that the VIP rooms are suspended over the main club floor to view the chaos that goes on below. As I reflect on the strange quality of Lindsay's voice, I realize that it is the voice of a young woman who, like many of her peers in or on the margins of the U.S. sex industry, has been thoroughly traumatized. It is the muffled voice of a girl straining to keep a life composed of too many vulnerable moments together.

Postscript: In October 2005, after this chapter was written, Lindsay returned to Montana to live with Tamara and Jaden. Tamara said that so far, things are going well.

DRUGS AND AIDS

Like so many teens in America, Paige and Lindsay coped with their troubled lives by self-medicating with drugs. Lindsay started with marijuana, alcohol, and meth, and later became a crack addict with the encouragement of her biological father. During her rebellious period, Paige used methamphetamines, or "crank" as her mother calls it, otherwise known as meth, crystal meth, tweak, or ice. The National Institute on Drug Abuse states that "behavior associated with drug abuse is now the single largest factor in the spread of HIV infection in the United States." While direct infection from injecting drug use accounts for 27 percent of U.S. cases, high risk behavior related to drug use is implicated in many other cases attributed to sexual transmission. Crystal meth is only the latest scare in the relationship between drugs and HIV.

The escalation of HIV infections among young gay men using methamphetamine began about five years ago. In July 2005 Jeffrey Klausner, San Francisco Department of Public Health director of HIV/STD prevention, told Toronto health officials who doubted the connection that they were "burying their heads in the sand." If they needed to be convinced, he said, "Just look around to every major urban area in the U.S., from San Francisco to Atlanta to Miami to Los Angeles and see the direct effect meth has had on continued transmission of HIV."

What is not as well known is that meth is as popular with straight men and women as it is with gays and that it is overwhelming many small American cities and rural areas. American heterosexuals are using meth for the same reasons gay men do. Meth makes the user "ravenously horny" and totally uninhibited. "I used to have the house and the Mercedes and a big job," one lawyer in San Francisco told reporter Michael Specter in his *New Yorker* article. "Then I fell into crystal. Oh, my God, it was great. I felt young and powerful and wonderful. And the sex. I was having sex I could have only fantasized about before."

In answering the question "Does crystal meth cause better sex?" California's AIDSHotline.org says "Meth stimulates your libido . . . can increase your self-confidence and lower your inhibitions. It also enhances sensation. If one uses crystal in a sexually charged situation, the effect will be heightened. For many people, sex under the influence of meth rapidly leads to an incredibly strong association between the two which is hard to break. One without the other is inconceivable." The Multicenter Crack Cocaine and HIV Infection Study Team also says that both crack cocaine and meth are associated with high-risk sex with multiple partners and no condoms.

Other drugs have the same effects. The use of alcohol—by far the most popular mood-altering substance among American teens and adults bar none—to loosen people up for sexual activity is so widespread that it is an American cliché. The National Institute on Alcohol Abuse and Alcoholism say that people with alcohol use disorders are more likely than the general population to contract HIV. The reasons for use are much the same as with meth and other drugs. Alcohol stimulates the libido and lowers inhibitions.

Drug use and HIV transmission have been closely tied since the earliest days of the epidemic for several other reasons. While meth is commonly eaten, it can also be snorted or injected, just like heroin, coke, and crack. Injecting users sharing needles and users sharing straws to snort drugs might also be sharing HIV and hepatitis B and C. Another important risk was also identified early in the epidemic. Male and female addicts often exchange sex for drugs with their dealers, pimps, and customers. Drugs and HIV are truly a vicious cycle. Recent research demonstrates that because they are depressed, people with HIV are more likely to abuse alcohol or other drugs at some time in their lives.

It was not hard for Paige to get hooked on crystal. Some experts say that it is impossible *not* to get addicted. Although it takes longer for smokers of the drug to get addicted, research suggests that injecting users will become addicted after just one use. Meth is a very seductive drug because it causes the release of all the dopamine in the brain—the chemical that makes people feel good. The high typically lasts for sixteen hours. After they come down, meth users become extremely depressed and often sleep for days because they have used up all their dopamine.

Meth and other addictive drugs artificially stimulate the brain's reward or pleasure center. They short-circuit users' survival systems so they have increased confidence in meth and rely less on the normal rewards of life. After weekend parties, users are often checked into hospital emergency rooms for treatment from dehydration because they forget to drink water. A one-time user described the drug to me as "instant nirvana" because it gave him a sense of enlightenment and power that he had long sought through Buddhist meditation.

A smokable form of methamphetamine, crystal is manufactured and sold around the world by a number of international cartels. But crystal is also easy and extremely profitable to make, selling for about fifty times the cost of the ingredients. Paige thinks that crystal meth became popular in Montana because the state has such a small population that there are many "wide open spaces where no one will notice the bathtub or the smell." During a recent speaking engagement at a small college in North Dakota, one of the professors complained to me that the end of his secluded driveway had become a popular drop off point for small-time crystal meth producers.

With a little determination, a recipe from the Internet, and some over-the-counter ingredients, you can cook up a batch in your back yard, provided the neighbors do not smell the cat-uriney gases given off when you cook it and you do not tip them off by trying to discard excess amounts of alcohol, ether, benzene, paint thinner, acetone, starter fluid, ammonia, iodine crystals, Draino, battery acid, Epsom salts, Coleman's fuel, propane cylinders, cold tablets, or bronchiodialators.

Over the past twenty years, Billings and other Montana cities have attracted drug dealers like flies, the latest in the influx of cowboys to this crossroads between upper Great Plains and the Rockies. Adventurers, explorers, trappers, traders, and miners drawn to it over the past two hundred years inhaled its open air deeply and dreamed of striking it rich. Drug dealers were no different.

Billings is a quiet little place, like many other small cities in the United States. It is home to the state's oldest institution of higher learning, Rocky Mountain College, affiliated with the United Methodist and Presbyterian churches and the United Church of Christ, with 800 students, and Montana State University, with 4,500 students. Paige says that "in Montana, unless you're a real nature-type person, there's really not a whole lot to do except for crystal meth, drinking, and having sex. There is a lot of it in Montana. They say it's the crystal meth capital of the United States. We have the Unabomber, the Freemen, all sorts of stuff here—and crystal meth is here, too."

Damien, the man Paige believes was responsible for infecting her with HIV, migrated to Billings from California in the early 1990s because "I had a couple of friends who lived there. They were from California. They were up there making a bunch of money and I thought, 'Well, let me go up and see what it's like.' They had a bunch of women involved. That's what got me up there, my friends that were already there, selling drugs and messing around with a bunch of women."

In 2002, when Paige learned she was infected, federal agents were gathering conclusive evidence for Damien's 2003 conviction on drug conspiracy charges. Billings was one of eight cities law enforcement sources said had the highest methamphetamine availability in the nation, the only smaller city in a list of much large ones (Seattle, Los Angeles, Honolulu, New Orleans, Memphis, Denver, and Sioux Falls). It was one of four (with Denver, Los Angeles, and Memphis) where the "Mexican connection" was increasing its hold, although authorities also noted that local production had increased in Billings.

Billings was a drug dealer's dream, Damien said. "Being a very small populated state, there's not a lot of drugs around. People that bring it there from other states, countries, or wherever they get it from tend to go to small places like that and distribute a bunch of it at a high price." Dealers can charge more for drugs in cities like Billings, he said, and his friends were taking advantage of the price differentials because demand exceeded supply. Meth was their main product, but they also sold crack and cocaine. "They wasn't really familiar with meth until people started bringing it out there. People were pretty addicted to that," Damien told me.

Damien was born in Banning, California thirty-one years ago, a relatively young community of roughly 25,000 souls half an hour east of Los Angeles and San Diego in Southern California. Half the population is white and 30 percent Hispanic. Only 8.5 percent of its residents are black, like Damien. About a sixth of the city's residents are foreign-born. Conveniently located between two of California's biggest cities and the Mexican border, Banning is a stopping point for migrants and drug traffickers.

Billings, four times the size of Banning, is a much less racially diverse city. Almost 90 percent of the residents are white non-Hispanic, and the proportion of black, Hispanic, and foreign-born residents is well under even Montana's low average. Incomes and housing values are below the state average too, although unemployment is much lower and education levels are much higher than in Banning. Crime rates in Billings are much lower, but both cities rank among the safest third in the United States. Billings is a conservative, clean, upright town, but like so many other small towns and cities in the United States, it has a dangerous alter ego named crystal meth.

Called "geeter" and "work" in Billings, crystal meth was brought into the city through organized sales structures that originated in towns on the Mexican border, like Banning, and in

Arizona, Texas, and Florida. Young adults between eighteen and thirty (Damien was twenty-seven when he met Paige) make up the sales force, but adolescents are the predominant users in Billings; in other areas of the country, older users are more common. Thirteen percent of Montana's high school students reported using meth in 2001, and 9 percent of the state's adults had used it sometime in their lives, rates a good deal above the national average. Billings scored the highest on all measures of drug severity in the federal government's twenty "Pulse Check" cities.

Federal agents said that meth was the most difficult drug to purchase in Montana, possibly because it is usually sold hand-to-hand, through networks of acquaintances at private parties, nightclubs, bars, and concerts. A dealer builds up friendly contacts with unsuspecting potential users, frequently at shopping malls, the most common connection point in Billings.

Dealers usually want cash, but some occasionally accept other modes of payment, such as sex, property, merchandise, or drug transport and other services. Beepers and cell phones keep dealers in contact with their suppliers and customers, which may explain why Damien's cell phone was always busy. Injecting the drug—which is the fastest way to get high as well as an excellent way to transmit HIV if the needles are not clean—was becoming more common in Billings at the time Paige was infected.

Like Billings, Montana, my hometown and its surrounding cities and villages have a population of 100,000. Touted as "Hometown USA" by its promoters, Glens Falls, New York, has been twice selected as the nation's "most typical" small city. It is halfway between New York City and Montreal and lies adjacent to the Village of Lake George, which attracts more than a million visitors a year. With negligible crime, reasonable employment opportunities, and the distinction of being *Golf Digest*'s number two ranking "golf town" in America, the "metro area" of Glens Falls has historically ranked in *Money Magazine*'s list of best communities in the country.

After hearing Paige's story, I felt relieved that my hometown was so different from Billings. Then someone corrected my myopia, pointing out that its location makes it an ideal hub for drug dealers transiting with illegal drugs brought over the border from Canada or imported and manufactured in New York City. I visited www.drug-rehabs.org's city list, where I learned that even Hometown USA is not exempt from the drug epidemic that rages across America.

In fact, the country's hometown is all too typical. According to the website, "Glens Falls City has long been home to numerous drug trafficking organizations. The city's large, diverse and multi-class population creates a demand that these organizations are more than willing to serve. It also acts as the source for organizations that smuggle drugs to other East Coast destinations and to Canada and Europe." The website says that drug programs and policing downstate have been successful, so "many drug traffickers are moving their illegal operations up to the city region to earn greater profits, elude law enforcement and avoid competition from rival drug groups."

In Glens Falls, multi-hundred-kilogram shipments of cocaine brought in by Colombia-based distributors are broken into smaller bundles by Dominicans for shipment to many other eastern U.S. cities. Our coke is smuggled in from large distribution centers on the Mexican border with Texas, Arizona, California, and Florida. "Mexican violators"—maybe part of the gang that operates in Billings?—"are prominent in this large-scale cocaine transportation, but are also becoming involved in local distribution. There are also links with Florida and Puerto Rico." Guess I don't have to go to the Bahamas anymore for the thrill of riding on a plane loaded with cocaine in the hand luggage!

Some of the purest heroin in the world can be bought on the streets of Glens Falls from Colombian, ethnic Chinese, and Dominican organizations, the site says. In some cases, it is the same folks who bring in the cocaine. Just like the guys in the Bahamas who take coke and heroin to Miami, they swallow heroin in condoms, fly to JFK, and drive straight up the Northway to Glens Falls. Heroin can be impregnated in plastic, formed into "common shapes," and recovered later by a chemical extraction process. The periodic influx of troll dolls into U.S. dollar stores could actually be just the latest Asian connection!

While so far Glens Falls seems to have escaped the notice of big-time methamphetamine dealers—meth is much less popular in the northeastern U.S. than heroin, coke, and crack—it seems that local labs are producing enough to supply local users, primarily gay men. When I told a teen friend what I learned on the website, she laughed. "Give me twenty-four hours and I can get you anything."

On a national level, America has both more injecting heroin users and the biggest population of cocaine users in the world. The use of heroin, cocaine, opium, and other illegal drugs has a long history in the United States—opium was grown for troop use by both sides during the Civil War—and containment has never been successful, but current levels of drug use are unprecedented. Meth also has a long history. It was first manufactured in Japan during World War II to juice up kamikaze pilots, and has been used by truckers for decades to stay awake at night or by laborers working an extra shift. Many American women get started on legal forms of meth in an effort to lose weight.

One-quarter of all Americans between the ages of twenty-six and thirty-four have used cocaine sometime in their life. The number of addicts is estimated conservatively at 2 million, but chronic users number 3.6 million according to the Office of National Drug Control Policy. The number of new cocaine users increased from 30,000 in 1975 to 361,000 in 2000. In 2001, 8.2 percent of high school students said they had tried coke at least once, and 5 percent of young adults ages nineteen to twenty-eight reported trying crack, a cocaine derivative, at least once.

The 2002 University of Michigan Monitoring the Future Study found that 1.7 percent of high school seniors had used heroin at least once, while in 2001, the national Youth Risk Behavior Surveillance System found 3.1 percent reporting at least one use. Males were slightly more likely to use heroin than females. Almost 600,000 Americans need treatment for heroin addiction. Some heroin injectors are shifting to inhalation, but two-thirds of users still inject.

The Partnership for a Drug-Free America's (PDFA) sixteenth national survey in 2003 found that of the 23.6 million American children in grades 7 to 12, 46 percent had tried illegal drugs at least once and 24 percent had used illegal drugs in the past thirty days. These figures were down slightly from reported drug use in 1999. Marijuana was the most popular drug, followed by solvents, ecstasy, cocaine and crack, methamphetamines, LSD, and heroin. The most commonly abused substances, however, were perfectly legal, at least if you are twenty-one or older in most states. More than three-quarters of high school students had tried alcohol and slightly more than half had tried tobacco.

Alcohol dependency is a problem for 15 million Americans. Half a million of these are children between the ages of nine and twelve. Twenty-five million Americans—one in ten—reported driving under the influence, including 23 percent of eighteen- to twenty-five-year-olds. Alcohol and alcohol-related problems cost the American economy more than $100 million in health care and lost productivity. Nearly one in four Americans admitted to general hospitals have alcohol problems, and the same proportion have been exposed to alcoholism in their families.

Problem drinkers receive plenty of reinforcement. Each year, the typical adolescent sees more than a thousand alcohol advertisements and several thousand fictional drinking incidents on TV. The industry spends more than $2 billion a year on advertising because Americans spend more than $90 billion on alcohol each year. The $5.5 billion spent on alcohol by students is more than they spend on soft drinks, tea, milk, juice, coffee, and books combined. In 2000, 7 million young people ages twelve to twenty said they were binge drinkers, or one in five under the legal drinking age.

Family stress and troubles are common drivers of substance abuse. Child substance abusers have a higher rate of child abuse than other young people. In women drug abusers of all ages, the prevalence of child sexual abuse ranges from 25 to 75 percent. In research on factors contributing to drug abuse, girls report more stress than boys, and report that they are more likely to spend their allowance on cigarettes, alcohol, and drugs. The average age at first use is twelve for alcohol and cigarettes and thirteen for marijuana.

More than half of students surveyed in 2004 by the PDFA said drugs are used, kept, or sold at their high schools, up 18 percent from 2002. One in six high school students interviewed in the 2003 study said that their parents used drugs. Forty percent of the parents surveyed thought it likely that their children would try drugs; teens whose parents believe this are three times more likely to try drugs than other teens. Only eleven percent of parents are lucky or deluded enough to say "Drugs are not a problem" for their children.

Young people are also abusing prescription drugs. After her son Daniel, a pre-law student at University of California–San Diego, died in 2005 when he took OxyContin and then drank alcohol at a fraternity party, Pamela Ashkenazy told *USA Today,* "Those kids who are high achievers are at risk. Parents think if they are raising kids in affluent homes, if their kids are getting good grades, nothing is wrong. Well, none of that protected him."

The 2004 PDFA survey found that one in five teens had abused a prescription painkiller to get high, and 6.7 million twelve- to twenty-five-year-olds took prescription drugs for nonmedical purposes. Of the illegal drugs, only marijuana, with 12.8 million users, was more popular. Almost half of middle and high school students surveyed in Detroit-area public schools had legitimate prescriptions for Ritalin, the stimulant used to treat attention deficit disorder, or other medications. One in five said they had sold or traded at least one pill.

Among illegal drugs, a 2004 survey of law enforcement agencies in five-hundred counties said that methamphetamine was creating the most social problems and the most rapid increase in crime. Crystal was responsible for one-third of the domestic violence among drug users, cocaine and crack for another third, and the rest of drugs the remainder. It accounted for a substantial increase in the nonviolent crimes of burglary, theft, and prostitution, and was escalating gang-related violence between rival sales groups.

Most of the methamphetamine that is not manufactured locally is trafficked through organized crime, particularly by the ultra-violent Mexican paramilitary commanders known as Zetas. The original cartel members are former Mexican army commandos trained by U.S. Army Special Forces to combat drug gangs, who now operate special training camps in the northern Mexican states. They provide the firepower and security for overland and seaborne shipments of drugs and alien workers, and are now embroiled in a bloody war for control so they can monopolize drug smuggling and human trafficking. In Mexico, the chemicals used to make the drug are not as strictly regulated and can be bought in huge quantities; most U.S. states have tried to control over-the-counter sales of the cold medicines that include meth's principle ingredient.

A Kansas deputy sheriff said that AIDS or no AIDS, "Once you use meth, your life is over." Ninety-eight percent of users become addicts, starting with an introductory hit of 5 milligrams and gradually needing larger doses to get high. Life can end quickly for some users. Toxicity typically occurs at 55 milligrams. In legally sold preparations, the drug is manufactured in 5, 10, and 15 milligram tablets.

Gram prices ranged from $20 to $40 in Seattle to $330 in Chicago, reflecting the profits of intermediate shippers and handlers like Damien. Prices in Billings in 2002 were $100 per gram for powder and $125 for crystal. One Montana judge said meth is typically sold in quarter-gram amounts for between $20 and $30. Big labs turn out thirty-five pounds per cook; amateur operations typically produce less than an ounce (about twenty-eight grams). At 2002 prices, an ounce could be sold for $2,800.

In Tulsa, Oklahoma, the meth epidemic has created a surge in orphans, a problem seen in many places where meth has hit hard. Leslie Nan Fishelman, a Vermont physician who worked a short time in Humboldt County on the north coast of California, worried that meth was entering her home state. She wrote her local Brattleboro paper, *The Reformer*, to say that "even 30 years of psychiatric practice did not prepare me for what I saw." Rural Humboldt, much like Vermont, has plenty of wide open space where methamphetamines are being manufactured. "The results are devastating to the area. The streets of downtown Eureka,

California are burdened by methamphetamine casualties, many of whom are literally raving mad from the drug. Crime, car break-ins, and petty theft are rampant."

Many of her patients who had started using the drug in the search for a little excitement had "lost jobs, homes, relationships, and often the custody of their children," and were now headed for prison. One patient, who kept using the drug "to keep from feeling worse" when he came down from his high, finally managed to kick his habit after a hospital stay, but is permanently troubled with paranoia and cannot sleep or hold a job. "His nervous system and his life were broken," Fishelman told her fellow Vermonters.

There are other costs as well. Montana has spent almost $2.6 million over the last five years cleaning up meth labs. One Montana judge said that he spent more than 60 percent of his time dealing with meth cases. Yellowstone County attorney Dennis Paxinos admitted to feeling overwhelmed by his caseload, up from 300 active felony cases in the 1990s to more than 1,000 in 2000 thanks to prosecution of meth dealers and meth-related burglary and violent crime. In 2002 the Montana Drug Enforcement Agency reported that 52 percent of all drug arrest involved meth.

The 2003 Montana Youth Risk Behavior Survey Report noted that 29 percent of state residents seeking treatment in chemical dependency programs were meth addicts. More than two-thirds of Montana women in prison are there on meth-related charges, not all of them from problem families. *Missoulian* reporter Michael Moore recounted the story of Jane Opartny, adopted daughter of a well-to-do Missoula, Montana family who as a child prodigy went to a top music college in Ohio to train as a concert pianist.

Freed from her "boring" family, Jane sought excitement and dabbled in alcohol until "partying had become my priority. I was just trying to get a reaction by being outrageous." When partying ruined her first marriage, she hung out with drug dealers and they introduced her to meth. It gave her the courage she had lacked. "I always had trouble being assertive and now I could be.

I'd walk into a room and people would notice me. That's pretty addictive, beyond what the drug actually does to you."

Jane started trading sex for drugs and dealing in 1998, and returned to Missoula with a man who picked her up hitchhiking. Fourteen years later she was high on meth twenty-four hours a day, downing OxyContin when she wanted to sleep. She used so much meth that she and her husband started cooking it. "At first people thought I was just a bag whore" who would turn tricks to get her drugs, but supplying drugs brought her attention from clients who would do anything to get their drugs—or, if they were caught, to plea bargain. Jane and her husband were arrested in 2003. Jane got a ten-year sentence but was released on probation in 2004, while her husband waits out forty-five years in prison. Perhaps some of President Bush's Christian foot soldiers will visit him, pray with him, and get him straightened out.

"What do advocating religious hiring rights, a $4 billion workplace retraining bill, and the war on drugs have in common?" asks Bill Berkowitz of *Dissident Voice*. "The short answer: Bring on the faith-based organizations!" In June 2003 the White House Office of Faith-Based and Community Organizations created by Bush asked that faith-based organizations—notoriously discriminatory in their hiring practices—be exempt from antidiscrimination statutes so they could exercise their "religious hiring rights" and hire anyone they please to spend the federal grants they were receiving. Follow-up legislative proposals granted an exemption from standard federal prohibitions against discrimination in hiring practices for religious organizations providing Head Start and workplace retraining services.

When President Bush was not as successful as he had hoped in getting direct congressional funding for his faith-based initiative, he decided to get the funding in other ways. In a move similar to the abstinence-only funding scam that is sending billions out to right-wing Christian businesses, Bush announced a new initiative to enlist religious youth groups in the war on drugs. Evaluation of the administration's earlier multimillion-dollar faith-based advertising campaigns showed that they "completely failed to slow down teen drug use." After a five-year ad campaign that cost the taxpayers almost $1 billion, the same number of teens still used illegal drugs. After seeing the ads, a number of teen girls *started* smoking pot, says Berkowitz.

Despite these failures, in 2003 the president announced a new slogan for his war on drugs: "Faith. The Anti-Drug," and built his anti-drug initiative around three tenuous premises, spelled out in a fact sheet entitled "Marijuana and Kids: Faith." According to the fact sheet, "Religion plays a major role in the lives of American teens"; "religion and religiosity repeatedly correlate with lower teen and adult marijuana and substance use rates and buffer the impact of life stress which can lead to marijuana and substance use"; and "youth turn to faith communities" for help with drug problems, but "most faith institutions [do not] incorporate significant teen substance abuse prevention activities."

The solution to this dilemma? Give them money! And, as with the purveyors of abstinence-only curricula, do not hold them accountable, so they can spend our tax dollars on anything they please. Including, we presume, the purchase of Bibles that repentant drug users can tuck under their pillows. A cornerstone of the president's vision for his anti-drug campaign is the use of "compassionate coercion" to get users into treatment. It "begins with family, friends, employers, and the community," and "also uses the criminal justice system to get people into treatment."

Barry Lynn, executive director of Americans United for Separation of Church and State, commented that "the Bush administration seems to think there's a 'faith-based' solution to every social and medical problem in America. The White House is ignoring vital constitutional safeguards. The Constitution calls for a separation between religion and government, not a merger."

Krissy Oechslin, assistant director of the Marijuana Policy Project, the country's largest marijuana policy reform organization, says that discussion about the effect of our drug laws is "conspicuously missing. You can talk all you want about prevention and reducing demand but the fact of the matter is, nearly 750,000 people were arrested for marijuana violations in 2001; nearly 90 percent of those were for simple possession." Faith-based deterrence conveniently ignored "significant ethical questions raised by the drug wars, such as whether kids should be put into prison for using marijuana."

PRISONS

Thanks to crystal meth, Montana has one of the fastest-growing prison populations in the United States. Drug convictions account for 20 percent of the U.S. state and federal prison population, compared to 8 percent in 1980, and they are growing fast. In 2001, 57 percent of federal incarcerations were for drug offenses. Such incarcerations are not only driving the growth of prison systems, but creating a virtual infection pump of HIV into the general population.

Most drug-related convictions target dealers, but many first-time and petty users are sentenced because they finance their drug use with small-time dealing. These and other revolving-door prisoners—on short stays with frequent returns—have high rates of HIV infection and either do not know or do not tell when they return to their old habits and partners on the outside.

On average, prison AIDS rates are six times higher than on the outside, but in Washington, D.C., New York, Massachusetts, and Nevada, infection rates in prisons rival those seen in Africa. "By choosing mass imprisonment as the federal and state governments' response to the use of drugs," said the National Commission on AIDS in 1991, "we have created a de facto policy of incarcerating more and more individuals with HIV infection."

Twenty-six percent of Americans living with AIDS have spent some part of their lives in our prison system. Many are HIV positive when they enter, but others are infected within the prison system itself. HIV is spread to other uninfected inmates by drug use, sex for money, and rapes, which continue on the inside. Our prisons are becoming larger and more deadly HIV infection pumps each year for other reasons as well. Not only does the United States have the largest and fastest-growing prison system in the world, but many prisons provide such poor health care that prisoners with HIV are not tested or treated.

Every ten minutes, another American disappears behind bars. At least 144 inmates a day are being added to our prison system, which already houses one-quarter of the world's prison population. One in every 142 U.S. residents is now in prison, five times the 1980 rate. We have the highest rate of incarceration in the world, with a prison population more than eight times as large as that of Italy, France, the United Kingdom, Spain, and Australia combined.

At the end of 2001, 2.1 million American adults were incarcerated and 6 million total lived in prison, in jail, and on parole or probation, three times the 1980 totals. The largest increase has been in nonviolent offenders, who now comprise more than half of all U.S. prisoners.

"The prison system looms so large on our political horizon that it is often difficult for Americans to comprehend its size and scale," says Justice Policy Institute (JPI), a nonprofit prison-research organization. Our nonviolent prison population is larger than the population of many of our states, and our total prison population is more than three times that of the European Union, although their overall population is about one and a half times ours. We lock up more than ten times the prisoners incarcerated in India, which is four times our size.

Americans adopted the "mass incarceration" approach to crime and drug control in the 1980s. Over the past twenty years, the number of Americans held in state and federal lockups has quadrupled, while the country's population has increased only 20 percent. The impact of this policy on crime and drugs is very hotly debated, and few outside of the administration would agree with Bush or Attorney General John Ashcroft that this approach is working in either the short or the long term. In fact, the war on drugs seems to be doing a better job of spreading AIDS than controlling drug use or crime.

Prison advocates say that the addition of about 75,000 new, hard-core violent repeaters to our population every year necessitates prison expansion and that the growth in prisons has caused a sharp drop in the crime rate. Law and public policy professor Michael Tonry scoffs, saying that you could lock up 1 million Americans at random and have the same effect on crime rates because nonviolent offenders are more than half of the total.

The relationship between incarceration and violent crime rates is puzzling. Many states, such as California, financed costly explosions in their prison populations but realized only a small drop in crime rates, while other states, such as New York, realized an even greater drop in crime rates by radically *reducing* their incarceration rates after initiating a community policing program. New York's homicide rate fell one and a half times that of California's in the 1990s, while California added nine times as many inmates per year to its prisons in the same period.

Prisons may be creating more criminals than they are rehabilitating. Time in prison and jail for nonviolent offenders is "profoundly damaging" says the JPI, and "their chances of pursuing a merely viable, much less a satisfying conventional life after prison are diminished by their time behind bars. The contemporary prison experience often converts them into social misfits and there is growing evidence that they will return to crime and other forms of deviance upon release." The RAND Corporation found that convicted felons who were incarcerated were significantly more likely to be rearrested after release than those placed on probation. Nonviolent offenders are jailed for crimes that involve no harm or threat to anyone, "warehoused . . . due to our inability—or our choice not to—sort out America's lingering social problems," say JPI experts.

Mass incarceration in the war on drugs has also turned out to be profoundly racist. "African Americans and Latinos comprise a growing percentage of those we choose to imprison," according to the JPI. In the 1930s, 75 percent of prisoners in state and federal facilities were white, representative of the overall population.

Now minorities account for three-quarters of all new admissions and more than half of all Americans behind bars, many more than in the population as a whole. It is also playing out as sexist. The fastest-growing segment of our prison population and the least violent is women.

To minority Americans, the motive for imprisonment seems to be something other than crime control. By 2004, incarceration had cost 13 percent of all African Americans their right to vote. In many states, one felony translates into permanent disenfranchisement, and the impact is devastating. Americans are rightly embarrassed that the world's largest democracy locks up and disenfranchises an inordinate number of its citizens. The results, if not the motive, are glaringly racist. Since 9/11 the drive to diminish the role of the courts in protecting civil rights could put more and more dissenters behind bars.

Not only is mass incarceration morally dubious, its public health implications are frightening. Substandard AIDS treatment in many prisons makes them ideal breeding grounds for drug-resistant superstrains of HIV. Prisons are infection pumps for other diseases as well. An outbreak of multidrug-resistant tuberculosis occurred in New York City in the early 1990s that cost the city $1 billion to control after prisoners were released. One-third of all Americans living with hepatitis C are in prison, which also creates ideal conditions for dangerous disease mutations. Our revolving-door prison system is repeatedly cycling prisoners—and their visitors and correctional employees—back to their communities, exposing family members and others outside the wall to dangerous diseases within.

Patrick Langan, the Bureau of Justice's senior statistician, says that the phenomenal growth of the U.S. prison system began in 1973, and since 1980, the prison population has increased by 6 or 7 percent each year. Langan says, "To sustain that level of growth, we are building the equivalent of a 1,000-bed prison every week." Langan believes that tougher drug laws do not account for the whole problem because the growth began before they were enacted in the 1980s. Much of it is due, he says, to recidivism, or repeat visits by the same prisoners.

Because we have failed to adequately develop other social systems to prevent crime and rehabilitate prisoners, many inmates go through the revolving prison door time and time again until they die. Bureau of Justice statistics show that since 1980, new court commitments dropped from 83 percent of total state prison admissions to 65 percent; returning parole violators increased to 35 percent. Two-thirds of all former inmates are back in jail within three years. The social and public health implications are mind-boggling. Demos Network senior fellow Sasha Abramsky writes that "there will be somewhere around 3.5 million first-time releases between now and 2010, and America will by then still be releasing from half a million to a million people from its prisons each year, not to mention hundreds of thousands more from short stints in jail."

In 1997 incarceration cost Americans more than $20,000 per prisoner, or $24 billion in total, exclusive of construction costs ($3.4 billion). When hidden costs like health care and other contractor services, administrative costs, and debt service on prison bonds are added, the costs are doubled, a Justice Policy Institute study has found. Even without the hidden costs, in 1997 Americans spent 50 percent more on prisons than on welfare, which serves 8.5 million people compared to 2 million in prisons and jails. We spent six times more on prisons than on child care, which serves 1.25 million children and one or two times that many parents. Most states are spending much more on prison construction and operation than on their college and university systems.

Although the nation spends more than $50 billion on the prison industry each year, few Americans feel that our communities are any safer than they were twenty years ago. More than 7 million American households, or 6 percent of the national total, are located in "gated communities," nestled behind walls and fences where access is controlled by gates, entry cards, key cards, or security guards. About 40 percent of new houses in California are behind walls.

Mass incarceration is a costly social and economic failure, but it has been a boon to the private companies that own and operate close to half of our prisons. Large, privately run, for-profit prisons house more than three-quarters of a million inmates out of the country's total of 2.1 million. This private "prison lobby" forced extensive prison building programs through many state legislatures in the 1990s. Prison growth benefits many: construction companies; employees; private companies that administer, maintain, provision, and staff facilities; and the owners and shareholders of these companies.

Paige's father Gordon, a Houston deputy sheriff who works nights in the county jail, describes his job as "warehousing lost souls." The prisoners are "people much like my daughter could have ended up being. Most of the African Americans I see have a mom, and they don't even know who dad is, a very similar scenario to what I was responsible for. I can't be a hypocrite. There but for the will of God goes she, and look at the terrible price *she's* paid for her activities. These kids needed discipline, they needed role models, and they don't have it. So what did they do? They went out and did something to get negative attention because negative attention beats no attention at all."

Gordon says "the young ones, seventeen- to twenty-one-year-olds, they're just angry at the world. They live impoverished lifestyles, and the only way to get ahead because you have no education is to deal drugs or steal things. And you can make a good living at that, so why in the world would you want to flip burgers at McDonald's? I understand the argument. Well, because one is legal and the other is illegal." The number of juveniles confined in jails and prisons skyrocketed from a little more than 2,000 to about 9,200 between 1991 and 1999, and most of the increased numbers were held in jail as adults.

Gordon says that prisoner HIV status is confidential, but "I'm sure many are HIV positive. In fact, some inmates have committed crimes simply to get their medications taken care of through the tax rolls. The medication, as you know, is very expensive. If you commit a crime and you go to jail, the government pays for it. I know for a fact that we have inmates that go to the infirmary twice a day, and at the exact same times when my daughter would be taking her stuff, they're taking theirs. I'm almost positive they're in the same situation.

"The recidivism is incredible," Gordon says, "especially around the holidays, because all their friends and family are in jail. Literally, sometimes the entire family is incarcerated. You pick up the mail and deliver it and you see it's going from one cell block to the next. That's all they know, the whole family. I would say easily 85 to 90 percent are African Americans in Houston. I would venture to say conditions are better than anything these people have had in their life. Their laundry is done twice a week. They're given three meals a day. We've got a dietitian who takes care of their meals. They get a fourteen-day assessment as soon as they're arrested, and if they need a special diet, they have a special diet.

"It doesn't get any better than that. Everything that you might envision a jail being, it's not that. The jails are clean. They clean up twice a shift. We've got trustee workers that are sweeping the floors and mopping. We have federal inspectors come in on a regular basis. Plus state-of-the-art gym, weight room. We keep it air-conditioned to control any kind of airborne germs. I freeze my butt off in there. It's really cold. My blood's too thin.

"Here they have their little subculture," Gordon says. "They go to recreation. They go to the clinic to see the nurse, which is usually something that they haven't done in years. If they went to a clinic at all, it was some government clinic where the lines are a mile long. They've got laundry day and the law library.

"They've got this time to get up and eat and that time to do this. Everything is really controlled and structured, and it's really a good thing for them. It's the first time they've had that. Even in high school, they basically did what they wanted. Well here they can't do that. All their decisions are made for them. We take them from one stage of their day to the next stage of their day and that's what they have to look forward to. The sun comes up and goes down."

According to criminal justice expert Jess Maghan, "Every state and county in the land now has fully equipped, air-conditioned, and awesomely modern correctional centers. These new architectural wonders, often juxtaposed against aging court houses, provide an incredible array of correctional services for inmates: law libraries, gymnasiums, counseling and education, and so on. The comparison of modern penal facilities with the poor condition of most public school and public recreational facilities in these communities is startling."

Maghan argues that the U.S. prison system is almost anything but a place in which those who have committed crimes can "pay their debt to society." They have become surrogate public housing, "an unwelcome extension of public welfare and other public dole programs." Prisoners are served by an array of skilled professionals, including librarians, legal staff, substance abuse and HIV/AIDS counselors, anger-management and parenting counselors, recreation supervisors, accreditation and affirmative action officers, and the like. With much lower education levels than the population as a whole, more than half of all prisoners participate in high school or college programs and attend English courses, and close to one-third get vocational education.

"At the same time," Maghan says, "there is a crisis of control. Gang warfare, turf disputes, racial tension, and institutional violence are rife." Threatened withdrawal of services and funding cuts by politicians currying public favor would "put our whole nation at risk." Maghan says that we must face the fact that "these are questions that can only be answered by social programs and other resources outside our prisons."

I spoke with Damien, the man whom Paige alleges was responsible for infecting her with HIV, after clearance from his case managers in the medium-security federal corrections center where he has been imprisoned since his drug conviction. He has a pleasantly quiet, deep telephone voice, almost seductive, and uses no street jargon. He was very patient, although he sounded tired. There were other voices in the background, and at times he spoke so softly I could hardly hear him.

He told me that he moved to Montana on July 4, 1992, fell into dealing, and "eventually I got myself in this situation where I am today." After dealing for about ten years, he was indicted in the U.S. District Court in Billings on February 6, 2003 on one count of conspiracy to distribute, five counts of distribution, and one count of possession with intent to distribute methamphetamines. Damien plea bargained and was sentenced to concurrent sentences of 27 years and six months on three counts and 20 years on the other four, after which he will undergo 5 years of supervised release.

Damien was not a small-time dealer. The sentencing document reveals that he and his codefendants were distributing about 50 grams of methamphetamine per month between 2001 and 2002. This kept hundreds of users happy and put about $3,000 in his pocket each month. Damien was probably not at the top of the local dealer's hierarchy, either. In 2004 the Billings newspaper reported on a conviction of thirteen Billings residents in a twenty-five-count drug-trafficking, money-laundering, and firearms conspiracy case. It said that the men and women charged had traveled to California to buy meth, but that two of the main dealers were from Washington State. Sentences for the man who apparently directed the operation were much more severe than Damien's.

Damien said that Paige was one of many women he knew in Billings and that they "dated for a short period of time. That was about it, as far as with her." He said that he was unaware that he was HIV positive until he "came to jail on this case. A few women said that they slept with me and apparently contracted it," so the prison's clinic staff suggested he get tested. He subsequently wrote a letter of apology to Paige's friend Amy (not her real name), who also believes he infected her. "I explained to her that I didn't . . . I didn't know that I . . . I was afraid to take the test when she took hers after Paige told her that she had contracted it."

I asked him how he felt about allegedly infecting the women in Billings. "That's a hard question," he said. "I felt bad. I know the girls that I did sleep with had slept with several men other than me, so I didn't see actually how they would put all the blame on me. So I'm a bit busted about that feeling, putting all the blame on me. While I was dating them, they were seeing other men. I know Amy wasn't, but as far as Paige, she slept with numerous men while we were dating. When she found out she was positive, Paige put the blame on me. She was supposed to go to the army or something like that and they tested her and found out she was positive, so she put the blame on me."

Damien never talked with Paige or wrote her. "I don't have any way to get a hold of her. I happened to get Amy's parents' address out of the phone book. I had a friend get it for me. I wrote her. I apologized and expressed to her how I felt. I felt I owed her an apology. Her sister wrote me back. I was expecting Amy to write me back, but her sister wrote me back. I still have the letter. She told me how her sister has changed her life, how much support she has from her family, and she doesn't hang around with losers like myself. Just things like that."

When I spoke with Amy afterward, she said she met Damien just after breaking up with her boyfriend of four years. She learned he had been unfaithful, so she was "feeling low, doing things I never would have normally done. I wasn't sleeping around." Damien looked "wholesome," and she did not know he was a drug dealer. She said the experience had helped her straighten up and make better choices.

Since then, she finished her bachelor's degree in human services and completed two internships with the Yellowstone AIDS Project as a community education volunteer. She wants to work in the AIDS field, but like many other under-funded human service organizations, YAP has no medical insurance, so she works in another agency that provides private insurance coverage for her AIDS drugs. Paige gets her drugs through Medicaid.

When Damien was arrested on drug charges, Paige's mother wanted her to formally accuse him of infecting her, but Paige refused. Montana is one of twenty-five states in which it is a misdemeanor or felony to knowingly or willfully expose or transmit HIV infection to another person. Although two highly publicized cases in New York and Missouri inspired a spate of legislation and prosecution in 1997 and 1998, it is still difficult to prove intent.

At least fifteen states have penalties for those who attempt to sell or donate HIV-infected blood with the intent of transmitting the virus, and other states make it illegal to sell or exchange non-sterile drug injecting equipment. Only a few states have penalties for deliberate transmission while incarcerated, but in Pennsylvania it is considered second degree murder. In other states, depending on the circumstances, deliberate transmission is variously considered a felony or second- or third-degree assault.

As a young man, Damien's life history was even more troubled than Paige's. He started selling drugs in California when he was fourteen to support himself. "My mom was on drugs, alcohol. I didn't have a father around at the time, so I was pretty much on my own. My grandmother raised me. Passed away of cancer in 1989." Damien said that after he started selling drugs, he smoked marijuana, but "I'd never done any other serious drugs besides ecstasy. That didn't happen until around 2000." He claimed that he had never been a meth user. Our conversation was cut short by prison time limits on phone calls. Although Damien agreed to call me back collect the next morning, I never heard from him again.

At about 10 o'clock that night, the phone rang. The woman on the other end of the line said that she was Damien's aunt from Mississippi and that he had sent her a letter asking her to contact me and find out what I was doing. After I explained, she sighed. "That poor boy," she said. "He's a good boy but he's gone wrong and I only hope that God helps him." Her deep voice was warm, gentle, polite, and friendly, with a slight southern accent.

While I had explained to Damien that I was interviewing him for a book about AIDS, he probably asked his aunt to call me because he is frantic with the idea that I might be after something else. Although convictions for purposive infection with HIV have not yet been successful in the United States, he probably suspected that I was an undercover agent investigating the possibility of charging him with that offense.

His aunt told me that she comes from a big family, with ten brothers and sisters, and that her sister, Damien's mom, had a hard time in life. Damien's mother had been "mixed up" after her husband abandoned her and ended up using alcohol and drugs. Damien grew up "pretty much on his own," and eventually ended up living with his grandmother, "a wonderful person" who did as much as she could for him but died when Damien was fifteen.

He then went to live with one of her brothers, a preacher with a church in Texas. The uncle had seen to it that Damien finished high school, but after that there was not much else he could do. Damien returned to Banning, where he got mixed up with "drug dealers." The aunt told me that she "continues to pray and trust God, but when the family's messed up it's kinda hard for kids to be good."

She said Damien learned he was HIV positive "after he was incarcerated, and when he told me, I just cried and cried. We cried and cried together," she said, and then they prayed. "I still pray to God for him," and she wonders what will happen to him. "I know he gets medicine in jail, but I wonder if it's very good. I know that Magic Johnson is okay, but that's only because he has so much money. The poor can't afford the drugs. They're very expensive."

Damien's aunt might be nervous about him because she knows about the ongoing struggle between Human Rights Watch and the Alabama Department of Corrections (ADOC). In 2004, ADOC acceded to a settlement in a federal lawsuit by 240 HIV positive prisoners challenging what Human Rights Watch calls "appalling conditions" at the Limestone Correctional Facility. Six months later, Human Rights Watch complained that Limestone had not yet complied with the court order to institute treatment for HIV positive inmates or to separate inmates with tuberculosis. In a letter to Alabama's governor in 2004, the organization said that Limestone's conditions were worse than prisons it had inspected in the former Soviet Union and Africa.

In 2003 an inspecting physician had reported numerous preventable AIDS deaths at Limestone and also warned that "without adequate infection control practices, the possibility of an outbreak of drug resistant tuberculosis" was acute, says Human Rights Watch. Conditions had improved very little by August 2005, when a physician sent in by Prison Health Services, the private company providing Limestone's medical services, to fix the HIV unit's problems resigned after she was suspended for filing formal complaints with her company. Dr. Valda Chijide said that the 300-bed HIV unit was "riddled with rats, where broken windows had been replaced with plastic sheeting that was falling apart." She said that nurses diagnosed patients and prescribed drugs without her supervision, and that her own prescriptions were ignored. Lab tests were lost or ignored, and inmates often "simply showed up unannounced" on the unit.

"Nobody was really making an effort to run an HIV clinic the way it was supposed to be," Dr. Chijide told *The New York Times*. None of the patients who had hepatitis C or tuberculosis were getting treatment, and the unit had no clerical support. "They would tell you one thing, but when it came down to it, they didn't provide any resources. Each day became a race to treat inmates in the infirmary, answer sick calls and hunt down missing medical records."

Prison Health Services, which provides health care for facilities in many states, has been implicated in eight preventable deaths in New York State prisons. New York's Department of Corrections complained it is frustrated by the company's lack of concern and failure to respond to complaints or discipline offending physicians and nurses, as well as to explain documented overcharging for services.

Damien's aunt is also old enough to remember Arkansas's River of Blood scandal. The Cummins State Prison Farm, sixty miles east of Little Rock, was the center of a "plasma farming" scheme run by for-profit companies that harvested blood from prisoners and sold it in the United States and abroad in the late 1970s and early 1980s. Called by inmates the Arkansas Blood Farm, Cummins prisoners were paid a little money or script for their blood donations by Pine Bluff Biological, which sold the blood to Health Management Associates.

The companies allegedly collected the blood using extremely dangerous and inhumane procedures and resold it at extremely high profit margins. Needles were alledgedly reused; blood from different prisoners was pooled; prisoners were repeatedly drained at frequent intervals, even those who were obviously sick; and some claim to have "donated" against their will.

The plasma was not tested, and at least 40,000 Canadians, mostly hemophiliacs, who got the blood from their Red Cross were infected with HIV and hepatitis C. Tainted blood products originating from the Farm were also traced to Spain, Ireland, and Japan. The program was cited repeatedly by the Food and Drug Administration and shut down in 1983, but the Arkansas Department of Corrections kept it running until 1994, when it became the last state program to stop selling its prisoners' blood.

Or Damien's aunt may have been thinking of the Tuskegee "experiment." World War I created an especially serious health crisis for black American soldiers and their families. Syphilis rates among black and white American soldiers during the war had been about equal, but rates among blacks soared to 252.3 per 1,000 by 1941, while rates among whites dropped to 17.4 per 1,000. The syphilis death rate for black men and women was more than three times than that of white men and women, because blacks were much less likely to seek treatment due to economic and cultural barriers. When they did seek treatment, it was from public clinics, which were more likely to report the results to public health authorities. During the same period, African American tuberculosis rates climbed to epidemic levels along with heart disease rates, differentials that persist today.

In 1932, U.S. Public Health Service experts initiated the Tuskegee study. Researchers withheld treatment from 400 black male prisoners to see how syphilis progressed, even after it became known in 1949 that penicillin could cure the disease. Treatment continued to be withheld from the men and their families even when the enormous systemic damage they sustained led to high death rates. The study was called to a halt only after a *New York Times* reporter exposed its chilling details in 1972.

Damien's aunt may fear for her nephew because she knows that many American prisons are not like the county jail where Gordon works. Many are virtual hell holes, where gangs run rampant and sexual and physical abuse are routinely used to control and intimidate prisoners. Chain gangs are legal in seven states, including Alabama, and more states are thinking about allowing them.

Human Rights Watch says that "many prisoners are targeted for sexual exploitation the minute they enter a penal facility" by their age, looks, and sexual preference. The organization, which has extensively documented mistreatment of prisoners in two reports, one on women and one on men, and says that "Rape was no aberrational occurrence; instead it was a deeply rooted, systemic problem. It was also a problem that prison authorities were doing little to address." A study of seven Midwestern prisons showed that 21 percent of inmates had experienced at least one episode of pressured or forced sex.

"Rapes are unimaginably vicious and brutal," said the Human Rights Watch report on male prisons. Many prisoners are used as sex "slaves" or "wives," forced to satisfy another prisoner's sexual demands and also to wash his clothes, massage his back, cook food, and clean his cell. They are also rented, sold, or auctioned off to other prisoners. According to Human Rights Watch, "It appears that the authorities' lack of response is premeditated. Rape is an effective, albeit ruthless, mechanism of inmate control."

Rodney Hulin Sr., who was working at a retirement home in Beaumont, Texas when Human Rights Watch interviewed him in 1997, said that his sixteen-year-old son had been sentenced to an eight-year term for arson in an adult prison. Older inmates at the Clemens Unit in Brazoria County, Texas immediately started to threaten and harass him.

Hulin's son died a year later. "My son was raped and sodomized by an inmate. The doctor found two tears in his rectum and ordered an HIV test, since up to a third of the 2,200 inmates there were HIV positive. Fearing for his safety, he requested to be placed in protective custody, but his request was denied because, as the warden put it, my son's abuses didn't meet the 'emergency grievance criteria.'"

For the next several months, Hulin continued, "my son was repeatedly beaten by the older inmates, forced to perform oral sex, robbed, and beaten again. Each time, his requests for protection were denied by the warden. The abuses, meanwhile, continued. On the night of January 26, 1996—seventy-five days after my son entered Clemens—he attempted suicide by hanging himself in his cell. He could no longer stand to live in continual terror. It was too much for him to handle. He laid in a coma for the next four months until he died."

Noting that "incarceration should not be a de facto death sentence for people living with HIV," Human Rights Watch has continually lobbied federal and state prisons to provide condoms and sterile syringes to inmates so that rape victims and drug users would not become HIV infected. It has also lobbied state governments to provide sterile syringes for drug users who are not incarcerated, and to stop the arrest, harassment, and search of drug users who obtain sterile syringes from state-authorized programs. Although almost all fifty states had enacted such a law to control HIV, some localities had "banned syringe exchange outright" in violation of the law, "forcing drug users to find syringes in trash cans, dumpsters, and shooting galleries." In some states, the law even prevents individuals from buying syringes at a pharmacy without a prescription.

On March 1, 2005, a private high-level commission organized by former attorney general Nicholas Katzenbach and former federal appeals court judge John Gibbons began a year-long study of prison violence. The commission's preliminary documentation showed that more than 34,000 assaults occurred annually in U.S. prisons; this is probably a low estimate because fear of retribution leads to underreporting. Katzenbach and Gibbons noted that there were no national standards for prisons, despite the fact that many were run by private contractors. "We seem to have a gap between our cherished ideals about justice and the realities of the prison environment," Katzenbach said. His commission's investigation was prompted in part by reports of misconduct by U.S. corrections officers in Iraq.

Guys like Damien leave wives and children on the outside every year, part of the ongoing baby-momma drama of Billings that is repeated all over the country. In 1999, the U.S. Department of Justice estimated that the parents of 1.5 million minor children were in state or federal prison, and others are in county jails and treatment programs. A little more than half of the children are African Americans, a quarter are white, and a quarter Hispanic.

Damien told me he married a Billings woman who now lives in Oregon. "We're kind of separated right now," he said. "I haven't spoke with her in about a month. I believe the marriage is coming to an end. I think she's dating. I know she talks about other guys. Other than that I don't know what she's doing. She changed her number and I don't know her new number. I have her address but that's it." He had been married once before. "I have a son and a daughter, ten-year-old daughter, eleven-year-old son," he said, his voice lifting. "Live in California with their mother. I met my kids' mother in Montana. She's originally from California, but I met her in Montana. That's where my two kids were born."

Prisoners' children live in single-parent or foster families. More than half of the parents are violent offenders or drug traffickers. More than three-quarters are repeat offenders, 60 percent had used drugs in the month before their incarceration, 25 percent had a history of alcohol dependence, 14 percent had mental illnesses, and 70 percent had no high school diploma. Like Damien, during their repeated jail sentences many had lost touch with their families, although more than half had been living with their children before they went to jail. Two-thirds said that they tried to maintain contact with their children by phone, mail, or personal visits. Damien is allowed 300 minutes a month of telephone time in 15-minute increments.

Of the 1.2 million citizens in state prisons in 2000, slightly more than 76,000 were women. North Carolina child development specialist Karen DeBord says that incarcerated parents worry about maintaining their legal parenting rights and must depend on friends and families to support their children and bring them for visits. Parents in jail worry that someone will replace them and their children will forget about them. Children of incarcerated fathers are usually cared for by their mothers, but if the mother is in jail, her children are usually sent to other relatives or placed in foster care.

The social and economic situation of children with incarcerated parents typically declines. Children are often deceived about their father or mother's whereabouts, and the trauma they suffer emerges later in their own dysfunctional family situations. Many parents in jail often have severe behavioral and emotional problems, which they pass on to their children. Some states, such as North Carolina, are trying to help men in jail develop better parenting skills in an effort to cut the vicious cycle.

The United States, with about 5 percent of the world's population, houses about 25 percent of its prisoners. It also contains half of the world's psychiatric and psychological practitioners. Prison mental health funding has both increased at explosive rates since 1970. Mental health expenditures jumped 770 percent between 1970 and 1999 while the inmate population rose 550 percent.

Prisoners are managed with drugs. All levels of the prison system increasingly rely on psychotropic drugs to control inmates because most corrections officials have abandoned hope for rehabilitation. Daniel Harr, an inmate turned writer, claims that "it is commonplace to see 50—even 60—percent or more of a prison population sleeping in their bunks for twenty-two hours a day due to the effects of psychotropic drugs they're being fed like candy." In many cases, use of drug combinations exacerbate the inmates' aggressive behavior.

In his 2002 State of the Union address, President Bush told Americans, "When the gates of the prison open, the path ahead should lead to a better life," calling America "the land of the second chance." Stuart Taylor, writing in the *Atlantic Monthly*, disagrees, saying that "there may not be much of a second chance for the tens of thousands of nonviolent offenders and others who are relatively harmless when they enter prison but deeply scarred—in many cases on their way to becoming career criminals—when they leave 5, 10, or 20 years later.

"One of the reasons is a push by Attorney General John Ashcroft and congressional Republicans to give Ashcroft's Justice

Department nearly complete control of the sentencing process and force federal judges to act as rubber stamps, in order to ratchet up the already excessive prison terms for a wide range of federal crimes." Ashcroft, a diehard member of the Christian Right, holds weekly Bible study classes at the Department of Justice offices for his employees.

The Bush administration's Christian justice gang was furious when the Supreme Court ruled in January 2005 that judges do not have to follow federal sentencing guidelines established in 1986 to help judges attain some comparability in their sentencing. The Court said that making the guidelines mandatory violated Sixth Amendment rights to a jury trial because a judge had to make factual decisions that could add to prison time. Although 86 percent of sentences given since that time fall within the range of the guidelines, in June 2005 the Justice Department urged Congress to approve new punishment guidelines to make sure federal judges cannot be too lenient.

Other, saner approaches could be more effective and less costly. Experiments with nutritional supplements in California prisons in the 1980s showed that inmate behavior improved and aggressiveness decreased with the simple addition of vitamins and minerals to their food. In the late 1990s, English researchers repeated the experiments and had the same results less than two weeks after prison diets were made more nutritious. "When inmate nutrition improves," writes Susan Freinkel in the May 2005 issue of *Discover Magazine*, "the number of fights, infractions, and other antisocial behavior drops by about 40 percent."

In 2000, then-Vice President Al Gore outlined a proposal to expand drug testing and treatment programs within U.S. prisons and in communities in order to "stop that revolving door once and for all. We have to test prisoners for drugs while they are in jail and break up the drug rings in our prisons." Gore proposed a "stay clean to stay out" parole system that would help former inmates get jobs.

In August 2005 Ohio governor Rod Blagojevich signed landmark legislation aimed at reducing the transmission of HIV from prisons into communities. The bill creates HIV/AIDS response officers in the Department of Health and Corrections; offers voluntary testing to prisoners; provides special case management and support to HIV-positive inmates to guide their reentry into the community; and expands free HIV testing in all high-traffic state offices, like driver's license bureaus and public assistance offices.

Only 15 percent of Ohio's population is African American, but blacks account for half of its new AIDS cases. "We are in a crisis situation with regards to the spread of HIV in the African American community. We need to act in an aggressive way to stop young black men and women from being infected," said state representative Connie Howard. "Emergencies require emergency measures."

RACE, POVERTY, AND CARE

In December 1988 Max Robinson died. He had served on the Chicago desk of ABC's *World News Tonight* and was the first black news anchor on any American national television network. Robinson was an icon of black advancement: good-looking, well dressed, intelligent, remembered in a *Vanity Fair* article as having a "steely, unadorned delivery, precise diction, and magical presence." By color, Max was in the AIDS epidemic's minority at that time, one of 4,123 African Americas in the national total of 17,119 AIDS-related deaths.

The *New York Times* obituary noted that he had an "unforced, authoritative manner" and was "blessed with a commanding voice and a handsome appearance." Newsman Peter Jennings recalled that "in terms of sheer performance, Max was a penetrating communicator. He had a natural gift to look in the camera and talk to people." Robinson could talk Received Standard English better than most white men, a facility which evoked "general surprise," and which allowed him admission to white America's economic and social mainstream. When he walked the streets of Chicago, black mothers would point him out to their children and tell them to "talk just like Max."

But Max had a bone to pick with the mainstream. In February 1981 he became the center of a national controversy and was called on the carpet at ABC when he told a college audience that networks, including his own, discriminated against black journalists and that the American media in general was a "crooked mirror" in which "white America views itself." And Robinson's death confronted America in another way: he was one of the first homosexual men to die of AIDS, a threat to both white and black beliefs about acceptable sexual behavior.

Although Max was in the minority by his color, he was in the majority of early AIDS deaths in the United States because of his sexual preference and behavior. Before 1990, male homosexuals—mostly whites—had the highest annual incidence of AIDS or new cases diagnosed each year. Now the two trends in the U.S. AIDS epidemic that Max represented are coming together with a horribly macabre result.

Although they comprise only 13 percent of the population, more than 50 percent of all new AIDS cases are among black Americans. In June 2005 the Centers for Disease Control reported that the epidemic's overall increase was driven by a 47 percent increase among young gays and that 60 percent of them were black. Many men who have sex with men are on the down low, and do not identify as homosexuals, and have sex with women as well as men.

As a result, while 45 percent of the blacks who are HIV positive are men who have sex with men, 27 percent of African American men and women are infected heterosexually. Many HIV-positive men are circulating through the prison system and back to their families, and many who are uninfected before they enter the prison system become infected there.

The rate of new AIDS diagnoses among African Americans was almost 10 times that of whites and three times that of Hispanics. HIV infection rates increased so rapidly in its communities of color in the late 1990s that Los Angeles declared a health emergency in 2000. The rapid growth of new infections among African Americans has changed the color balance of existing cases. In June 2005 the Centers for Disease Control reported that 47 percent of all Americans living with AIDS are black, 34 percent are white, 17 percent are Hispanic, and 2 percent come from other backgrounds.

HIV rates for African American females were nineteen times the rates of white females and five times the rates of Hispanic females. For black women, heterosexual contact is the top cause of infection, followed by injecting drug use. Although AIDS is the tenth leading cause of death for white women, it is the third highest cause of death for African American women and the fourth leading cause of death for Latinas.

Authorities said that the latest epidemic wave stemmed from an increase in machismo, violence against women, and rape. Mass imprisonment of American black males is having a cruel effect on both rural and inner-city black communities. On any given day, one in twenty-one black males of any age and one in ten between ages twenty-five and thirty-four are in prison or jail.

These high rates of imprisonment not only have drastic effects on HIV transmission but also destroy family and community structure, says Marc Mauer, a leading authority on race and incarceration. Fifty percent of all African American households with children under eighteen are headed by black women, who suffer disproportionately from all the problems of single parent households including poverty.

Mauer says, "The movement toward mass incarceration is also affecting our democratic processes in ways that are increasingly profound." Forty-eight states prohibit felons from voting while incarcerated, and at least ten prohibit any felon, even those who have finished their sentences, from voting ever again. About one in seven African American males cannot vote. That's 4 million Americans, 2 percent of the voting population overall and 13 percent of the African American population. In many states, voting rights can be reclaimed only by a gubernatorial pardon. The United States is the only developed country that allows complete and permanent disenfranchisement of felons. In some European countries where it is believed that criminals can be reformed, felons are allowed to vote from their cells.

Disenfranchisement is changing American politics in several ways. Researchers have demonstrated that since 1972, six Senate races and one presidential election would have had different outcomes. They estimated that felon disenfranchisement cost Gore 30,000 to 80,000 votes in Florida, which lost him the state and the election.

Harvard Political Review writer Tobias Snyder says that "the high rate of African-American disenfranchisement tends to weaken the expression of African-American voting preferences, causing some to wonder whether felon disenfranchisement is tenable under the Voting Rights Act of 1965." Andrew Schapiro, a Harvard Law School research fellow, believes that "criminal disenfranchisement is an outright barrier to voting that, like the poll tax and literacy test, was adopted in some states with racially discriminatory intent and has operated throughout our nation with racially discriminatory result."

In black communities, disenfranchisement contributes to a sense of alienation because it erodes their ability to redress injustices through the political process. Mass imprisonment and automatic disenfranchisement are creating a powerful community of potential violent people who are disinterested in and disaffiliated from the political process. Criminologist Scott Minerbrook says that child abuse, the threat of gangs and street violence, and an ineffective juvenile justice system are combining to create killers and thieves without remorse or fear of punishment, killers and thieves who owe no allegiance to the population as a whole.

Other restrictions of federal benefits reinforce this vicious cycle of alienation. In 1996 the federal welfare reform law permanently banned drug felons from food stamp eligibility to prevent the coupons from being used as currency. This precaution was not needed when the benefits program went online, and seventeen states had opted out of the restriction in part or in total by mid-2004. The California Narcotics Officers Association said that the ban was "not only silly but increases the probability that the individual will return to the same illegal drug behavior that got them in trouble in the first place." Many convicted drug offenders are in treatment, and denying them food assistance makes it less likely that they will reintegrate into their communities or society as a whole.

Coupled with disenfranchisement, these kinds of restrictions also lead to widespread suspicion about government HIV/AIDS policy that has a serious impact on HIV spread. A 2004 national survey found that the majority of blacks believe that "a lot of information about AIDS is being held back from the public" and 53 percent believe that an AIDS cure has been found but is being withheld from the poor. Fifteen percent of those surveyed believe that AIDS is a form of genocide against blacks. Three-quarters of men who believed the AIDS conspiracy theories were much less likely to use condoms regularly. Blacks also believe that AIDS, like syphilis, is part of a deliberate strategy to reduce their numbers.

To further tip the balance in their favor, since 1997 the Christian Right has been trying to enlist mainstream African Americans to their cause. It has had little success. Ralph Reed, then executive director of Pat Robertson's Christian Coalition, repacked the coalition's legislative agenda into an outreach program to black Americans called the "Samaritan Project," but it was a nonstarter. Promise Keepers, a once-powerful Christian men's movement, declared that "everyone of any race or status who walks through the door is loved and is part of God's creation and family." This was a nonstarter with black and white men alike.

Then, in 2003, the Christian Right tried to enlist black Americans in their movement against gay marriage. "For this mother-of-all wedge issues," says Bill Berkowitz, "right-wing opponents are trying to convince mainstream and traditionally Democratic Party–oriented African Americans that gays are sullying the history of the civil rights struggle in the U.S." Right-wing foundations are bankrolling a number of conservative black organizations, radio show hosts, and intellectuals to enlist black voters.

This divide-and-conquer approach to hate-mongering has had little success because, Berkowitz says, many black leaders were having a hard time forgetting that Pat Robertson's Christian Coalition and Jerry Falwell's Moral Majority consistently opposed civil rights legislation and supported apartheid in South Africa. It was also hard for black leaders to swallow the fact that "the workforces at 'evangelical institutions' were staunchly segregated" so that less than 10 percent of their employees were minority Americans.

The "racial reconciliation" advocates of the Christian Right also failed to give any credence to the institutional basis of racism in America, which they interpret as simply a matter of individual prejudice. "Ironically, this failure to acknowledge any sweeping material or ideological basis for racism enables [the Christian Right's] periodicals to print articles on the evils of racial prejudice and then follow them up with calls to repeal affirmative action, support immigration moratoriums, and oppose multicultural curriculums in schools," says *Colorlines Magazine* writer Andrea Smith.

Beverly Tatum, president of Atlanta's Spelman College, says that "Racism, like other forms of cultural oppression, is not only a personal ideology based on racial prejudice, but a *system* involving cultural messages and institutional policies and practices as well as the beliefs and actions of individuals. In the context of the United States, this system clearly operates to the advantage of whites and to the disadvantage of people of color." Racism—prejudice plus power—leads to differential "access to social, cultural, and economic resources and decision making." Ultimately, it reduces the quality and length of life itself.

Dorothy Height, president of the National Council of Negro Women for thirty years and recipient of both the Presidential Medal of Freedom and the Congressional Gold Medal, said that white Americans still see blacks as "problem people" rather than as fellow citizens. Despite the advances of the civil rights movement, blacks in America have failed to achieve anything like equality in terms of access to resources. The median net worth of a white American in 1998 was $81,700; the median net worth of an African American was $10,000. The pattern of disparity is similar for Hispanics and Native Americans.

Poor people still have much lower educational levels and get caught in a spiral of poverty that affects all aspects of their lives, including their health. Single mothers receiving welfare are the poorest segment of the population but they are far from alone. The United States leads industrial nations with the largest proportion of its population in poverty: 20 percent of its children, 12 percent of its adults, including 37 percent of its single mothers. Gains continue to accelerate for the upper 25 percent of United States income earners, however, so income is becoming increasingly concentrated. The 3.6 percent of households with wealth levels over $500,000 now have almost 60 percent of the nation's wealth.

On March 11, 2005, America's mainline Protestant church officials used extraordinarily harsh language to condemn the Bush administration's proposed budget, saying that it would "be truly devastating for people living in poverty—in this country and around the world." Condemning the budget proposal as a "moral outrage," church leaders expressed concern over the state of Bush's soul, and warned him that he would suffer the fate of eternal damnation, like the rich man who ignored Lazarus lying at his door.

"This budget neglects and exacerbates our nation's health care crisis, and fails to honor the commitments our nation has made to combating poverty and disease," said one of the church officials. "Such a budget is not a reflection of the compassionate values of our nation," the clerics said, and "compels us to stand boldly and firmly" against cuts in food stamps, Medicaid, veterans' health benefits, and other human services "in order to support military might, war spending and tax cuts for the wealthy and corporations."

Despite the condemnation, in October 2005 congressional Republicans renewed their drive to reduce Medicaid and Medicare funding by as much as $12 billion over the next five years. Although they argued that cuts in social services for the poor were essential to pay for hurricane damage and the war in Iraq, they continued to pursue estate tax cuts to benefit the rich. Their primary cost reduction target, Medicaid, is the last-resort health care option for millions of children, pregnant women, the disabled, elderly, and working poor. Republicans also proposed cuts in food stamps for 300,000 families, billions of dollars of reductions in student loans, and elimination of pension guarantees and unemployment insurance.

Many of the gains in inner-city programs realized during the Clinton administration, including reduction of crime and violence, expansion of public health and services for the poor, and containment of HIV/AIDS, have been reversed since the Bush administration took office. Passage of the Republican-sponsored Personal Responsibility and Work Opportunity Reconciliation Act in 1996 dramatically altered cash assistance for poor families with children. This harsh law made it clear that "politicians make decisions that are not based on research and experience," said DHHS assistant secretary Peter Edelman, who resigned when President Clinton signed the law.

While the law dramatically increased the proportion of poor women who are working, many of these women are still below the poverty level and still need government assistance. Because they were employed, many lost public health insurance coverage for themselves and their children, and their health suffers as a consequence. In 2005, researchers studying the long-term effect of the law found that "recipients face worsening health and deepening health burdens that already limit participation in work."

Persistent health disparities in all chronic diseases between whites and all other races have bred widespread discontent and suspicion about the intent of government among nonwhite Americans. Mary Thomas, the sixty-year-old former president of the Pima Nation, says that failure to deal with type 2 diabetes, which Thomas and a high proportion of fellow Native Americans have, is because "they're not really wanting us to get well." Besides African Americans and Latinos, the country's 3 to 4 million American Indians and Alaska Natives are also experiencing a dramatic rise in HIV/AIDS, and have the highest rate of HIV after blacks and Hispanics, according to CDC data. Their AIDS-related death rates are also higher because of late diagnosis and lack of treatment and care.

The mother of a twenty-one-year-old Native American woman in Fort Lauderdale, Florida, told *Vibrant Native Life* reporter Victor Parachin that her daughter caught HIV in a moment of youthful indiscretion. "A parent could not have wished for a more loving, talented, and motivated child. You cannot imagine the toll her death has taken on our entire family. Our heartbreak and sorrow have been overwhelming."

Most HIV-positive Native Americans and their families are in cities, because few Native Americans still live on reservations, where access to services and testing are very low. The Yellowstone AIDS Project, where Paige works, provides routine outreach to the northern Cheyenne reservation, and similar programs are provided by AIDS service organizations in other states.

Like blacks and Hispanics, longtime disparities in access to care, education, and social opportunities has left Native Americans at higher risk of all chronic and life-threatening diseases, not just AIDS. A 2005 report from the Agency for Healthcare Research shows that on average, the health status of all racial and ethnic minority groups is worse than that of whites, especially if they are poor.

A higher proportion of Native Americans, blacks and Hispanics lack health insurance, receive lower quality health care, have fewer prevention measures for all diseases, and have lower access to childhood vaccinations. In these minority groups, violence, suicide, and homicide are higher. Femicide—the homicide of women—is the leading cause of death for African American women ages fifteen to forty-five and the seventh leading cause of death among women overall, largely from abusive relationships.

Beulah Ramsey, a sixty-one-year-old grandmother in Raleigh, North Carolina, has suffered mightily at the hands of a racist system. In an early 2005 conversation with Sarah Avery, a reporter for the Raleigh *News and Observer*, Beulah described her childhood. The oldest of ten children, she grew up among New York City's poor. Like many migrants from America's rural South to the big cities of the North in the 1940s and 1950s, Beulah's family "moved from one place to another, never quite outrunning the mice and roaches that crawled over them at night." By sixteen, Beulah rebelled and became pregnant with her first child. Responsible for her nine brothers and sisters, she thought, "If I was going to take care of babies, I figured they ought to be my own."

Streetwise, long-legged, and beautiful, Beulah easily drew the attention of men, who left her with six more children but no economic support. She worked as a home health aide, nurse's assistant, and hotel maid, and in the 1960s snorted heroin for the first time. Although she had used alcohol and smoked pot, heroin fixed her in a twenty-year downward spiral. Eventually she lost custody of her five oldest children. In 1982, "tired of everything—life itself," she completed a residential treatment program and never injected drugs again. But her past had already caught up with her.

In 1988 Beulah learned that she was HIV positive. She was in the first cohort of HIV-infected people in the United States, mostly gay white men. While Beulah was an oddity at the time, she is typical of the epidemic's second wave. The disease is ravaging black families in poor inner cities and rural areas alike. Two of Beulah's brothers have died of AIDS, another son is living with it, and her daughter recently contracted it.

After living with HIV for fifteen years, Beulah stopped her medication because she believed that she was cured. Three months later she nearly died, losing forty pounds in two weeks. Not only was her strategy a personal failure; when it is repeated by thousands of AIDS patients like her, it gives rise to drug-resistant strains of HIV. The fear that such strains may break loose reached near hysteria in 2005 when carriers with a "super-virus" HIV that killed them in less than a year were discovered in several American cities. HIV strains that are resistant to many known AIDS drugs have been on the rise in recent years throughout the United States, due in part to patients quitting their medications. One-quarter of Americans with HIV are infected with such strains.

Beulah Ramsey's story is being repeated in thousands of rural communities across the country, where heterosexual sex is the dominant form of transmission to women. Although the AIDS epidemic is spreading fastest in inner cities, which look frighteningly similar to hard-hit parts of Africa, it is also rising in rural areas because their residents believe they are immune. Damien's aunt said that poor girls are being taken advantage of in many small communities. She tells me about the girl who plays piano at her church, "who was a good girl, but this fellow came to town and he took advantage of her." He knew he was HIV positive, she said, "but he still took advantage of her." The girl is taking HIV drugs, but Damien's aunt was not sure how she pays for them. "Medicaid, maybe," she said.

This is the typical pattern for a second-wave epidemic. The number of HIV-positive individuals in groups that are infected early eventually gets large enough to spread the infection to people who have contact with them: occasional drug users, clients of commercial sex workers, prisoners and their families, unsuspecting partners and spouses who do not know enough about the disease to protect themselves. Overlapping sexual relationships accelerate the spread of HIV, sending the virus out in a sexual chain letter.

University of North Carolina AIDS researcher Dr. Peter Leone said that poor women feel powerless to protect themselves because they rely on men for support and are afraid to demand condom use. He added, "Almost a quarter of the women learned about their HIV status when they went in for prenatal screening. A third reported that they had a monogamous relationship," and did not use a condom because they trusted their partner. Like Paige, the bad news came when many of these women were trying to turn their lives around.

Leone's colleague, Dr. Adaora Adimora, says that fighting poverty would go a long way toward curbing the epidemic. "Poverty affects your choices," she explains, pointing out that often it is a vicious circle. "It affects where you live, where your children go to school and who you mix with. It affects the type of education you get, and that affects the type of jobs you qualify for, and that affects how poor you are." A person juggling two or three sexual relationships is common in poor African American communities, wherever violence, joblessness, and prison reduces the number of eligible men. Women may accept relationships with men they suspect are not monogamous in the hope that they will change their partner's behavior.

Many Americans living with AIDS depend on public sources for their health care, housing, and food. If they were not poor before they got HIV (like Beulah), multiple illnesses, the cost of medications and health care, and loss of jobs and income push many into poverty (like Susan Howe). For each

HIV-positive person, the cost of care, treatment, and social support is high. Beulah's care and medications cost $35,000 per year, including $530 a month in federal disability and $550 a month for her rent.

North Carolina, which enjoyed a decline in new cases from 1995 to 2000, is now seeing the number of new cases rise to their former levels. In that state alone last year, taxpayers spent $145 million on Medicaid for people living with AIDS. Of that amount, the state spent $65.4 million on AIDS medications, $9.7 million on doctors, $6.6 million on case management, $2.8 million for emergency room visits, $1.3 million for hospice care for the dying, and $1.2 million on hospitals.

In February 2005, North Carolina's health director, Dr. Leah Devlin, told the Raleigh *News and Observer* that the state was not getting the support from Washington that it needed to fight the disease. She argued that federal funding goes disproportionately to urban areas, and federal budget allocations were ignoring the fact that the disease is hitting more and more rural states, especially in the South.

Devlin said, "Responding to this epidemic is complicated by the fact that the public health system we depend on to fight this battle is shrinking in many communities. The vulnerability of the public health infrastructure was highlighted on 9/11." Instead of improving it, the government took resources away from health care to fund emergency preparedness and antiterrorist activities, leaving the nation poorly protected from infectious diseases like AIDS, and even from bioterrorism.

A year later, the U.S. Department of Health and Human Services announced that it planned to redirect resources from metropolitan areas with successful HIV/AIDS programs to states that are "lagging behind," including more rural states where the epidemic is hitting hard. If Congress shifts AIDS resources to rural areas, the country's urban AIDS programs will be devastated, city health authorities argued. Boston officials said that prior federal cutbacks had an extremely negative effect on their programs, and the city was seeing increases in risky sexual behaviors and in syphilis, signals of increased HIV transmission.

Disease expert Laurie Garrett, who analyzes the security implications of AIDS and other diseases for the U.S. Council on Foreign Relations, said that the administration and Republican lawmakers were "playing a nasty game of political football with AIDS" to "aid and comfort the religious right." Although Bush claims to have made an "unprecedented effort" to fight HIV/AIDS in the United States, funding for domestic programs are not keeping up with epidemic growth, which rose by more than 30 percent in 2003. Internationally, the $15 billion in foreign aid the president promised in 2004 was slow to roll out and is now threatened by competing allocations to the war in Iraq and to repair the damage caused by Hurricanes Katrina and Rita.

In 2004 President Bush made a special one-time allocation of $20 million to clear the lists of people waiting for AIDS drugs across the country. The allocation covered one year of medications, but people with the disease must stay on medication the rest of their lives. The small increases being considered for the Ryan White act funding will force many off their medications again in 2006, with implications not only for their health but for the development of drug resistant strains of HIV. California Representative Maxine Waters requested a huge increase in the Minority AIDS Initiative for 2006 to compensate for cuts in other programs.

If Medicaid, the largest payer for AIDS drugs, is cut, even more people living with AIDS will be unable to pay for their medications. Medicaid costs rose $300 billion in 2004, driven by a surge in enrollment of newly diagnosed AIDS patients, of employees whose private health insurance was discontinued, and by rising drug costs. Many HIV-positive Americans quit their medications if they become too expensive. The disease is hitting many individuals who have unstable incomes, homes, unsure relationships with doctors and health care systems. They are forced by cuts in assistance "to chose between their rent and their meds," a trap in which Paige says that more and more of her clients fall.

Congress is also considering cuts in the Housing Opportunities for People Living with AIDS (HOPLA) initiative. This will be devastating to people living with AIDS, who need housing to stabilize their lives and return to productive employment. Susan Howe, who has lobbied Congress to increase HOPLA funds, says, "They are trying to cut our housing, the HOPLA funding, which would put us into the shelter system if we live in a big city. I don't know what would happen in the rural counties—they probably wouldn't have any housing—but in the big cities, they have HUD. In Pittsburgh, where I live, the waiting lists for housing are two to four years. There are periods where they will not take any applications at all. In New York, the waiting list is eight years. Eight years! In San Diego it's five years."

While treatment has been successful since the early 1990s, close to half of all Americans living with AIDS still get no modern treatment. Women are particularly disadvantaged in this respect. Cost, access, diagnosis, awareness—all of these are among the causes, along with the side effects and inconvenience patients face in taking the AIDS medications available in this country.

But the lion's share of the responsibility rests with our drug companies, which have blocked the import of newer drugs developed in other countries that are cheaper and easier for patients to take while refusing to lower their prices and profits. The U.S. taxpayer foots an annual bill for AIDS medications of $10,000 or more per patient, while the annual cost for patients taking more sophisticated medications in developing countries is about $300. We pay the highest prices for prescription medicines of any country in the world.

Drug prices are high for one reason only: to support the industry's enormous profits. Independent Congressman Bernard Sanders of Vermont, who holds the state's only seat in the U.S. House of Representatives and is likely to become the Senate's first Independent Senator next year, used the drug industry's own Fortune 500 numbers as raw data in an analysis that showed that the top seven pharmaceutical companies had profit margins almost twice as high as the next most profitable U.S. industry. Drug companies took in more in pure profit than the top seven auto companies, the top seven oil companies, the top seven airline companies, and the top seven media companies.

Pharmaceutical companies have been the most profitable sector of our economy for three decades, ranking at the top of all of *Fortune Magazine*'s measures of profitability. Frank Clemente, of Public Citizen's Congress Watch, remarked in 2001 that "During a year in which there was much talk of sacrifice in the national interest, drug companies increased their astounding profits" by 32 percent when other industries declined by 53 percent. Clemente attributed this to "advertising some medicines more than Nike shoes" and lobbying campaigns that keep U.S. congressmen safely in drug company pockets, extending "lucrative monopoly patents. Sometimes what's best for shareholders and chief executive officers isn't what's best for all Americans."

Vermont's Sanders says that "for the last year, the pharmaceutical industry has used scare tactics to try and stop real prescription drug legislation from passing in Congress. One of its most deceitful and shameless claims is that real reform will somehow stifle research and development and make their business unprofitable." In fact, analysis of the industry's own data shows that it spends much more on advertising than on research and development. A 2003 University of Minnesota study found that of every $100 drug companies spend, $31 is spent on marketing, advertising, and administration, while $13 goes for research. Drug companies are the fifth largest buyer of U.S. television time, spending $6.5 billion in 2004 alone.

Even Senate Majority Leader Bill Frist admitted that drug ads increase health care costs and asked companies to put a two-year voluntary delay on advertising for new drugs, saying "A lot of direct-to-consumer advertising is misleading. This . . . advertising can oversell hope. It could oversell results. And it can undersell the risk." The American Medical Association (AMA) refused to back the proposed delays on advertising, despite rising concerns about the dangers of certain heavily marketed painkillers and antidepressants. They said it infringed on the pharmaceutical industry's rights to free speech and increased awareness of certain ailments.

The AMA's position was more than a little self-serving. Arthur Kuebel, who worked for more than thirteen years "detailing" drugs, or promoting them to physicians, said that doctors were paid $250 to $2,500 by drug companies to promote Vioxx at professional 'roundtable' discussions and large dinners. Nine of ten drug researchers, many of them doctors, are financially linked to the drug industry, and six of ten researchers receive corporate funding for their research.

Recognizing the dangerously close relationship that drug companies have with doctors, advocates are lobbying for company disclosure of expenses higher than $25 on gifts, meals, or entertainment purchased for doctors or other health care professionals who prescribe medications. A spokesperson for the American Association of Retired People said that "Such disclosure would reveal how much money companies spend persuading doctors to prescribe high-priced, brand-name drugs."

When Congress was searching for a way to fund hurricane repairs in the South, Vermont's Sanders suggested a unique solution. He said that if Congress was willing to stand up to the pharmaceutical industry and demand drug price controls, the country could more than pay for the hurricane damage with the savings it would reap on Medicaid and Medicare drug bills, and still have enough left over to fully fund both programs' benefits.

The artificially high cost of drugs leaves American AIDS patients unable to afford treatment, exposing us all to the lethal possibility of mutual, drug-resistant superstrains of HIV. It also creates a huge financial burden and an artificial ethical crisis for the U.S. taxpayer. We search our consciences and budgets for a way to provide needed drugs to a quickly expanding HIV-positive population in the face of persistent Medicaid cuts while drug company profits soar.

The typical U.S. patient with HIV/AIDS must take handfuls of drugs daily. Patients using newer, equally or more effective treatment regimens manufactured in developing countries take one or two pills a day. Fixed-dose combinations (FDCs) were being used in other countries for five years before the U.S. Food and Drug Administration finally approved the one-pill-a-day treatment for use here. FDCs combine two or three different types of AIDS drugs together in potent combinations so patients have an easier time stomaching the medicine and remembering to take their daily doses. They boost patient compliance, which means patients are less likely to stop taking their drugs, reducing the opportunity for drug-resistant strains of HIV to develop. Big drug companies lobbied the Food and Drug Administration to delay their introduction here until they could develop their own copycat versions.

When Abbott Laboratories announced it was increasing the price of Norvir five-fold in 2004, Aetna Insurance Company filed a class action suit, accusing the company of violating antitrust law. Patients are "being forced to pay higher prices for Norvir than would otherwise occur in a fair and competitive market," said the company. Activists responded with a new push to remove the federal government's trade protections for U.S. drug companies so that cheaper generic drugs could be imported.

It was not until large pharmaceutical companies started experiencing competition from third world producers in the late 1990s that the world understood two important things about AIDS drugs: they could be produced inexpensively, and they could be manufactured in forms that were easy to take. Susan Howe says that in the first year she was diagnosed, 1996, there were not many medications available.

After she lost almost half of her T cells in the first year, her doctors gave her only a year to live and offered her free medications through a pharmaceutical company trial. At first she refused. The drug they offered her required that she maintain a strict eating schedule. She told her doctors, 'Oh, that'll never work. If I have to die in a year, I have to die in a year. But I'm using food to cope right now. You can't tell me I can't eat. I just thought, 'Well, if I have to die, I'm going to die with cigarettes and I'm going to die eating cake!'" After six months, she agreed to take a "cocktail" of AZT and 3TC. Her doctors told her that said most patients adjust to the drugs within a month.

"I never quit throwing up for a year. But now I'm fine. I hung in there a year. It was like being pregnant. It was like morning sickness twenty-four hours a day. It was a horrible year. Because when you're depressed and you're sick on top of it, you never get out of bed except to go to the bathroom. All your clothes are dirty and your house is a mess because you can't stay up long enough to clean it because you're sick to your stomach and you're going to throw up if you move. You say, 'What kind of life is this? I don't want to live.' You get to a very bad place. That was a very hard year for me. The blessing was I did get through it. I don't get sick to my stomach from AZT anymore, and I've been on AZT and 3TC and they never had to add that other drug. Why take it if I'm not allowed to eat? Now they want me to stop taking these drugs and I'm saying, 'No,'" Susan told me. "I was really angry for a while. I asked them, 'Are you just trying to help the government?'"

When HIV is diagnosed early, patients may not have to start medications immediately. Doctors have also learned how to adjust drug combinations and dosages so people on the drugs do not get as sick. The CD–4 count of people on HIV medications has to be tested periodically so that if they develop resistance to one combination of drugs, they can start another one. New HIV combinations develop within individuals who acquire two types. A drug user, for example, can get the B subtype from sharing needles and C from a sexual contact. Predominant types can also shift. During vaccine trials in Thailand, the dominant subtype, B, was almost completely replaced by subtype E in the test group in only a few years.

Paige, diagnosed five years after Susan, is taking newer medications. She says "My health is excellent. When I was first infected, I drank a lot just to try to deal with the pain of it. That affected my numbers a lot, so I quit drinking. I try to eat healthier, stay away from the fast food. I have an undetectable viral load, less than fifty copies in a teaspoon of blood. The meds have reduced it, and the virus is undetectable. I have over nine hundred T cells. I've been doing very, very well on my medication. I take nine pills a day: three Kaletra in the morning and three at night, one Combivir in the morning and one at night, and I take an antidepressant at night to fight off the effects of the Kaletra and Combivir, the insomnia. This is my second regimen. I started on Sustiva and Combivir, but the dreams were just too weird on the Sustiva. The hardest part is keeping an appetite. I've lost a lot of weight from the medication."

The Food and Drug Administration is now being slammed for pervasive corruption and manipulation of the drug approval process to protect drug producers. It's alledged that the FDA fast-tracked scientific reviews, approved drugs with dangerous health effects, and slowed approvals for competitive drugs that would reduce company profits. David Graham, a senior scientist with the FDA's Office of Drug Safety, told the press in February 2005, "I know the FDA is responsible for 100,000 people being injured." The Agency ignored the advice of its own safety experts, Graham charged, and it is trying to have the evidence "swept under the rug." In testimony before the Senate, Graham said the system is "broken" and incapable of preventing dangerous drugs from coming on the market. Now, with the Bush administration's budget cuts, the FDA will reduce all of its inspection programs that review drug and food safety.

With the help of our government and the World Trade Organization (WTO), the big drug companies are blocking development of treatment innovations by nonwestern pharmaceutical companies. Our pharmaceutical industry has repeatedly squelched innovation by third world producers and blocked access to drugs for millions of people living with AIDS in other parts of the world. Poor countries have had to fight for the right to manufacture or purchase low-cost AIDS drugs to keep their infected citizens alive. In 2000 the United States allied itself with the pharmaceutical industry to threaten economic sanctions against Brazil, South Africa, Zimbabwe, and other countries using less expensive generic versions of anti-AIDS drugs to reduce treatment costs. After a media and e-mail campaign led by Médecins Sans Frontieres (Doctors Without Borders), public indignation was so intense that pharmaceutical giants dropped their lawsuits to stop the countries from purchasing low-cost generics.

Our brazen intimidation of developing country governments tarnished our humanitarian image and raised UN hackles. In 2001 the UN Commission on Human Rights declared that access to medicine was an essential human right and asked member states like the United States to "refrain from taking measures which would deny or limit equal access" to HIV/AIDS drugs and actively "facilitate access" of poor countries to drugs, including their manufacture. In March 2002 WHO included generic AIDS drugs on its approved list of medicines, and the European Union and United Nations Children's Fund (UNICEF) agreed to finance generics produced in other countries.

Big U.S. drug companies still refused to accept the idea that they should not be the only ones making life-or-death decisions about access to these drugs. Brazil was so intimidated by the United States and the WTO that it refused to sell its generic AIDS drugs to other Latin American countries. When a thirty-six-year-old Honduran mother of four died in 2002 because she could not afford drugs, the Pan American Health Organization stepped in to negotiate an average 55 percent price reduction from five brand name manufacturers and even better deals from generic producers. In 2004, the Bush administration tried to derail a successful treatment program in Botswana, an African country in which close to a third of the population of 1 million are HIV positive. Botswana refused to be bullied, arguing that if it bought expensive U.S.-made AIDS drugs instead of low cost generics it would not be able to afford to provide treatment to all of its citizens.

While our pharmaceutical industry intimidates innovative generic drug manufacturers in developing countries, it is not developing many new or innovative drugs itself. Marcia Angell, former editor of the *New England Journal of Medicine*, says in her new book, *The Truth About the Drug Companies: How They Deceive Us and What to Do About It*, that very few new drugs produced by our companies are innovative. Most of the truly new ones are developed by federally funded research programs in universities. Our pharmaceutical companies produce mainly copycat drugs, many with harmful side effects that are not properly regulated by the FDA, Angell says. Three of the most popular medications available today in the United States are produced by a small pharmaceutical company that had to innovate to be competitive.

When large pharmaceutical companies threaten and manipulate smaller drug manufacturers in developing countries, they are squelching the potential for development of new drugs and threatening the future of us all. Peter Rost, M.D. is a drug industry whistle-blower who reported widespread tax-dodging frauds at Pfizer, where he worked until a few years ago. He said that drug company manipulation of Medicare drug benefits and their attempt to stop American consumers from buying their drugs in Canada "have antagonized grannies all over the U.S." He says the industry's claim that patients are getting substandard drugs by ordering over the border is a falsehood.

State governments trying to control their healthcare expenditures have been trying to force a showdown with the Bush administration, Congress, and the FDA for more than a year by helping consumers buy drugs abroad. Jonathan Oberlander, a University of North Carolina expert, says that the idea of saving millions of dollars by importing drugs is "catching fire," making it hard for the Bush administration to "hold onto this issue. This out-and-out state revolt against federal policy is a sea change in American health politics."

Governor Rod Blagojevich of Illinois said that he finally decided to launch a state website to help consumers buy cheaper medications abroad without FDA approval in 2004. "It's been a frustrating experience working with the FDA," he says. "They've acted more like the guardian of the drug companies and their anti-free-market price structure instead of protecting the health and safety of American consumers." A team sent by Blagojevich to investigate drug safety procedures in Canada and six European countries found that the United States no longer held the "gold standard" on drug safety. "Frankly," he said, "I don't think our safeguards are as good as other countries."

Vermont Governor Jim Douglas sued the FDA after it rejected the state's plan to run a pilot to show how importation from Canada could be handled safely. The Minnesota Senior Federation, a grassroots group, sued nine drug companies for antitrust conspiracy, and fourteen California pharmacies have sued fifteen manufacturers, claiming they conspired to charge

Americans "artificially higher prices" than those charged for the same drugs abroad.

State lawmakers meeting in Charleston, West Virginia to discuss how they can control health care costs and drug prices in late October 2005 told the press that they have been intimidated by lawsuits and intensive lobbying by the Pharmaceutical Research and Manufacturers of America, or PhRMA. "It has done everything it could to knock us off our stride," said Massachusetts state Senator Mark Montigny. "The only way to beat them is through good state legislative work." The new federal Medicare drug program that begins January 1, 2006, Montigny said, will leave senior citizens confused, uninsured patients with even lower access to drugs, and drug companies with higher profits.

Rapacious drive for profits, disregard for human lives lost to out-of-reach drug pricing, and questionable research and lobbying practices have cost the drug industry whatever respect it formerly had from the American public. Only 44 percent believe drug companies serve consumers well, according to the latest Harris polls. Big tobacco, the most reviled industry, is rated only 14 percentage points lower. Two in three Americans think that drug prices are "unreasonably high" and 60 percent favor federal price controls.

Kurt Furst, who earned $600,000 as a federal and state drug industry lobbyist for G.D. Searle, Pfizer, and Merck, quit "in disgust" four years ago after he was involved in a drug industry lobbying deal that hurt "the poorest, sickest people in Florida. I realized I couldn't look at myself in the mirror and justify what I was doing for a living." Furst said that what ethics the industry had went out the window with television advertising. "It overwhelmed everything." Lobbying also changed, he said, as the industry developed fake grassroots organizations to front their interests. But the worst, he said, "is the manipulating of groups, like families of mental health patients, to say with absolutely no evidence that a government policy is going to take away a drug from them, and to do it in a way that truly terrifies them."

Why is our government willing to sacrifice our health so big drug companies can maintain their huge profit margins? The reason is simple, and if it occurred in a foreign country, we would be screaming about government corruption and company bribes. Here we call it lobbying. In the last five years, U.S. pharmaceutical companies have spent more than $800 million for federal lobbying and in federal and state campaign donations.

Providing AIDS treatment to all of a country's HIV-positive citizens who need it is not only a sound humanitarian measure, but can actually control the spread of HIV and stop the epidemic in its tracks. It is also affordable in countries where the drug industry does not have a stranglehold on the government. In 1996, Brazil decided that it would provide medical treatment to all of its citizens infected with HIV, ignoring the bullies—the U.S. government, our pharmaceutical industry, the WTO, and the World Bank—who tried to stop it. By 2002, Brazil had proven conclusively that antiretroviral treatment not only made HIV-positive individuals feel better, but also reduced their viral load, preventing at least half of the new infections projected for 2002 and turning the nation's epidemic clock back to 1995. Treatment averted 146,000 hospitalizations between 1997 and 1999 because it caused dramatic reductions in opportunistic infections.

Best of all, savings gained by the Brazilian government from treatment more than covers the cost of the drugs because Brazil manufacturers its own low-cost antiretrovirals. It spent $954 million providing free AIDS drugs from 1997 to 2001, but saved more than $1 billion. This does not include the indirect economic impact of the program. Patients who were too ill to work recovered and became productive again. Family members remained at work. And children were not orphaned.

Had every country in the world followed suit, HIV would have been tamed world wide. Had our government followed Brazil's lead instead of bullying it on behalf of our pharmaceutical companies, many more Americans would be alive, healthy, and uninfected. Giving lip service to the need to trim government fat in the name of protecting and promoting individual rights, this administration is allowing the profits and incomes of the richest Americans to grow while cynically pursuing the breakdown of many essential social services for the poor. The result is widespread exposure to the spread of dangerous diseases, foremost among them HIV/AIDS.

A FAMILY OF LIFE

Limits in federal spending have forced many people living with AIDS to rely on their families and friends for care. Unfortunately, many of them are not as lucky as Paige, and are too afraid to tell their friends and family because of the stigma of the disease. Families are also scattered, or their members are unable to help.

Sometimes it is easier for family members to let go than to help people living with AIDS cope with their many problems. Damien is not sure of the whereabouts of his second wife. Paige's adoptive father lives in Billings, but he has cut her off completely. Two of Beulah's sons who live nearby are not around much, although one lived with her until recently. Last year, Beulah planned a big Thanksgiving dinner for her family, cooking the food she had obtained with the help of local agencies. She told her math tutor during a study session for her GED, "I'm going to cook turkey, and macaroni and cheese, and turnip greens." When the big day came, she prepared the whole dinner and then sat down to wait for her family to come. Only one of her sons showed up. She tried again at Christmas at the urging of her caseworker, who brought her a Christmas tree. Two days after the holiday, Beulah was still waiting for her granddaughter to open the doll she had bought with money she had managed to save.

AIDS support organizations like the Yellowstone AIDS Project exist in every state. Although they get some federal support, they rely on hardworking volunteers to raise money to help meet their clients' needs. Lauren Swanberg, Paige's youngest sister, organized one such event in early August 2005, a pet walk that netted $5,000 in donations and helped raise community awareness.

Susan Howe says that the HIV/AIDS organizations that her doctor recommended were essential lifelines for her. After he told her she was HIV positive, he said, "'Now, Susan, I know you live alone. I do not want you going home and committing hari kari. These are five phone numbers I want you to call before five o'clock.' [It was about quarter to four.] Susan called all of the agencies he recommended, and their immediate response and continued support over her first year probably saved her from depression and suicide, the fate of many newly diagnosed Americans with AIDS.

"I was rather overwhelmed. I was in shock. I was just doing whatever anybody told me to do," Susan said. The agency care and support she received gradually restored her health. "I was very taken by the people who dedicate themselves to us," she said. "They don't have the disease. It is their career, their income, their agency's income, and their federal grants that they're fighting for, and there are times when I will speak up if they make a suggestion that favors them if it's against the consumer. But beyond that, we are very blessed in Pennsylvania. It may be their jobs and their grants and their Ryan White money, but they really do work together and they do have our well being at heart. They'll come to the healing weekends, and they serve in many other ways. We are very blessed. They're dedicated to us, beyond the call of duty."

Websites like Tom Donahue's Who's Positive provide an online community for those who are computer literate. He wants to become "a national organization that reaches out to youth and in doing that, I foresee bringing other HIV-positive youths on board. We're launching a new outreach program called 'Infected/Affected, Real Stories/Real People.' Who's Positive is fund raising to begin a 24/7 emergency HIV-positive youth hotline. It can be done. It's going to be done. It's probably going to cost us a couple of thousand dollars a year. Now, if somebody calls and our answering service picks up and decides it's an emergency, they will contact me on my cell phone."

Susan also coped with her first years of living with AIDS by providing help to dying gay men in the Pittsburgh area. "All these men were dying. I guess God wanted me to be their nurse. I thought, 'But, geez, God, I would have been their nurse without all this! You didn't have to go here, but okay.' So I'm taking care of all these wonderful, wonderful men, who reminded me of my son. Their partners couldn't find anyone to take care of them who wasn't afraid of them. They didn't have money for help, so they would call me. Then I would stay with them until they died. But their families had abandoned them, or they had no money. So I just cared for them. I was very happy when the meds came out because people stopped dying so much. It really was too hard for me."

Susan says that the anguish of people dying of AIDS is heartrending. "If they're dying and having fevers—you know, if you've had any kind of STD, it really, really comes on strong at the end—it's horrible, the infections are rampant, so people will be sweating to death and freezing. You're bathing them and then wrapping them in towels constantly to give them comfort because that's all that you can do. I've taken a rosary—and I'm not even Catholic!—and placed it on someone's chest and tried to say it. 'My dear mother of God,' I've prayed, Come down here right now because Jim needs you and I don't know what I'm doing. Hurry up and send Jesus too!'" She laughs.

"You just do whatever you can think of doing," Susan continues. "You sing them their favorite song. You know, these gay men loved musicals, so I would sing them their favorite show tunes. Whatever you have to do. Whenever anybody said anything about gay couples, I'd say, 'You know what? I took care of a man. He lived on the fourth floor. His partner would come home after working long days, and he would carry him down four flights of stairs to the street, put him in a wheelchair—they had no car— and he would wheel him in that wheelchair to another part of the city where his group was so he could see friends before he died. He'd wait in the waiting room. He'd wheel him back home after group, and he would carry him back up those four flights of stairs. And he had a bad back.' I'd say, 'Now, that's love. That's more love than I've seen in some marriages.'"

Susan has become an AIDS activist, like Tom and Paige. But "I quit all the fighting until they called me to go to D.C. They wanted me because, they said, 'They won't be able to dismiss you. We need somebody that will make them sit up and say, 'Oh, my God! My child could come home from college with this. It might hit our family. Maybe we'd better pay attention. Maybe we'd better not be so mean to these AIDS victims. It might hit our family.' Who knows?"

"People with AIDS are sick people. But in Washington, because these senators and representatives—even churches—like to think, 'Well, you're a prostitute. Or you're gay, or you're a drug addict and you're from prison, and you asked for this.' Now they won't come out and say that, but that's where they are. So they sent me to Washington because they wanted someone who was not black, who was not a drug addict, who was not from prison, who did not get this in a way that they could say, 'It's your own fault.'"

Because she's a preacher's daughter, I asked Susan to give me a prayer to say for people with AIDS in the United States. To my surprise, Susan answered, "I can't do that. I don't do the prayer for people with AIDS in the United States. Here's what happened last year." She explains that her sister, who lives in Delaware and is head of a hospital laboratory, led a Methodist mission to Africa to set up a lab so people could get HIV treatment. "They decided to go over and build a lab for this community where people are living underneath pieces of paper, for God's sake." Susan wanted to go to help, but she couldn't leave the country for more than a month because she would lose her Supplemental Security Income.

"In the fall, we're all getting together and my sister brings the pictures of her visit. And I'm just so sad that I couldn't go and help somehow. Well . . . she has a picture . . . of these two little boys in the middle of this dirt road and it's night time and they're trying to build a fire with two sticks. They're about two and three years old. They're trying to build a fire with sticks because their mother is in the hospital, and she's dying of AIDS. In Africa, when your family is in the hospital, you are responsible for feeding them. They will take care of you as well as they can with whatever meds they have. But they cannot feed them. If they die of starvation, they die of starvation. Here's two little baby boys, two and three years old, in the middle of the night, trying to start a fire so they can cook something for their mother who is dying of AIDS.

"Every day I pray for those two little boys," Susan says. "Every day of my life, that picture burns in my brain. How lucky I am. How blessed I am. How lucky we all are here in America. But we are part of a whole world of people who are not as blessed as we are. I've been a Christian a long, long time. And all these people in Washington, who tout that they are Christians . . . well, personal piety is no replacement for social justice. We have been blessed here in America. A lot of people have been blessed because of our economy, and they have risen to the top. There are people who need our help—who need their help—and they look at the poor as a burden."

Susan says that the fight for Americans affected by AIDS is an inclusive struggle, one that is in the self-interest of all of us. "I've learned to love people I used to be afraid of," she says. "All the drug addicts and the people from prison, I'm now running around defending. People from prison can't get into the HUD system because they're felons. They will have nowhere to go. Can you imagine getting out of prison, and you have AIDS, and you cannot access any support system? Now would that make you warm as a criminal, or would that maybe send you back to your old behavior so you can live? So you can get back in prison where somebody will house you and feed you. And what might you have to do to get back in there? And who will be harmed? Are we safer by taking away their housing?"

Stigma still stalks the HIV-infected, sometimes coming from where they expected the most assistance. According to the Reverend Kelvin Redmond, pastor of the Body of Christ Church in Raleigh, North Carolina, AIDS has not been a priority for many black churches although it directly affects the lives of many church members, whether they are infected or not. The Reverend Dr. Enoch Holloway of the Friendship Chapel Baptist Church in Wake Forest, North Carolina, said that many black churches have allowed stigma to fester rather than address it directly. "If someone gets cancer, the church lends a hand and prays. HIV? They're not going to publicize it to anyone." Although black churches nationally rallied against the "death of a race" due to the crisis of drugs and violence in their communities, some are less able to deal with an infection that will have much more severe demographic consequences.

But not all churches are listening to Christian Right dogma about how HIV is a "rightful and cleansing plague." Father Lynn Edwards, the Catholic priest who founded Sheperd Wellness Community in Pittsburgh, says, "in 1987, my heart was broken seeing so many people dying of AIDS. Today my heart is broken seeing so many people from all walks of life trying to live with this disease." The Reverend Holloway says that his church, which runs an AIDS mission with the Alliance of AIDS Services in North Carolina, is fighting the ignorance and stigma surrounding the disease. "Providing compassion for people is perfectly in line with the will of God," the reverend said. "Jesus himself said He came for those who needed a physician and not for those who are well. And if anybody needs a physician, it's those living with HIV."

Cuts in Medicaid and other public programs will affect people living with AIDS in many serious ways. "You live out of food banks and the grace of other people," Susan Howe says, "and you're at the mercy of the government. On one hand, I am really grateful to live in America. When you look at Africa, wow! The government has sort of taken over the job of family, and ultimately, they've done a good job of taking care of us. This used to be the job of the family, to take in someone sick. In the Old Testament, in Bible times, you would take in your sick parents, and you would take care of old people, and you would take care of women who were alone and take care of children. That's how society was then.

"We're so industrial now that children move away and nobody takes care of their parents," she continued. "Nobody's taking in the sick ones, and nobody's taking care of the mothers of children. It's just not happening. So, on one hand, I'm grateful that our government has done this. Compared to Africa, it's a lot. On the other hand, if you look at Canada, you see that we could take much better care of our people. The Medicaid problem is only hiding a bigger problem, which is that we need national health care."

Beulah Ramsey decided to go public so she could help other HIV-infected people and their families. In a November 2004 radio program and on World AIDS Day, December 1, she addressed a multifaith service at Raleigh's Temple Beth El. "Tonight I add my voice to the voice of millions of other women who are living with HIV/AIDS," she told the congregation. "My silence cannot protect me. Your silence cannot protect you. I cannot be silent anymore."

AIDS kills three times more people *each day* than died in the World Trade Center attack on September 11, 2001, and if we count those infected *each day*, it is five times more lethal. The disease is a pervasive security threat because it leads to growing poverty, food insecurity, economic and social collapse, deaths among the armed forces and police, increased criminal violence, and sudden power imbalances.

At a November 2002 Washington dinner honoring UN Secretary General Kofi Annan for his diplomatic work in obtaining sanctions against Iraq, then U.S. Secretary of State Colin Powell surprised the guests when he switched the focus from Baghdad and declared that the most serious problem facing the world today is not terrorism but the HIV/AIDS epidemic. AIDS is a not a future threat, it is destabilizing our entire planet right now and will have far worse consequences than any event a terrorist could ever invent.

Even if a cure is found tomorrow, the toll of death and suffering by 2010 will far exceed any other recorded human catastrophe, any other previous epidemic, natural disaster, war, or incident of genocidal violence. On a time line extending from

A.D. 0 to 2010, three huge spikes of death loom. Two are just past the middle: the Black Death, which killed 93 million people worldwide by the early 1500s, and the decimation of Native Americans by waves of multiple diseases brought by their European conquerors in the 1500s, which killed about 90 million people.

At the other end of the time line looms the impending disaster of AIDS, which will have killed or infected at least 130 million people by 2010. Everything in between is dwarfed by these gigantic disease disasters, including World War I, which killed 10 million people, the 1918–1919 influenza epidemic, which killed 20 million, and World War II, which killed 50 million people. Other events we commonly think of as catastrophic look relatively small next to these giants. The Vietnam War, for example, took 5 million lives on both sides, and the U.S. Civil War 600,000.

The United States has always been near the top of the list of countries infected by HIV/AIDS. This is a travesty because we have the resources to stop our epidemic, unlike many developing countries with large numbers of infected people. The early failure to contain the spread of AIDS among gays, minority, and low income populations is now being further impeded by race, class, gender, and intergenerational conflict, leading to increased spread of HIV. HIV/AIDS continues to spread despite high literacy and education levels and the affordability of anti-HIV drugs because of poverty and economic inequality, racism, systemic violence, the commodification of women, and religious-based political denial.

In the meantime, our government is busy turning the heat up on the pressure cooker by adopting regressive social and economic policies that heighten concentration of wealth and remove basic social safety nets. It is a travesty that the richest, most well-informed country in the world has such a huge AIDS burden. It is also a sign that things have gone very, very wrong in the social, political, and economic affairs of this country.

Although President Bush declares that "America is a free society, which limits the role of government in the lives of its citi-

zens," he can certainly make an exception to this rule in order to
meddle in and worsen the private lives of teens, women, and families. But when it comes to big business, including the pharmaceutical industry, the sex sector, or the prison lobby, the
government does not seem to give a damn.

Unless we act, the future is not bright. Although medical science responded rapidly in the early stages of the AIDS epidemic,
progress in developing a cure or a vaccine has come to something
of a standstill. Besides an impressive ability to mutate, AIDS may
behave like other epidemic diseases have in the past, switching
the manner in which it is transmitted. Imagine, for a moment, if
AIDS became a respiratory infection and could be transmitted by
a sneeze like the bubonic plague did when it became the Black
Death in 1347. "No rule of nature contradicts such a possibility,"
says Joshua Lederberg, former president of Rockefeller University. "The proliferation of AIDS cases with secondary pneumonia
multiplies the odds of such a mutant, as an analogue to the emergence of pneumonic plague."

Long-term control of the disease requires individual and social change, a coming to maturity of our personal and social
ethics, the commanding of personal sexual urges, and reduction
of deep-seated addictions. We must learn to speak clearly and
without shame about our problems so we can be more frank
about protecting our young people. Curbing the epidemic also
requires governmental behavior change and change in economic
systems. Above all, it requires a paradigm shift—the kind of
change human beings find hardest to make—a change in our
basic understanding of how things work, an acknowledgment of
how deeply and intricately all systems of this earth are intertwined in ways much more subtle than our intellect is able to
comprehend. Arriving at that kind of paradigm change requires a
fundamental honesty, looking at and responding to the world as
it really is.

The question of what to do about HIV/AIDS in America will
not be resolved by science alone. We already know at least nine
ways to prevent further spread of the disease and how to respond
to its victims. Although a vaccine could avert total global disaster,

it is far in the future and a little beside the point. We can stop this disease with prevention and treatment but hesitate because of the cost and questions of morality. We must address severe inequities in the distribution of income, protect human rights, and provide access to care.

A successful human response to the HIV/AIDS epidemic must, in the end, be composed of equal parts of science and economics and humanitarian concern for our future. AIDS may be the most serious challenge we have ever had to face, stretching our capacity to feel as well as think, our ability to balance scientific genius and economic considerations with our fundamental humanity in the face of human suffering and loss. The response must be measured in small steps and little ways, in acts of kindness and salvation by ordinary people, as much as it is in giant steps of Nobel Prize-winning ingenuity.

History tells us that epidemics last a long time. HIV/AIDS will be around for at least the next two or three hundred years. The trajectory of HIV/AIDS growth that started in the late 1980s will continue until the middle of the twenty-first century, with peaks and valleys occurring at different times on different continents. Then, after a long plateau, there will be a long drop, and AIDS will stabilize worldwide at a lower level and be with us permanently as an endemic, chronic disease.

What will the epidemic look like as it gets worse? What will it feel like? What impact will it have? Imagine yourself in the middle of the Black Death, which killed one-quarter to one-third of the world's population during the fourteenth and fifteenth centuries. It completely changed social, economic, and political systems, religions, art, architecture, and the nature of interpersonal relations. HIV/AIDS will have the same effect over the next twenty to thirty years. Recent reports from Africa say that the much-anticipated worst day has already arrived on that continent. In another ten years, it may be America's turn.

Paige says "I still lead a pretty normal life, but I have to think about different things than other people do. I've taken my diagnosis as a heads up." Maybe it's time that we take a heads up and begin to think in different ways about our social issues and the value of all members of the American family. Gordon, her biological dad, says "I don't think AIDS should be political at all. I think that politics should be put on the shelf. It should be looked at realistically. The best thing that we can do as a nation, as men and women, is lead by example." So far we have not presented an example to the world as a nation that can handle its social problems well. Instead, we are known as people that refuse to help, care, or even constructively think about our tired, weary and downtrodden—about all the members of our national family.

Tom says that "The most positive thing about being positive is the ability to be able to use your positive status in a positive way. If there is no cure in my time," Tom said in one of his recent speeches, "I think about the day my family learns of my end, the end of my journey, the end of my fight. I hope that from this day forward you take this fight to whomever you can, using your voices loud as you can to encourage others to join this fight, and one day, we will be able to say that all of us who used our voice made a difference in saving lives."

This American family portrait of AIDS includes all of us. The people you have met in this book are working to confront the injustices of our society and make changes happen that will slow the growth of AIDS in America. But they cannot do it without us, without our compassion and our care. They need our help to make our country a place that is safe for all of us and for our children. They need our voices to realize the American vision of democracy and equality, to ensure that our government makes sane and just decisions that protect our health and our rights.

How can we be more proactive in confronting the epidemic? First of all, we need to be aware of what our epidemic looks like, and what is causing it to spread. The purpose of this book is to help people become more aware of the changes taking place in America that are contributing to the growth of HIV/AIDS.

Second, we need to fight against the administration, its Christian Right backers, and any politicians who have allowed the epidemic to take off in recent years. Only we can preserve our civil rights. We must believe they are worth having.

Last, more of us need to become pro-active in our social thinking and politics, to know what is going on, so we do not let the minority ruin what is great about our country and take away our hard-won freedoms. The stories in this book are about Americans who could be you or me. AIDS can happen to *any* American. Let us work to stop the epidemic in its tracks and reclaim our right to a government that is of the people, by the people, and for the people.

"You know, this struggle is a blessing, because we get to know what's really, really important," Susan says. "None of us have control. None of us! We are all in the same boat, in the same stormy sea, and we owe each other a terrible loyalty. Life is no respecter of political parties and money in the bank. No! Life can be out of control, but it's what makes you part of the human race. We are all bonded. We all belong to each other. I would rather be the one in the shelter than be the one on Capitol Hill or the one with money in an account. I would rather be the one who knows how special each person is. This is our family. A family of life."

FOR FURTHER READING

PRIMARY SOURCES: THE INTERVIEWS

I conducted one or more lengthy telephone interviews with the following people: Paige and all of her family members, Susan Howe and Cathy Frye, and "Damien" and his aunt. I had brief interviews with Dr. Carlos del Rio of Emory University and with Debbie Hendricks of the Montana State Health Department. All the stories in the book are true, whether they are my own experience or that of someone else, including those specifically noted below which were taken from press reports or online sources.

SECONDARY SOURCES

Introduction

Radical Christian Right: Any of Michael Moore's work; former President Jimmy Carter's *Our Endangered Values* (Simon & Schuster, 2005); Al Franken's *Lies and the Lying Liars Who Tell Them: A Fair and Balanced Look at the Right* (Penguin/Plume, 2003), Mark Crispin Miller's *Cruel and Unusual: Bush/Cheney's New World Order* (W.W. Norton and Company, 2004), Cornel West's *Democracy Matters: Winning the Fight Against Imperialism* (Penguin Books, 2004), *Power Shift: Knowledge, Wealth, and Violence at the Edge of the 21st Century* (Bantam, 1990; see especially "Yearnings for a New Dark Age" and "The Global Gladiators"). The changing nature of the country: Molly Ivins and Lou Dubose's *Bushwhacked: Life in George W. Bush's America* (Vintage Books/Random House, 2004). American Conservatism: *Michael Adam's Fire and Ice: The United States, Canada and the Myth of Converging Values* (Penguin Canada, 2003). For more sources on the Christian Right, see Chapter 6.

Chapter 1: Paige's Story

Stories of HIV positive individuals: www.whospostive.com; www.poz. com, or "HIV/AIDS Positive Stories" on www.hivaids.webCentral.

com.au or www.positivewomen.au.org. Children born HIV-positive: J. Dee, 2005, "I was an AIDS Baby," *The New York Times Magazine,* June 26, 2005, p. 34–60. Magic Johnson: *My Life: Earvin Magic Johnson* (Random House, 1992). Personality and health, including HIV: "Is Your Personality Making You Sick?" *Health,* May 2005, p. 254. Yellowstone AIDS Project: www.yapmt.org. International, national, and state AIDS organizations, hospitals, and clinics: www.thebody.com/hotlines.html. April, 2005 AIDS March on Washington: "The Campaign to End AIDS Shows Off Its Power," at www.poz.com/articles/1_48.shtml. On AIDS activist training: "The Next Wave," www.hwadvocacy.com. Campaign to end AIDS: www.endaidsnow.org.

Chapter 2: The Changing Demographics of AIDS

U.S. statistics: "Diagnoses of HIV/AIDS—32 States, 2000–2003," *Morbidity and Mortality Weekly Report,* December 3, 2004, www.cdc.gov. Global statistics: www.unaids.org: *AIDS Epidemic Update* (December 2005) or *Reports on the Global HIV/AIDS Epidemic.* June 2005 CDC press conference announcing that HIV infections in the U.S. totaled more than a million, including comments by Dr. del Rio: AP report, "HIV/AIDS Infections Surpass 1 Million in U.S." carried by major U.S. newspapers in all major cities and *USAToday,* www.usatoday.com, "AIDS, STDs continue to hit hard in southern United States," *The Nation's Health,* June/July 2003, p. 9. Future predictions: K. Stanecki, 2004, *The AIDS Pandemic in the 21st Century,* www.usaid.gov; N. Eberstadt, "The Future of AIDS," *Foreign Affairs,* 81, no. 6 (November/December, 2002), pp. 22–45; and D. Gordon et al., "The Next Wave of HIV/AIDS: Nigeria, Ethiopia, Russia, India and China" (National Intelligence Council, September, 2002), ICA 2002–04D.

AIDS vaccine: UNAIDS, the International AIDS Vaccine Initiative—www.iavi.com, and AmfAR, www.amfar.org, M. Specter, "The Vaccine," *The New Yorker* February 3, 2003, p. 54; SRI Media, "AIDS Vaccine Dramatic Findings," February 24, 2003, www.srimedia.com; J. Cohen. Therapeutic vaccine: M. Barr, "Vax is Back," www.poz.com/articles/_11.shtml. Post-exposure prophylaxis: R. Minnich, "PEP on the Down Low," www.poz.com/articles/_56.shtml.

U.S. sexual behavior: W. Mosher et al., *Sexual Behavior and Selected Health Measures: Men and Women 15–44 Years of Age, United States, 2002,* U.S. Department of Health and Human Services, Centers for Disease Control, Advance Data No. 363, September 15, 2005. Bestiality: J. Sullivan, "Enumclaw-area animal-sex case investigated," Seattle Times, July 15, 2005, www.seattletimes.newsource.com; and "Has 1 in 8 people had sex with an animal?," www.straightdope.com.

AARP 2004 study of sex in older Americans: Susan Jacoby's "Sex in America," *AARP Magazine*, July/August 2005, p. 63. Jon Roberts' story and other information on drug addition in older Americans: R. Karaim, "Calling It Quits," *AARP Bulletin*, March 2008. Older Americans: "AIDS Rate Surges in People 50+," *Bulletin of the American Association of Retired People*, May 2004; M. Cichocki, "HIV Over 50," www.aids.about.com/cs/aidsfactsheets/a/seniors.htm; A. Semuels, "Worry Grows About Seniors and HIV/AIDS," *Pittsburgh Post-Gazette*, June 28, 2005, www.postgazette.com, National Association on HIV Over Fifty—www.hivoverfifty.org. High school and college students: "HIV, HIV Counseling, & AIDS," www.huhs.harvard.edu/ Health_Information; "HIV/AIDS Cases Increasing at Southern Universities," *WRUF News*, March 11, 2004, www.am850.com; AP report, "Black colleges seek to stem HIV cases: Stepping up safe-sex education after spike in infections," www.msnbc.msn.com. CDC, "HIV Transmission Among Black College Student and Non-Student Men Who Have Sex with Men—North Carolina, 2003," *Morbidity and Mortality Weekly Report* August 20, 2004, "Trends in Sexual Risk Behaviors Among High School Students—United States, 1991–2001," *MMWR* September 27, 2002, www.cdc.gov/mmwr; H. Weinstock et al., "Sexually Transmitted Diseases Among American Youth: Incidence and Prevalence Estimates, 2000," *Perspectives on Sexual and Reproductive Health*, v 36(1), p. 6.

Breaking news: Global AIDS Alliance, www.globalaidsalliance.org, and the "Daily HIV/AIDS Report" of the Kaiser Family Foundation AIDS website, www.kaisernetwork.org. AIDS timelines: www.cbsnews.com/htdocs, www.avert.org/hist; or Aegis's "So Little Time," www.aegis.com. Early history: Randy Shilt's *And the Band Played On* (St. Martins, 1987); J. Mann and D. Tarantola, eds., *AIDS in the World II: Global Dimensions, Social Roots, and Responses* (Oxford University Press); D. Ward, *The AmFAR AIDS Handbook: The Complete Guide to Understanding HIV and AIDS* (W.W. Norton and Company, 1999).

HIV tests: www.orasure.com/oraquick. For 800 hotlines for HIV/AIDS testing and counseling, check the white pages of your telephone book. Information on prevention and testing: "A False Sense of Viral Security: HIV/AIDS and Hepatitis C Risks are Medical, Not Moral," *The American Legacy*, Winter 2005, p. 12.

Sexually transmitted diseases: "Medline," National Library of Medicine, www.nlm.nih.gov/medlineplus; American Social Health Association, www.ashatd.org/stdfaqs/' "Trends in Reportable Sexually Transmitted Diseases in the United States," "Tracking the Hidden Epidemics: Trends in STDs in the United States 2000," "Most Teens Not Provided STD or Pregnancy Prevention Counseling During Check-Ups," www.cdc.gov; E. Stewart, "Entering a New Relationship on a

Healthy Notes," Women's Health, www.womenshealth.about.com; "Sex, sun, sea and STIs," www.health24.com; M. Ginty, "What to Ask Your Gynecologist," *Ms. Magazine*, August 2000; "Six Nerve-Wracking Questions," www.bupa.co.uk/health_information; American Health Consultants, "Check STD Screening: Room for Improvement?" *Contraceptive Technology Update*, 2003, p. 1; J. St. Lawrence et al., 2002, "STD Screening, Testing, Case Reporting, and Clinical and Partner Notification Practices: A National Survey of U.S. Physicians," *American Journal of Public Health*, v92 (11), p. 1784; M. Hogben et al., 2002, "Sexually Transmitted Disease Screening by United States Obstetricians and Gynecologists," *Obstetrics and Gynecology*, v100(4), p. 801. History: A. Fairchild et al., "The Myth of Exceptionalism: The History of Venereal Disease Reporting in the Twentieth Century, *Journal of Law, Medicine & Ethics*, Winter 2003, v31(4), p. 264; "STDs: Yesterday and Today," *World and I*, March 2004, v 19(3); K. Testerman, "Promiscuous Plague," *World and I*, March 2004, v 19(3), p. 26; A. Brandt, *No Magic Bullet* (Oxford University Press, 1985); C. Quetel, *History of Syphilis* (Johns Hopkins University Press, 1990); R. Davidson and L. Hall, eds., *Sex, Sin and Suffering: Venereal Disease and European Society since 1870* (Routledge, 2001); "Roots of Black Syphilis Epidemic in World War I," *New York Amsterdam News*, 1997, v88(18), p. 13; J. Knowles, "Notes on the History of the Condom," Planned Parenthood Federation of America, 2003 (ww.plannedparenthood.org/articles/condomhistory.html); J. Cutler and R. Arnold,1988, "Venereal Disease Control by Health Departments in the Past: Lessons for the Present," *American Journal of Public Health*, v78(4), p. 372; D. McBride, *From TB to AIDS: Epidemics among Urban Blacks Since 1900* (State University of New York Press, 1991).

Chapter 3: The Homosexual Demographic

Tom Donahue: www.whospositive.org, J. Haber and A. Maloney, "Pennsylvania: Former Penn State Student's Billboard Raises AIDS Awareness," www.aegis.com/news/ads/2004. Craigslist.com: A. Rostow, "The hottest spot online," *The Advocate*, August 16, 2005, www.advocate.com. HIV in gay men: "HIV/AIDS Among Men Who Have Sex with Men," "HIV Prevalence, Unrecognized Infection, and HIV Testing Among Men Who Have Sex with Men—Five U.S. Cities, June 2004-April 2005," and "Patterns of Sexual Behavior Change Among Homosexual/Bisexual Men—Selected U.S. Sites, 1987–1990," www.cdc.gov/mmwr. Public attitudes: "U.S. Public Opinion Polls on Homosexuality," www.religioustolerance.org, Dale Carpenter's "After Santorum," www.indegayforum.org, the "Prevalence of Homosexuality: Brief Summary of U.S. Studies": www.kinseyinstitute.org. Colonel Ronald Ray and Judith Reisman: D. Radosh, "Why Know?" *The New Yorker,*

December 6, 2004. "Anal Sex Statistics: How Common is Anal Sex?," www.analsexyes.com.

Sexual identity: "Genes, not genitalia, key to gender," www.health24.com/new/Sexuality/1–944, 30915.asp, and S. Lovgren, ""Sexy" Smells Different for Gay, Straight Men, Study Says," *National Geographic News*, www.news.nationalgeographic.com/new/2005; E. Spillane, "Same-sex but not 'gay'," *The Advocate*, August 16, 2005, p. 34, www.advocate.com; or R. Young and I. Meyer, "The Trouble with "MSM" and "WSW": Erasure of the Sexual-Minority Person in Public Health Discourse," *American Journal of Public Health*, July 2005, v 95(7), p. 1144. Anne Fausto-Sterling: *Sexing the Body* (Basic Books, 2000) and *Myths of Gender* (Basic Books, 1992), *Discover*, "Why Do We Know So Little About Human Sex?" (June 1992, pp. 28–30); B. Colemen, "Uncovering the real truth about down low brothers," *Court Bouillon*, April 25, 2005, www.ducoutbouillon.com, *On the Down Low: A Journey Into the Lives of "Straight" Black Men Who Sleep with Men* by J. L. King (2004, Broadway Books);. B. Lichtenstein, 2000, "Secret Encounters: Black Men, Bisexuality, and AIDS in Alabama," *Medical Anthropology Quarterly*, v 14(3), p. 374.

Drug use: Michael Spector's *New Yorker* article, "Higher Risk: Crystal meth, the Internet, and dangerous choices about AIDS" (May 23, 3005), "Gay men use Viagra recreationally," www.health24.com; E. Brown, "Crystal Ball," *New York*, April 29 2002; K. Ernst, "AIDS, Sex and Drugs: Gay activists are preaching the wrong message," from the *City Journal* February 18, 2005, www.city-journal.org; for the more scientific perspective on risky gay sexual behavior, see the June 2003 issue of the *American Journal of Public Health* (v 93, no. 6).

Christian Right on homosexuals: see www.hatecrime.org. Human Rights Watch 2001 study of U.S. gay teens, *Hatred in the Hallways*: www.hrw.org/reports/2001. The HRW fact sheet on *Lawrence v. Texas*, www.hrw.org/press/2003; www.en.wikipedia.org.

Chapter 4: Teen Sex and Abstinence

Planned Parenthood on the Christian Right: *White Paper: Adolescent Sexuality* and *Abstinence-Only "Sex" Education*, www.plannedparenthood.org. HIV and sex in teens: "HIV/AIDS Among Youth," www.cdc.gov/hiv/pubs/facts/youth.htm; W. Mosher et al., *Sexual Behavior and Selected Health Measures: Men and Women 15–44 Years of Age, United States, 2002*, U.S. Department of Health and Human Services, Centers for Disease Control, Advance Data No. 363, September 15, 2005; "Multiple Sexual Partners Among U.S. Adolescents and Young Adults, *Family Planning Perspectives* v 30(6) p. 271, www.agi-usa.org/pubs/journals; "Teens see oral sex as less risky," www.health24.com; L. Stepp,

"Study: Half of All Teens Have Had Oral Sex," *Washington Post*, September 16, 2005; M. Burford, "Girls and Sex: You Won't Believe What's Going On," *O Magazine*, November, 2002; *The Sex Lives of Teenagers: Revealing the Secret World of Adolescent Boys and Girls* (Dutton, 2000). *A Global Generation Gap: Adapting to a New World*, February 24, 2004, www.pewglobal.org/commentary.

Abstinence-only education: AP, May 2005, "Study: 'Abstaining' Teens Still Risk STDs," www.foxnews.com/story, "Virginity Pledgers More Likely to Engage in Risky Sexual Behavior," www.siecus.org, P. Bearman and H. Bruckner, 2000, "Promising the Future: Virginity Pledges as they Affect Transition to First Intercourse," Columbia University Institute for Social and Economic Theory and Research. Christian Right position: "Focus on Social Issues: Abstinence Policy," www.family.org. Congressional study: *The Content of Federally Funded Abstinence-Only Education Programs*, prepared for Henry A. Waxman, www.democrats.reform.house.gov; D. Bagby, "Abstinence-only curricula faulted for false data; M.A. Woodbury, "Misled by Sex Ed: Abstinence-Only Programs are Riddled with Wrongs," *Health*, May 2005, p. 120; T. Henneman, "Sex, lies, and teenagers, *The Advocate*, August 16, 2005, p. 58; E. Kaplan, "Bushed to the Limit," www.poz/articles; "Keeping Our Youth 'Scared Chaste' SIECUS Curriculum Review," www.siecus.org; J. Marcotty, "State's abstinence-only sex education doesn't work any better, report says," Minnesota AIDS Project, www.mnaidsproject.org/policy; "ACLU Criticizes the CDC for Proposed Changes in Guidelines on AIDS-Related Materials," August 17, 2004, www.aclu.org/HIVAIDS; C. Wright, "Programs don't affect teens' sexual activity," *The Nation's Health*, December 2002/January 2003, p. 21; Human Rights Watch, 2002, *Ignorance Only: HIV/AIDS, Human Rights, and Federally Funded Abstinence-Only Programs in the United States*, www.hrw.org. CDC on HIV in male adolescents: www.cdc.gov. On www.4parents.gov: Human Rights Watch, "Letter Urging Removal of Government Website Censoring Critical HIV Prevention Information," www.hrw.org; "National Public Health Professionals Find HHS' 4parents.gov Website Inaccurate and Ineffective: Site Includes Multiple Inaccuracies, Misleading Information, and Biases," www.siecus.org; "NOW Cheers Investigation of Deceptive Federal Government Website," August 17, 2005, www.now.org/issues/health.

Teen pregnancy: "Teenagers in the United States: Sexual Activity, Contraceptive Use, and Childbearing," www.cdc.gov; www.teenpregnancy.org; "Not Just Another Single Issue: Teen Pregnancy Prevention's Link to Other Critical Social Issues," February 2002, www.guttmacher.org; "Teens See Oral Sex as a 'Casual Alternative' to Intercourse, Study Shows," www.mtv.com/new/articles, April 6, 2005.

Policy and Economic Analysis: the Advocates for Youth Report, *Teenage Pregnancy, The Case for Prevention*, www.advocatesforyouth.org/publications/coststudy; P. Fagan, "The Decline of Teen Marriage is a Serious Problem" in the *Opposing Viewpoints* Resource Center, www.galenet.galegroup.com; O. Starr, Jr., "Teen Girls Are Easy Prey for Over–20 Predators," *Insight*, May 3, 1999, reprinted in T. Roleff, ed., 2001, *Teen Sexuality: Opposing Viewpoints* (San Diego: Opposing Viewpoints Series), K. Moore and A. Driscoll, "Most Teens Sex Partners Are Close in Age," and E. Zorn, "Premarital Teen Sex is Normal," from the same volume of the *Opposing Viewpoints* series.

Teen risk behavior: "Substance abuse, alcohol linked to unprotected sex," *The Nation's Health*, April 2002; p. 15, "Protecting Teens: Beyond Race, Income and Family Structure," www.allaboutkids.umn.edu; "Wisconsin Youth Risk Behavior Survey," www.dpi.state.wi.us/dpi; M. Talbot, "Best in Class: Students are suing their way to the top," *The New Yorker*, June 6, 2005, p. 38. Censoring of textbooks: P. McMasters, "Trying to shut out the light by banning books," www.freedomforum.org. "Bio textbook censored," www.thefileroom.org. Kaiser Family Foundation 2000 survey of parents: www.kaisernet.org. Dr. Kimber McKay and Montana sex education: E. Bader, "Abstinence-Only Education," www.zmagsite.zmag.org; "Montana's Teen Pregnancy Rate Drops more than 30 Percent in 20 Years," www.siecus.org.

Chapter 5: Women at Risk

Francis Priddy: "AIDS Taking on a Female Face," www.cbsnews.com; statistics on women: UNAIDS's December 2004 *AIDS Epidemic Update*, www.unaids.com; "Women Increasingly Bearing the Burden of HIV/AIDS, Study Finds," summarizing the Henry J. Kaiser Family Foundation's 2002 study, *Key Facts: Women and HIV/AIDS*, both available from www.kaisernetwork.org. "HIV/AIDS among Women," www.cdc.gov;. www.unaids.org or www.who.org for news from the Global Coalition on Women and AIDS, their Technical Update on Gender and HIV/AIDS, the 2004 global report, *Women and HIV/AIDS: Confronting the Crisis*, Access to HIV drugs: "A Globally Effective HIV Vaccine Requires Greater Participation of Women and Adolescents in Clinical Trials," www.unaids.org.

U.S. history: D. Rowland, 2004, *The Boundaries of Her Body: The Troubling History of Women's Rights in America*, (pub, date); "Women Gain Votes (Some Even Matter)," *New York Times*, May 12, 2005, E. Kolbert, "Firebrand: Phyllis Schlafly and the Conservative Revolution," November 7, 2005, *The New Yorker. Roe v. Wade:* People's for the American Way's "Another Brick from *Roe*'s Wall" and "Reproductive Rights," www.pfaw.org. American opinion on abortion: C. Lake, "The Polls

Speak: Americans Support Abortion," *Ms. Magazine*, www.ms-magazine.com/summer2005/polls.asp. Emergency BC pill: NOW, August 19, 2005, "Will Young Women Have Access to EC?," www.now.org/issues/abortion; L. Fraser, "The RU–486 Abortion Pill Should Be Available to Women" *Opposing Viewpoint*, www.galenet.galegroup.com. Birth control: *The Unfinished Revolution in Contraception: Convenience, Consumer Access, and Choice*, "The Role of Contraception in Reducing Abortion," "Abortion in Context: United States and Worldwide," "Revisiting Public Funding of Abortion for Poor Women," and "Lessons from Before *Roe:* Will Past be Prologue?" www.guttmacher.org/pubs.

Pharmacists' conscience:, "Pharmacists Do Not Have the Right to Determine Women's Health Care and Childbearing Decisions," "NOW Supports Legislation Protecting Women's Right to legal, Safe Birth Control," and NOW President Kim Gandy's testimony to the House Committee on Small Business Hearing on Freedom of Conscience for Small Pharmacies, July 25, 2005, www.now.org. Microbicides, M. Gross, "HIV Topical Microbicides; Steer the Ship or Run Aground," J. Vail, et al., "Improving Topical Microbicide Applicators for Use in Resource-Poor Settings," and "Acceptability of a Microbicide Among Women and Their Partners in a 4-Country Phase I Trial," July 2004 *American Journal of Public Health*, v 94(7).

Annie Laurie Gaylor: "The Religious War Against Women" and "Why Women Need Freedom from Religion" at www.ffrf.org; "Annie Laurie Gaylor: Women's rights fading in the U.S.?" *Detroit Free Press*, August 6, 2005, www.freep.com/voices. Iraq's new constitution: August 26, 2005 statement of NOW President Kim Gandy, "On Women's Equality Day in the U.S., NOW Advocates for Iraqi Women's Rights, www.now.org/press.

Justice Robert's record: "Supreme Court Nominee John Roberts: An Incomplete Record that Gives Cause for Concern," American Association of University Women, www.aauw.org; "President Bush Nomination to the Nation's Highest Court is an Extreme Disappointment," www.siecus.org; People for the American Way, "Right-Wing Groups Claim Roberts 'Firmly in the Mainstream,'" www.pfaw.org. Public confidence in the Supreme Court: "Supreme Court's Image Declines as Nomination Battle Looms: Court Critics Now on Both Left and Right," Pew Research Center, www.people-press.org. Bush on Social Security: T. Bethell, "The Gender Gyp: No wonder women are worried about Social Security," *AARP Bulletin*, July-August 2005; B. Basler's "We Love Social Security: President Bush is proposing a dramatic change that could divided generations," *AARP Bulletin*, March, 2005, p. 10; J. Erickson, August 19, 2005, "Social Security: The Fight of a Lifetime," www.now.org/issues/economic/social.

U.S. statistics on rape: M. Koss, 2000, "Acquaintance Rape: A Critical Update on Recent Findings with Applications to Advocacy," www.vip.msu.edu, or her "Rape is a Serious Problem," *Opposing Viewpoints*. Comparative national statistics on rape and other crimes: www.nationamaster.com. Domestic abuse: "CDC Reports the Health-Related Costs of Intimate Partner Violence Against Women Exceeds $5.8 billion each year in the United States," www.cdc.gov; www.cdc.gov/ncipc/factsheets/svfacts.htm; M. Gallagher, "Domestic Violence Trials are Rare," *Albuquerque Sunday Journal*," May 1, 2005, p. 1; "Facts on Family Violence and Sexual Assault," National Mental Health Association, www.nmha.org; Johns Hopkins University School of Public Health and the Center for Health and Gender Equity (CHANGE at www.genderhealth.org), *Ending Violence Against Women, Population Reports Issues in World Health*, Series I, No. 11; Amnesty International, "Women's Human Rights," and "HIV/AIDS and Violence Against Women: An International Perspective," www.amnestyusa.org; CDC's National Violence Against Women Prevention Research Center, www.vawpresentioin.org;, U.S. Department of Justice Office on Violence Against Women, www.ojp.usdoj.gov/vawo; Family Violence Prevention Fund, "Domestic Violence is a Serious, Widespread Social Problem in America: The Facts," www.endabuse.org; "Men's Voices, Men as Allies," in *Men Can Stop Rape*, www.feminist.com; G. Gellert, *Confronting Violence: Answers to Questions About the Epidemic Destroying America's Homes and Communities* (American Public Health Association, 2002); S. Maman et al., "HIV-Positive Women Report More Lifetime Partner Violence," *American Journal of Public Health*, (2002) v92 (9); "Violence Against Women's Act Needs Your Support" (August 2005); "Don't Let the Bush Administration Role Back Family Leave!" (March 17, 2005); "Supreme Court Leaves Women More Vulnerable to Domestic Violence" (June 28, 2005), and "NOW Supports Real Assistance for Women Escaping Family Violence and Poverty" (June 24, 2005), www.now.org/press;. S. Lane et al., "Marriage Promotion and Missing Men: African American Women in a Demographic Double Bind," *Medical Anthropology Quarterly*, v 18(4), p 405; G. Kaplan et al., "The Health of Poor Women Under Welfare Reform," *American Journal of Public Health*, July 2004, v 95(7); "Poverty," in Houghton Mifflin's "Reader's Companion to U.S. Women's History," www.college.hmco.com/history/readerscomp/women; "Welfare Law and the Drive to Reduce 'Illegitimacy,'" www.guttmacher.org.

U.S. income disparity: W. Niekirk, July 24, 2004, *Chicago Tribune*, "Riches in a few hands: In surprise statement, Greenspan says concentration of wealth a worry," www.freepublic.com/ or: www.money.cnn.com. Poverty statistics: *Income, Poverty, and Health Insurance Cover-*

age in the United States, 2003, www.census.gov; D. Leonhardt's September 1, 2005, *New York Times*, "U.S. Poverty rate rose in 2004, even as economy grew," www.iht.com; *Reading between the Lines: Women's Poverty in the United States, 2003, Legal Momentum*, www.legalmomentum.org; J. Johnson, "U.S. Census finds more are poor but number lacking health insurance remains steady," *San Francisco Chronicle* August 31, 2005, www.sfgate.com; K. Christopher et al, "Women's Poverty Related to Men's in Affluent Nations: Single Motherhood and the State," Joint Center for Poverty Research, www.jcpr.org; United Nations Population Fund, *The Promise of Equality: Gender Equity, Reproductive Health and the Millennium Development Goals*, www.unfpa.org/swp/swpmain.htm. U.S. budgetary allocations: www.database.nationalpriorities.org. Edelman's resignation: A. O'Connor, *Poverty Knowledge: Social Science, Social Policy, and the Poor in Twentieth-Century U.S. History* (Princeton University Press, date?); G. Koretz " . . . And the Home of the Poor," *Business Week online*, March 12, 2001, www.businessweek.com.

Social security changes: T. Gray, "Pension Roulette: Millions of Americans are losing promised benefits," *AARP Bulletin*, July-August 2005. Wage inequality: L. Berg, "Jon Roberts' Dismissive View of Pay Equity," August 19, 2005, and "Bush Wins the CAFTA Battle, Women and Poor Workers Pay the Price, "August 2, 2005, www.now.org/issues. Wal-mart: L. Featherstone, *Selling Women Short: The Landmark Battle for Worker's Rights at Wal-Mart* (Basic Books, 2004); R. Greenwald *WAL-MART: The High Cost of Low Price*, film released in November 2005; J. Randall, "Wonderful world of Wal-Mart," February 21, 2003, www.news.bbc.co.uk/1/hi/world/americas/2787951.stm; "Wal-Mart Settles Consumer Class Action for $7 Million," January 23, 2004, www.consumeraffairs.com/news04; J. Schmidt, "Local Wal-Mart Class-Action suit is a shot across the bow of employers," www.startribune.com. CEDAW: "Women's Discrimination Now a Global Concern," an Inter Press Service August 5, 2004 update from the more liberal www.religiousconsultation.org. Women's sex drive: E. Yoffe, "Passion, Interrupted: Can a dab of testosterone make life sexier?" *Health*, May 2005; A. Newitz, "The Coming Boom: Big Pharma has made billions pumping up the male population." *Wired* July 2005; M. Bryner, "For Women, a World of Turn-Ons," *Psychology Today*, July/August 2005.

Chapter 6: Marriage, Family and the Courts

Statistics: L. Rouse, *Marital and Sexual Lifestyles in the United States: Attitudes, Behaviors, and Relationships in Social Context* (Haworth Press, 2002); www.census.gov; www.nationmaster.com; S. Nock, *Marriage in Men's Lives* (Oxford University Press, 1998); S. Coontz, *Marriage: A History* (Viking, 2005); M. Small, *What's Love Got to Do with It? The Evo-*

lution of Human Mating (New York: Bantam Doubleday Dell, 1995); G. Althen, *American Ways: A Guide for Foreigners in the United States* (Intercultural Press, 2003); C. Zimmer's "Take My Wife, Please," *Wired*, November 2004. "Marital success can be predicted," www.health24.com; "C. Rush, "Revealed! 101 Secrets to a Happy Marriage," www.magazines.ivillage.com/redbook/sex/happy/articles. Cohabitation: "Breaking Cohabitation's Curse," and "Continental Shift," July/August 2005 *Psychology Today*. Gay marriage: M. Fitzgerald and A. Cooperman, "Marriage Protection Act Passes: House Bill Strips Courts of Power Over Same-Sex Cases," Washington Post July 23, 2004, www.washingtonpost.com; "Marriage Equality Back in the Spotlight," www.pfaw.org; and J. Schaeffer, "For Gay and Lesbian couples, a New Wrinkle at Tax Time," People for the American Way, www.pfaw.org. Christian right viewpoint on marriage and the courts: G. Stanton, 2003, "New Jersey Court Strongly Affirms Marriage," Citizen Link, www.family.org; J. Bergman, "Darwin's Teaching of Women's Inferiority," *Impact* No. 249, www.icr.org/pubs/imp/imp–249.htm. Teen suicide rates: "Suicide and America's Youth," www.1-teenage-suicide.com; R. O'Connor, "Teen Suicide," www.focusas.com/Suicide.html. Mixed race marriage: P. Wallenstein, *Tell the Court I Love my Wife* (Palgrave Macmillan, 2002); R. Moran, *Interracial Intimacy: The Regulation of Race and Romance* (2003, University of Chicago Press).

Victorian sex: H. Horowitz, *Rereading Sex: Battles over Sexual Knowledge and Suppression in Nineteenth-Century America* (Alfred A. Knopf, 2002); M. Sweet, *Inventing the Victorians: What We Think About Them and Why We're Wrong* (St. Martin's Press, 2001); J. MacKenzie, *The Victorian Vision: Inventing New Britain* (London: V&A Publications, 2001). *Esquire*, May 2005, "Women, 2005" *O, The Oprah Magazine*, June 2005, "Ah, Men!"; Z. Hughes, May 2005, "5 Mistakes That May Be Keeping You From the Altar," and "Sisters, Beware! Are You Really 'The One' or Just One of Many?" *Ebony*. N. Foston, "10 Ways to Tell if He's the One," April 2005 *Ebony*; K. Chappell, "For Brothers Only: Don't Blame Mama!" May 2005 *Ebony*.

Supreme Court cases: J. Toobin, "Sex and the Supremes: Why the court's next big battle may be about gay rights," *The New Yorker*, August 1, 2005; People for the American Way, "Celebrating the Right to Privacy: 40th Anniversary of *Griswold v. Connecticut*" and "40th Anniversary of Griswold Highlights Threat to Privacy Rights from Future Supreme Court Nominees," www.pfaw.org.

Christian Right and the Dominionists: C. Miller *Cruel and Unusual: Bush/Cheney's New World Order* (W.W. Norton and Company, 2004); G. Monblot, "Their beliefs are bonkers, but they are at the heart of power, *The Guardian* April 20, 2004, www.guardian.co.uk; J. Lampman, July 7, 2004, *Christian Science Monitor*, "Mixing prophecy and politics," "Fundamentalists: Profile Report," www.religoiusmovements.lib.virginia. edu; "Fundamentalist Christianity," www.en.wikipedia.org; R. Perlstein, "The Jesus Landing Pad: Bush White House checked with rapture Christians before latest Israel move," May 18, 2004 *Village Voice*, www.villagevoice.com; C. Berlet and J. Hardisty, "Drifting Right and Going Wrong: An Overview of the U.S. Political Right," S. Nakagawa, "Race and the Religious Right," www.eserver.org/race; "The Christian Right, Dominionism, and Theocracy," "On the Road to Political Power and Theocracy," "Theocratic Dominionism Gains Influence," "Behind the Culture War to Restore Traditional Values," "Contemporary Assaults on the Freedom of Expression," and "Dances with Devils," www. publiceye.org; "The Rise of the Religious Right in the Republican Party," www.theocracy.watch.org; Leigh Schmidt, *Restless Souls: The Making of American Spirituality from Emerson to Oprah* (HarperCollins, 2004) and D. Sweeney, *The American Evangelical Story* (Baker Academic, 2005).

Chapter 7: The Sex Trade

Troubled adolescents: E. Currie, *On the Road to Whatever: Middle-Class Culture and the Crisis of Adolescence* (Metropolitan Books, 2004); Statistics: *Opposing Viewpoints* books on child abuse and juvenile justice, www.galenet.galegroup.com; U.S. Department of Health and Human Services National Clearinghouse on Child Abuse and Neglect Information, the *Third National Incidence Study of Child Abuse and Neglect* (1996), and their chart book, *Child Maltreatment 2000*; R. Bolen and M. Scannapieco, 1999, "Child Abuse is a Serious Problem," *Social Service Review* v73, p. 281; D. Finkelhor and R. Ormrod, *Offenders Incarcerated for Crimes Against Juveniles*, U.S. Department of Justice, 2001; American Humane Association and the National Committee for the Prevention of Child Abuse; "Teens at Risk, Essays and Articles," eNotes, www.enotes. com/teens-risk; National Runaway Switchboard, www.nrscrisisline.org; www.childrenofthenight; "Welcome to Boot Camps for Teens," www.bootcampsforteens.com; J. Franzen, "The Retreat: Fellowship, a youth minister, and me," *New Yorker* June 6, 2005. On the nature of today's adolescent crisis, see "Teens at Risk, Essays and Articles" at eNotes, www.enotes.com/teens-risk.

Erotic dancing and prostitution: F. du Plessix Gray, "Dirty Dancing: The rise and fall of American striptease," *The New Yorker*, February 28, 2005; J. Raphael *Listening to Olivia: Violence, Poverty, and Prostitution* (Northeastern University Press, 2004; T. Friend, "Naked Profits: The employees take over a strip club," *The New Yorker*, July 12, 2004; www.prostititionresearch.com; A. Kiraly, "Eyes wide shut: Brothel owner Ken Green spreads the legal prostitution gospel," www.lasvegasmercury.com; R. Dalla, "Exposing the 'Pretty Woman' Myth: A Qualitative Examination of Female Streetwalking, www.findarticles.com; N. Bode, "Prostitution horror for young women," *New York Daily News*, www.nydaily.news.com; A. Loinaz, "From Cradle to Street," www.villagevoice.com; B. Roche et al., "Street Smarts and Urban Myths: Women, Sex Work, and the Role of Storytelling in Risk Reduction and Rationalization," *Medical Anthropological Quarterly*, v19(2); "The 1996 National Sexuality Survey," *Family Research Report* October/November 2004, www.familyresearchiinst.org; *Revolving Door: An Analysis of Street-Based Prostitution in New York City*, www.sexworkersproject.org; M. Scott, 2002, *Street Prostitution, Problem-Oriented Guides for Police Series No. 2*, U.S. Department of Justice, www.coops.usdoj.gov; J. Nichol, *Prostitution, Polygamy, and Power* (University of Illinois Press, October 2002); *Opposing Viewpoints* on pornography, sexual addiction, rape, sexual violence, and trafficking, www.galenet.galegroup.com; Prostitutes' Education Network at www.bswan.org. Las Vegas sex scene: www.menshealth.about.com. R. Mead; "American Pimp: Dennis Hof's enterprises in Nevada," *The New Yorker*, April 23, 2001.

Adult entertainment industry facts: CBS news report on "Porn in the U.S.A.," September 5, 2004, www.cbsnews.com/stories; J. Harder, "Porn 500," www.insightmag.com; "Are Sex Workers Coming to New York for the RNC?," August 17, 2004, www.democracy.now; "Hookers and Haulers, *Discover*, 2000, v 21(5); V. Nelson, "Prostitution: Where Racism and Sexism Intersect," in the *Michigan Journal of Gender and Law*, 1993, v1; J. Potterat, "Pathways to Prostitution: The Chronology of Sexual and Drug Abuse Milestones"; and M. Medrano, "Childhood trauma and adult prostitution behavior in a multiethnic heterosexual drug-using population," www.findarticles.com; "Best.Phone.Sex.Ever," *Wired*, July 2005, D. McGinn "Skin City: They dropped out of Silicon Valley to reverse engineer netflix and reinvent themselves as the princes of DVD porn," *Wired*, November 2005; A. Lane, "Oral Values: Inside Deep Throat," *The New Yorker*, February 28, 2005; "The Home Team: Thy Pitcher's Wife," *The New Yorker* June 6, 2005, p. 36.

Male-female power differentials: A. Dworkin, 1993, "Prostitution and Male Supremacy," www.nostatusquo.com/ACLU; Fear Us, "Pornography Causes Sexual Violence," in the *Opposing Viewpoints* series, www.fearus.org. Harvard controversy: J. Wolcott, "Caution: Women Seething" in *Vanity Fair*, June 2005, www.vanityfair.com; A. Ripley, "Who Says a Woman Can't be Einstein?" *Time*, March 7, 2005; A. Pearson, "Rape Culture: It's All Around Us," *Off Our Backs* v 30, August 2000 (also in the *Opposing Viewpoints* series). The "right" of boys to rape girls: "Teen Dating Abuse Alarmingly High, Study Says," June 10, 2005, report of a national survey conducted by Teenage Research Unlimited with funding from Liz Claiborne, Inc.; www.mtv.com/new/articles, P. Smith et al., "A Longitudinal Perspective on Dating Violence

Among Adolescent and College-Age Women," *American Journal of Public Health* July 2003, v93(7). Alan Guttmacher Institute, *In Their Own Right: Addressing the Sexual and Reproductive Health of American Men*, www.guttmacher.org; L. Hammar, "Fear and Loathing in Papua New Guinea: sexual health in a nation under siege," in *AIDS in Oceania*, L. Butt and R. Eves, eds.

Trauma of prostitution: www.sexindustrysurvivors.com; J. Parker, "How Prostitution Works," "Between the Hammer and the Anvil: Working with Complex Post-Traumatic Stress Disorder in a Hostile Environment," and "Brain Damage," www.prostitutionrecovery.org; T. Quan, *Diary of a Manhattan Call Girl* (Crown Publishing, 2001) and "An Upscale Call Girl Speaks Out on Safe Sex" in *Opposing Viewpoints*, www.galenet.galegroup.com.

Trafficking: A. Harrison, "Hooker's Unite! San Francisco sex workers are on a mission to decriminalize prostitution here and across the country," www.sfbg.com; www.bayswan.org; U.S. Department of State, *Trafficking in Persons Report*, www.state.gov/tip/rls/tiprpt/2004; Human Rights Watch www.hrw.org; the Coalition Against Trafficking in Women, www.action.web.ca/home/catw; A. Safo, May 17, 2005, "Human Traffickers Make US$32 Billion Profit" at www.allafrica.com/stories; AP feature, "New York targets immigrant slavery in 'human trafficking' bill," www.jamaicaobserver.com; R. Estes and N. Weiner, *Study of child sex trafficking in the U.S., Canada, and Mexico*, University of Pennsylvania School of School Work,2002, restes@ssw.upenn.edu; D. Shirk and A. Webber, 2004, "Slavery Without Borders: Human Trafficking in the U.S.-Mexican Context," *Hemisphere Focus*, v 12(5), www.csis.org; the U.S. Department of Health and Human Services Administration for Children and Families' Campaign to Rescue and Restore Victims of Human Trafficking website, www.acf.hhs.gov.

Child pornography: "Internet child porn fuels abuse: UN" www.abc.net.au/news; the U.S. Department of State "The Facts About Child Sex Tourism" www.state.gov; V. Silverman, "U.S. Law Enforcement Targets Child Sex Tourism," www.tokyousembassy.gov. HIV outbreak in the porn movie industry ; P. Harris, April 18, 2004, "HIV scare hits US porn industry," www.guardian.co.uk/aids/story, "US porn industry rocked by 4th HIV case," www.news-medical.net; R. Jablon, "Porn industry at standstill after stars test HIV positive," *The Scotsman*, April 17, 2004.

Contribution to national economies: L. Lim, ed., *The Sex Sector: The Economic and Social Bases of Prostitution in Southeast Asia* (International Labour Office, 1998); L. Murthy, "Illegal Sex Business Adds to National Incomes" (Indian Press Service, 1999); M. Ditmore, "Addressing Sex Work as Labor," and L. Agustiin and J. Welden's "The Sex Sector: A Victory for Diversity," www.swimw.org/aslabor.html Baby Mama Drama: www.abclocal.go.com; Daz Dillinger lyrics, www.lyricsdepot.

com. Sapphire Club: www.sapphirelasvegas.com. Christian Right's view: B. Shapiro's *Porn Generation: How Social Liberalism is Corrupting Our Future* (Regnery Publishing, 2005).

Chapter 8: Drugs and AIDS

Statistics: "Surveillance for Certain Health Behaviors Among Selected Local Areas—United States, Behavioral Risk Factor Surveillance System, 2002," www.cdc.gov; National Survey of American Attitudes on Substance Abuse VIII: Teens and Parents, the National Center on Addiction and Substance Abuse (CASA) at Columbia University, www.casacolumbia.org; U.S. Substance Abuse and Mental Health Services Administration, "State Estimates of Substance Use From the 2002–2003 National Surveys on Drug Use and Health," www.oas.samhasa.gov; *Opposing Viewpoints'* articles on substance abuse., www.galenet.galegroup.com; Office of National Drug Control Policy, "Pulse Check" reports; www.whitehousedrugpolicy.gov; Partnership for a Drug-Free America studies, www.drugfree.org; www.drug-rehabs.org, National Institute of Drug Abuse, www.nida.nih.gov. Alcohol abuse: National Institute on Alcohol Abuse and Alcoholism, www.niaa.nih.gov; A. Stueve and L. O'Donnell, May 2005, "Early Alcohol Initiation and Subsequent Sexual and Alcohol Risk Behaviors Among Urban Youths," *American Journal of Public Health*, v 95(5); Institute for Intergovernmental Research, www.irr.com; Human Rights Watch, 2003, *Injecting Reason: Human Rights and HIV Prevention for Injection Drug Users*, www.hrw.org; United Nations Office on Drugs and Crime, 2004, *World Drug Report*, www.unodc.org.

Crystal meth: E. Feizkhah, "Ice: From Gang to Bust," www.time.com/time/pacific/magazine; "National Trends of Methamphetamine," www.kci.org; "Crystal Meth Ingredients," www.totse.com; "Crystal meth ingredients being pulled from shelves," www.vancouver.cbc.ca; "Toxicity, Methamphetamine," www.emedicine.com; "Meth use 'absolutely everywhere' in county,'" www.chronotype.com; "Meth's march challenges drug war," www.theledger.com; D. Leinwand, July 24, 2005, "Counties say meth is top drug threat," *USA Today*, www.usatoday.com; www.methwatch.com; K. Zenike, "The orphans of methamphetamines strain foster care, July 12, 2005, *The New York Times*, www.iht.com. Meth in Montana: "How to Spot a Meth Lab," "The Seductiveness of Meth," www.kblg.com; "City man admits meth plot role in Montana," www.drug-rehabs.org; Meth-Free Montana, www.methfreemt.org; C. Johnson, "Billings Man faints in hearing on meth charges," and L. Harper, "We don't need it. . . . We don't want it," *Billings Gazette*, www.billingsgazette.com; www.drugtest123.com. J Opartny: M. Moore, www.editorialmatters.lee.net. Mexican connection: "Invasion USA: Mexican drug commandos expand ops in 6 U.S. states," www.worldnetdaily.com. Drugs and AIDS: AIDSHotline, www.aidshotline.org; B. Edlin, et al., 1994, "Intersecting Epidemics: Crack Cocaine Use and HIV Infection among Inner-City Young Adults," The New England Journal of Medicine, v331(21); www.content.nejm.org. Daniel Ashkenazy: D. Leinwand, "Prescription abusers not just after a high," *USAToday*, May 27, 2005, p. 3A.

Information on Billings, Banning, or any other U.S. city: www.city-data.com. Glens Falls: www.cityofglensfalls.com. Criticism of Bush approach: B. Berkowitz, "Faith-Based Drug Wars: Bush Recruits Religious Youth Groups as Ground Troops for the 'Drug Wars'," *Dissident Voice*, August 21, 2003, www.dissidentvoice.org.

Chapter 9: Prisons

U.S. prison system: S. Borgia, *Courtroom 302: A Year Behind the Scenes in an American Criminal Courthouse* (Alfred A. Knopf, 2005); T. Rosenbaum, *The Myth of Moral Justice: Why Our Legal System Fails to do What's Right* (HarperCollins, 2004), C. Rathbone, *A World Apart (Random House*, 2005); S. Abramsky, *Hard Time Blues: How Politics Built a Prison Nation* (St. Martins, 2002); *Opposing Viewpoints* on the criminal justice system and mass incarceration, www.galenet.galegroup.com, including P. Street, "Racism Undermines the U.S. Judicial System." and J. Maghan, 2002, "Prisons Do Not Coddle Inmates" in *Opposing Viewpoints*;, "So Who's NOT in Jail? U.S. Prisons taking in 700 new inmates weekly," "U.S. Prison Population tops 2 Million: 1 in 142 US residents now in prison," and "Go to Jail! Go Back to Jail! Prison recidivism rates highest ever," June 2002, www.usgovinfo.about.com; "State Prisons' Revolving Door: A Too-Obvious 'Emergency,'" www.latimes.com; M. Stout and T. Whittle, "Every 10 minutes, another American disappears behind bars," Freedom Magazine, www.freedommag.org, Justice Policy Institute, www.justicepolicy.org; U.S. Department of Justice website, www.usdoj.gov; H. El Nasser, December 15, 2002, "Gated communities more popular, and not just for the rich," *USA Today*, www.usatoday.com.

HIV and health in prisons: October 2005 issue, *American Journal of Public Health*, especially the editorial, "Standing in the Gap" by H. Treadwell and J. Nottingham; "U.S. correctional health needs major improvements," *The Nation's Health*, November 2005; E. Kantor, "HIV Transmission and Prevention in Prisons," February 2003, www.hivinsite.ucsf.edu; "PlusNews Web Special on HIV in Prisons," www.plusnews.org. Needle exchange, see "Cities Can Declare Health Emergencies: In Fight against HIV/AIDS, New Jersey to Allow Needle Exchange," *The Nations' Health*, January 2005, p. 14.

Legal issues: American Civil Liberties Union, "State Criminal Statutes on HIV Transmission—2004," and T. Lange, November 2003 report, "HIV & Civil Rights: A Report from the Frontlines of the Epidemic." www.aclu.org/HIV/AIDS; www.poz.com; www.avert.org; National Conference of State Legislatures, www.ncsl.org/programs/health/hivpolicy.htm. American Bar Association, AIDS Coordination Project, www.abanet.org/AID.

Alabama's Limestone Prison: A. Liptak, "Alabama Prison at Center of Suit Over AIDS Policy," *The New York Times* October 26, 2003; "*New York Times* Examines Doctor's Experience Caring for HIV-Positive Male Inmates at Alabama Prison," www.kaisernetwork.org; S. Bailey, "Programs Urged for HIV/AIDS Inmates," *The Birmingham News* September 22, 2003, www.schr.org; "Alabama Agrees to End Egregious Treatment of Prisoner Living with HIV/AIDS," and "Inhumane Prison Conditions Still Threaten Life, Health of Alabama Inmates Living with HIV/AIDS," Human Rights Watch, www.hrw.org; Arkansas River of Blood scandal: "Canadian Red Cross Pleads Guilty to Distributing HIV-, Hepatitis C-Contaminated Blood in 1980s," June 1, 2005, www.medicalnewstoday.com; S. Parke, "Blood Money," www.archive.salon.com; "Blood Trail: Prison Blood Products Used in Canada after U.S. Deemed Practice was Unsafe," www.freerepublic.com or www.info-implants.com; "Clinton & the killer blood," www.prorev.com; P. Likoudis, "Two Crimes, 1,500 Miles Apart, Aimed at 'Tainted Blood' Investigators," *The Wanderer* June 10, 1999, www.lifesite.net; AP, "High Risk Blood Traced to US," May 11, 1995, www.aegis.com; A. Mozes, "Tainted Blood Supply Spread HIV/AIDS in Poor Nations," Reuters Health, 2002, www.rense.com; J. Chamberland et al., "HIV Screening of the Blood Supply in Developed and Developing Countries," *AIDS Review* (2001) v3. Tuskegee Experiment: S. Reverby, *Tuskegee's Truths: Rethinking the Tuskegee Syphilis Study* (University of North Carolina Press, 2000); "Roots of Black Syphilis Epidemic in World War I," *New York Amsterdam News*, 1997, v88 (18), p. 13; J. Cutler and R. Arnold, "Venereal Disease Control by Health Departments in the Past: Lessons for the Present," *American Journal of Public Health* (1998) v78 (4); D. McBride, D, *From TB to AIDS: Epidemics among Urban Blacks Since 1900* (State University of New York Press, 1991).

Rodney Hulin's story: Human Rights Watch, 2001 *No Escape: Male Rape in U.S. Prisons*; also see their 1996 report *Sexual Abuse of Women in U.S. State Prisons*, www.hrw.org; *Ill-Equipped: U.S. Prisons and Offenders with Mental Illness*, 2003, and N. Gordon, "Rape used as control in U.S. prisons," www.natcath.com. Prisoners' families: C. Mumola, Incarcerated Parents and Their Children, Bureau of Justice Statistics Special Report, www.usdoj.gov; "What Happens to Children?" Child Welfare

League of America, www.cwla.org; Karen DeBord, "Incarcerated Fathers: Extending their Parenting Knowledge tot the Outside,"
www.ces.ncsu.edu.

Katzenbach commission: J. Smith, "Commission to Study U.S.
Prison Conditions," *Washington Post*, March 2, 2005, www.washington-
post.com. Ashcroft and uniform sentencing guidelines: W. Anderson,
"Ashcroft and Justice: Mutual Exclusives," August 30, 2002, www.truin-
justice.org, D. McCullagh, "Perspective: Ashcroft's worrisome spy
plans, www.news.com, and H. Thomas, 2003, "No Mercy in Ashcroft's
Brand of Justice," www.commondreams.org. Bush quote on the gates of
prisons: from S. Taylor, "Ashcroft and Congress are pandering to puni-
tive instincts," *Atlantic Monthly* www.smirkingchimp.com. Other approaches to prisons: "Gore calls for drug testing to 'stop revolving door'
at U.S. prisons," www.archives.cnn.com; J. Briggs, "New law to focus
on HIV in Blacks: Infection rate tied to prison population," *Chicago Tribune* August 19, 2005, www.chicagotribune.com, and "Governor Blagojevich signs legislation to fight the spread of HIV/AIDS among
African-Americans," www.illinois.gov.

Chapter 10: Race, Poverty, and Care

HIV/AIDS in African Americans: "African Americans Disproportion-
ately Affected by STDs," December 5, 2000, and "HIV/AIDS among
African Americas, www.cdc.gov; "HIV/AIDS is Devastating Chicago's
African American Community" (and similar analyses on the impact of
AIDS on New York, Connecticut, New Jersey, Massachusetts), Health
Watch, 2005, www.hwatch.org; African American attitudes on
HIV/AIDS: Rand Corporation-Oregon State University Study results
reported in the February 1, 2005 issue of *Journal of Acquired Immune
Deficiency Syndrome*. HIV/AIDS among Hispanic populations, see
www.LibertadLatina.org (see, for example, "United States-Latina
Women and Children At Risk"). AIDS and Native Americans, see V.
Parachin, "How to Talk with Kids about Tough Issues," *Vibrant Native
Life*, Autumn 2002, p. 4. Pima chief Mary Thomas quote: J. Wheel-
wright's "Native America's Alleles," *Discover,* May 2005; "Native Americans and HIV/AIDS," University of Oklahoma Health Sciences Center;
"Project brings AIDS testing to Mont reservation," November 21,
2003, and "HIV/AIDS called 'time bomb' on reservations, January 12,
2004," "High HIV/AIDS Rate among Native Americans," June 14,
2003, www.indianz.com; E. Puukka et al., 2005, "Measuring the Health
Status Gap for American Indians/Alaska Natives: Getting Closer to the
Truth," *American Journal of Public Health*, v 95 (5).

Racial and gender disparities: "Wealth and Poverty," www.pbs.org/
peoplelikeus/resources/stats.html; G. Singh, 2003, "Area Deprivation

and Widening Inequalities in US Mortality, 1969–1998," *American Journal of Public Health* v 93(7); Agency for Healthcare Quality Research, *2004 National Healthcare Disparities Report,* www.qualitytools. ahrq.gov; February 11, 2005 *Morbidity and Mortality Weekly Report,* www.cdc.gov/mmwr; S. Riolo et al., 2005, "Prevalence of Depression by Race/Ethnicity: Findings from the National Health and Nutrition Examination Survey III," *American Journal of Public Health,* v 95(6), p. 998; "Health Status of American Indians, Alaska Natives still lagging behind," *The Nation's Health,* June/July 2005; B. Lichtenstein, 2003, "Stigma as a barrier to treatment of sexually transmitted infections in the American deep south: issues of race, gender and poverty," *Social Science and Medicine,* v 57(12), p. 2435; G. Herek, G., et al., "HIV-Related Stigma and Knowledge in the United States: Prevalence and Trends, 1991–1999," *American Journal of Public Health* (2002) v92 (3); C. Denny, "Disparities in Chronic Disease Risk Factors and Health Status Between American Indian/Alaska Native and White Elders," *American Journal of Public Health,* v 95 (5), p. 825.

African American communities: O. Williams and C. Tribbs, *Community Insights on Domestic Violence among African Americas: Conversations About Domestic Violence and Other Issues Affecting Their Community* (Office on Violence Against Women, U.S. Department of Justice, 2002). M. Mauer, 2002, "The Expanding Prison System is Socially Unjust," and S. Minerbrook, 2002, "Juveniles are Becoming Ruthless," *Opposing Viewpoints* series, www.galenet.galegroup.com. Felons disenfranchisement: T. Snyder, 2004, "Felon Factor: Racial implications of disenfranchisement," www.hrponline.org; D. Mitchell, "The New Invisible Man: Felon Disenfranchisement Laws Harm Communities," www.bad.eserver.org; "Food Stamp Ban is Silly and Dangerous," May 14, 2004, *Sacramento Bee,* www.democrats.assembly.ca.gov.

Christian Right and African Americans: A. Smith, "Devil's in the details: Andrea Smith Scrutinizes the Christian right's 'race reconciliation' movement," *Colorlines Magazine,* Spring 2002; B. Berkowitz, March 29, 2004, "Religious Right Plays the Race Card," www.alternet.org; "Project 21: A Laughable Attempt to Redefine 'Civil Rights,'" www.pfaw.org; S. Nakagawa, "Race and the Religious Right," www.eserver.org. Structural racism: B. Tatum, *"Why are All the Black Kids Sitting Together in the Cafeteria?" And Other Conversations About Race* (Basic Books, 1997); C. West, *Race Matters* (Vintage Books, 1994); N. Pal Singh, *Black is a Country: Race and the Unfinished Struggle for Democracy* (Harvard University Press, 2004); S. Begley "The Roots of Hatred," *AARP Magazine,* May/June 2004; "Learning Series: Genes, Race and Medicine," *Discover* magazine's March 2005. Dorothy Height: see "Dorothy Height: Honoring the Diversity of America," www.nwhp.org., or her biography on www.thehistorymakers.com; www.congressionalgoldmedal.com.

The October 2005 Medicaid fight: www.moveon.org; "Proposed cuts to Medicaid may harm the most vulnerable" (April 2005), "Medicaid cuts could have dire impact on the disabled" and "Uninsured working adults face barriers to health care," (June/July 2005) *The Nation's Health*; B. Basler and C. Hudnall, "Living in a House of Cards: What will happen to the millions of uninsured when Medicaid cuts kick in?" *AARP Bulletin*, April 2005.

Beulah Ramsey was the subject of a long study by Sarah Avery in the Raleigh, North Carolina *Sunday News and Observer*, February 6, 2005. This is also the source on the North Carolina budget and cost of care comes from and the quotes from Peter Leone, Adaora Adimora, and Leah Devlin. More stories: Community HIV/AIDS Mobilization Project, www.champnetwork.org; PBS cover story, "AIDS and the African-American Church," www.pbs.org/wnet/religion and ethics/wee519/cover.html. Children with HIV: L. Wilson et al., 2005, "The Economic Burden of Home Care for Children with HIV and Other Chronic Illnesses," *American Journal of Public Health*, v 95(8); "The New Face of AIDS: Why is HIV preying on minority women, and what can America do about it?" from *Newsweek*, www.msnbc.msn.com; "HIV Transmission Among Black Women—North Carolina, 2004," February 4, 2005, www.cdc.gov/mmwr.

HIV superstrains and drug resistance: New York City Department of Health press release, February 11, 2005; M. Santora and L. Altman, "Doctors Discover new HIV Strains: Virus is Resistance to Nearly All Drugs," *International Herald Tribune*, February 12, 2005, www.iht.com; "HIV Drug Options Exhausted," March, 2005, www.allafrica.com/stories/2005-310-0023.html. See also "Advancing on AIDS," *Discover*, v 12(3), March 2000; Laurie Garrett': "Bush Administration's HIV/AIDS Cuts Cater to 'Religious Right,' Opinion Piece Says," June 1, 2004, www.thebody.com;.also see her books: *The Coming Plague* (Farrar, Straus and Giroux, 1994) and *Betrayal of Trust* (Hyperion, 2000).

AIDS in rural areas: "Rural HIV/AIDS Bias Persists: Lincoln Nebraska," November 14, 2003 CBS News, www.cbsnews.com/stories/2003. Church reaction, see "The Church and the drug crisis: ministers mobilize against 'The death of a race'," 1989, www.findarticles.com; "An Open Letter to President George W. Bush from Black Church Leaders," June 14, 2005, www.globalaidsalliance.org or go to the *Los Angeles Times* website. Maxine Waters' comments" "Congresswoman Waters and 117 Other Members of Congress Seek Increased Minority AIDS Initiative Funding," Press Release from Waters' office, May 12, 2005, www.globalaidsalliance.org. Administration policy: include "HHS Proposal to Cut Ryan White Funding for Highly Affected Metropolitan Areas is 'Irresponsible and Unfair,'" August 18, 2005, www.kaisernetwork.org/daily_reports; E. Jacobs, "Further cuts for Ryan

White funding," www.baywindows.com; "Bush plan would shift Ryan White funding to rural areas," July 29, 2005, www.advocate.com; Senate Subcommittee Approves $10M Increase in Ryan White Funding for FY2006," www.medicalnewstoday.com; T. Murphy, "Work With Me!," www.poz.com/articles; Housing Works AIDS Advocacy website, ww.hwadvocacy.com; U.S. Department of Housing and Urban Development, "HIV/AIDS Housing: The Need for HIV/AIDS Housing Assistance," www.hud.gov; "Facts on Housing for People Living with HIV/AIDS," www.aidshousing.org; "Ensuring Adequate Housing for New Yorkers with HIV Disease," www.gmhc.org; J. Milby et al., "To House or Not to House: The Effects of Providing Housing to Homeless Substance Abusers in Treatment," *American Journal of Public Health* v 95(7).

Drug industry: M. Angell, *The Truth About the Drug Companies* (Random House, 2004); C. Lubinski, 2004, "An Overview of AIDS Drug Access in the United States: Examining the Pharmaeconomics of U.S. AIDS Drug Access," and B. Huff, 2002, "Patient Care Squeezed by Soaring Drug Prices," www.thebody.com; P. diJuston, "Under the Influence: As corporate funding of drug R&D grows, so do the pro-industry results," *Wired*, May 2003. AIDS drug innovations: L. Whitehorn, 2005, "One a Day: You've Come A Long Way," www.poz.com. For the Gilead Company story, "A Glimpse into the Future: Interview with Norbert Bischofberger, Ph.D.," go to www.hivpositivemagaizne. com/meds.html, which also has an overview of HIV Medications.

Bush administration's role in blocking of drugs in developing countries: M. Desvarieux et al., "Antiretroviral Therapy in Resource-Poor Countries: Illusions and Realities," *American Journal of Public Health* v 95(7), "India beats global drug firms at their own game," March 21, 2004, www.busienss.timesonline.com, M. Cohen and G. Schiff, "Ban on generic drugs will prove to be a fatal mistake," *Chicago Sun-Times*, May 5, 2004; R. Weissman, "U.S. Pharmaceutical Companies and the U.S. Government Have Blocked the Availability of Drugs in Developing Countries," *Opposing Viewpoints*, www.galenet.galegroup.com; J. Cohen, "Drugmakers Test Restrictions on Generics in U.S. Programs" Science October 8, 2004, v 306(5694), www.globalaidsalliance.org.

Bernie Sanders' study: "New Figures Prove Pharmaceutical Industry Continues to Fleece Americans," www.bernie.house.gov. Drug company lobbying and whistle blowers: M. Ismail "Drug Lobby Second to None: How the Pharmaceutical Industry Gets its Way in Washington," www.publicintegrity.org; "Defeating AIDS Means Changing the Course of History," wwww.whoint.whr/2004; P. Barry, "States Defy FDA on Drug Importation," *AARP Bulletin*, October, 2004;,P. Barry, "The Insiders," *AARP Bulletin*, November, 2004; and W. Melillo, "Drug Cos. Work to Stave Off Legislation," *Adweek*, July 11, 2005, p. 6.

For the White House attack on condoms distribution, see People for the American Way's story "House Cuts Funding for International Family Planning: White House Pressure Played Role," www.pfaw.org; G. Carter, April 2002, "Fighting Back Against Pharmaceutical Company Greed," www.thebody.com; M. Gladwell, "High Prices: How to think about prescription drugs," *The New Yorker,* October 25, 2004, p. 86; B. Koerner, "Born Again: What's the fastest, cheapest way to develop a wonder drug? Recycle an old one," *Wired,* June, 2003, p. 106; or J. Davenport, "How Big Pharma Finds Its Next Fix," *Wired,* June 2004, p. 34; P. Barry, "The Real Value of Drugs: Evidence-based research is fast emerging," *AARP Bulletin,* March, 2005, p. 16. State versus federal position: L. Messina, AP, "State lawmakers host prescription drug summit," October 21, 2004, www.boston.com; "Drug Importation risky, costly to regulate, U.S. task force says," *The Nation's Health,* February 2005; E. Becker, "Bush Scaling Back Dollars for Third World," *The New York Times,* January 29, 2004.

Drug access and vaccines, see World Trade Organization, "TRIPS: Counsel Discussion on Access to Medicines, Developing Country Group's Paper," June 19, 2001, www.wto.org; K. Baldwin, "Latin American AIDS Activists Turn on Brazil," Reuters, May 25, 2002; SRI Media, "HIV/AIDS: TRIPPS and President Bush's 'Emergency Plan for AIDS Relief'" (February 11, 2003, www.srimedia.com); World Health Organization and World Trade Organization, *WTO Agreements and Public Health,* (2002, www.wto.org); O. Jablonski, "Accelerating Access: Serving Pharmaceutical Companies and Corrupting Health Systems," (Act Up-Paris, May 14, 2002); S. Gottlieb, "Drug Companies Maintain 'Astounding' Profits," *British Medical Journal,* May 4, 2002 at www.bmj.com/cgi/contents/full); SRI Media, "AIDS Drug Will Cost Each Patient $20,000 a Year," February 24, 2003, www.srimedia.com; R. Carroll, "African's AIDS drugs trapped in the laboratory: Kenya has the pills. Now the fight is on to get them to the people," *The Guardian,* May 21, 2003.

FDA controversy: "Criticism of FDA Prescription Drug Approval Process, Boston Globe," April 12, 2005, www.medicalnewsonline.com; K. Greider, "Vioxx: Downfall of a Superdrug," *AARP Bulletin,* November, 2004; L. Richwine, October 4, 2004, "Arthritis Drug Recall Sparks Criticism," www.vascularweb.org; M. Rath, April 12, 2005, "Criticism of FDA Prescription Drug Approval Process," www.drrathresearch.org; or see the 60 Minutes February 16, 2005 story, "FDA: Harsh Criticism from Within," www.cbsnews.com, or "Drug Researcher Testifies: The System is 'Broken,'" www.ombwatch.org; the *USA Today* story by Julie Appleby, "Budget cuts FDA safety checks," www.usatoday.com; M. Davis, January 4, 2005, "Merck Mess Shows FDA's Flaws," www.thestreet.com; R. Mishra, "AMA calls for total drug-trial disclosure," *Boston Globe* June 16, 2004, www.boston.com; B. Huff, May/June 2004, "Abbott's Norvir Price Hike is Bad Medicine" and May 2004, "Aetna Files Class-Action Lawsuit Against Abbott over 400% Price Increase of Antiretroviral Drug Norvir," www.thebody.com; M. Dahir, April 23, 2004, "Allow imported HIV/AIDS Drugs," the *Washington Blade*, www.washblade.com.

Brazil's program; A. Vakhovskiy, "Winning the War on AIDS, Brazil Style," *Dartmouth Free* Press, August 10, 2001; J. Galvao, "Brazil and Access to HIV/AIDS Drugs: A Question of Human Rights and Public Health," and A. Berkman et al., "A Critical Analysis of the Brazilian Response to HIV/AIDS: Lessons Learned for Controlling and Mitigating the Epidemic in Developing Countries," both in the *American Journal of Public Health* July 2005, v 95(7); T. Smart, "Brazil's HIV/AIDS programme is a model for the rest of the world," *HIV/AIDS Treatment in Practice*, v 53 August 18, 2005, www.nam.org; "Brazil Spurns US Terms for AIDS Help," *The Guardian* May 4, 2005, www.guardian.com.uk; J. Levi, "Ensuring Timely Access to Care for People with HIV Infection: A Public Health Imperative," *American Journal of Public Health*, (2002) v92 (3).

Conclusion

HIV future: J. Lederberg:, "Pandemic as a Natural Evolutionary Phenomenon," in *In Time of Plague: The History and Consequences of Lethal Epidemic Disease*, M. Arien, ed. (New York: New York University Press, 1991.

INDEX